The
Place of
Grammar
in
Writing
Instruction

The Place of Grammar in Writing Instruction

PAST

PRESENT

FUTURE

edited by
Susan Hunter
and Ray Wallace

Boynton/Cook Publishers
HEINEMANN
Portsmouth, NH

Boynton/Cook Publishers, Inc.
A subsidiary of Reed Elsevier Inc.
361 Hanover Street
Portsmouth, NH 03801-3912
Offices and agents throughout the world

Copyright © 1995 by Boynton/Cook Publishers, Inc.

Library of Congress Cataloging-in-Publication Data

The place of grammar in writing instruction : past, present, future /
   edited by Susan Hunter and Ray Wallace.
    p.   cm.
    Includes bibliographical references.
    ISBN 0-86709-352-8 (paperback)
    1. English language—Rhetoric—Study and teaching. 2. English language—Grammar—Study and teaching. I. Hunter, Susan, 1948–
II. Wallace, Ray.
  PE1404.P56 1994
  808'.007—dc20   94-38896
                                                   CIP

Editor: Peter R. Stillman
Production: Renée M. Pinard
Cover design: Julie Hahn

Printed in the United States of America on acid-free paper
99 98 97 96 95 EB 1 2 3 4 5 6

Contents

Introduction: Reexamining the Place of Grammar in Writing Instruction

Ray Wallace

In developing this collection, the contributors—compositionists first and foremost—felt it was time to look more closely at where our profession stood on the issue of grammar instruction at the college level and at how we had reached this position. The contributors also felt that as a profession we needed to answer some difficult questions we have been avoiding for some time. Was it simply enough to claim that we didn't teach grammar because research "showed" that it does not improve writing? Why, when in 1986 George Hillocks in *Research on Written Composition* seemed to dismiss the study of grammar as having no effect on the composing process, had others spent so much time writing so many articles, textbooks, and handbooks focusing on error, style, and editing? While grammar exercises might indeed not make students better writers, should our classes involve no grammar instruction at all? Did our composition classes really include no grammar instruction? Had grammar instruction been dropped because we were not willing to go along with the gatekeeping role that had historically been part of the mission of English departments? Did writing teachers face a dilemma in their classrooms when they could not find a place for grammar instruction among the currently preferred ways of teaching composition at the same time that they saw a need for it? Why were most future secondary teachers required to take a course in advanced grammar and yet did not have to take a course in the teaching of writing? If grammar was not important to the composing process, why were so many students sent to writing centers to work on syntactical "errors"? Was it enough to talk about composing without developing philosophies about the political nature of correctness, usage, style, and our roles as teachers of "service" courses?

In 1945, the National Council of Teachers of English appointed a Commission on the English Curriculum to study these very questions. More than forty-five years later, they remained largely unanswered. The contributors to this volume decided that they—voices from the trenches—could offer some of these answers. Working with multiple definitions of grammar in this collection, the contributors have begun an important revision in our field.

When Richard Braddock, Richard Lloyd-Jones, and Lowell Schoer called for the abolition of grammar in the teaching of writing in the 1960s, compositionists began to revise their pedagogy to embrace the composing process and eventually to embrace as well liberatory, collaborative, social-epistemic principles—a revision often based on unsubstantiated research. Because of the traditional distinctions made among invention, style, and arrangement, modern composition theory had difficulty justifying instruction in grammar. Like style and arrangement, grammar is believed to be a feature of the product, and because the process approach emphasizes invention, grammar has no place in writing instruction. The modern refusal to include grammar in writing pedagogy is best seen as a reaction against its prominence in early composition history.

But while grammar exercises may indeed not make students better writers, should our composition classes involve no grammar instruction at all? Will the missing discussions of grammar prevent our students from becoming literate in ways sanctioned by the academy and the community beyond? We suspected that grammar instruction had just been driven underground and still occurred even when the dominant pedagogy of the classroom was not what James Berlin would call "current-traditional." In *The Chronicle of Higher Education*, July 1, 1992, Dennis Baron writes that "it still borders on the unethical to allow students to practice linguistic diversity unchecked" (B1). And, he goes on to claim, "English teachers cling tenaciously to the gatekeeping function served by the proper use of language" (B2).

We must scrutinize the maxim that there exists a large body of empirical research that proves that grammar instruction does not enable writing instruction. In the past ten years, some have claimed that statements by researchers were taken out of context and wrongly interpreted by those who stood to gain much by such a reading—they no longer had to instruct students in any of the increasingly complex (and sometimes boring) grammars. While compositionists seem to accept this maxim that grammar instruction should play no part in the teaching of writing, they both expect and are expected to help writers understand their composing processes *and* the importance of their linguistic and stylistic choices. Where do we turn for help to try to meet both these goals?

At first, the methods of teaching grammar in classical times did not seem likely to inspire us to pedagogical imitation. These methods depended on lists, lectures, exercises, and handbooks—not exactly considered to be innovative practice today. However, in classical times, learning grammar meant learning literacy, literary history, and critical thinking about literature. Now, learning grammar for most students means learning "how the structural system of a language combines with a vocabulary to convey meaning" (Corbett, *Little English Handbook* 5).

When we turn to such works as Constance Weaver's *Grammar for Teachers* or Rei R. Noguchi's *Grammar and the Teaching of Writing*, we find conflated positions. Weaver claims that

> There is little pragmatic justification for systematically teaching a grammar of the language, whether that grammar be traditional, structural, transformational, or whatever. On the other hand, it may be desirable or even necessary to use some grammatical concepts and terminology in helping students become more effective language users. Thus the teacher needs a fairly solid background in grammar in order to work with students. (89–90)

Noguchi concludes that writing teachers can teach less grammar more effectively if they concentrate on "teaching the minimal set of grammatical categories and . . . use these categories to treat a maximum number of the most serious stylistic errors" (34). In doing this, teachers will be teaching grammar for writers. The pro-grammar and anti-grammar camps that Noguchi identifies represent variations of a similar pedagogical position—that of teachers who assume that we teach writing *to* students.

Even our professional organizations—NCTE and its Commission on Composition—fail to address our dilemma: the "NCTE's Position on the Teaching of English: Assumptions and Practices" simply states that students should "learn grammar and usage by studying how their own language works in context." The Commission on Composition's "Teaching Composition: A Position Statement" valorizes process over product: " . . . writing teachers who write know that effective comments do not focus on pointing out errors, but go on to the more productive task of encouraging revision . . ."

Reconsidering the relationship between grammar instruction and writing instruction is fraught with problems. Noguchi warns us that we need to decide what grammar we are discussing. Baron reminds us that Americans use grammar as a demarcator of social class. Henry Giroux relates grammar to economics: American business and the myth of upward mobility for all demand certain "skills" of workers. Robert Connors and Andrea Lunsford alert us to community pre/misconceptions when parents and politicians lump an astounding number of disparate items under the heading "grammar" and even educators disagree about what constitutes "serious" error. As an issue related to writing instruction, however, the question of grammar's role(s) within the teaching of writing allows us to bring into view many of the commonplace myths about grammar, and having done so, to discuss what place these myths serve in maintaining a societal status quo.

Changes are occurring. The NCTE now has a Special Interest Group dealing with grammar and writing. Some of the contributors to this collection and those mentioned above, as active members of this interest group, are making other compositionists aware of its goals. Indeed, college teachers need to have the same level of awareness as their high-school-teacher peers regarding the important links between grammar instruction and the writing classroom. Hence, this collection is aimed at those primarily interested in writing instruction at the college level.

The following essays by specialists from all over the country and from a wide variety of areas in composition studies reevaluate the place of grammar—or grammars—in the teaching of writing and describe where we stand on the issue in the 90s, a decade of accepting cultural differences. These discussions about grammar will necessarily spill over into discussions of "standard" English and dialects, attitudes toward error and students' right to their own language, and class struggle. This volume provides a forum for teachers and researchers to explore further the place of grammar in the teaching of writing and to describe ways that grammar instruction has been, is, and should be used in our writing programs. The three sections allow for a progressive observation of the places of grammar in writing instruction. The contributors who explain past attitudes toward grammar instruction not only deal with history but all tell stories of, or strongly suggest, connections to the present. In the remaining two sections of the book, dealing with the present concerns toward grammar instruction and the future places of grammar in writing instruction, all the contributors use an expansive definition of grammar rather than a limiting one. Indeed, many of the writers in these sections show how they, as self-defined "informed practitioners" rather than traditional grammarians, use "rhetorical grammars" in their classrooms.

In the section on past attitudes toward grammar instruction, Cheryl Glenn, Jon Olson, Gina Claywell, Richard Boyd, and Garry Ross discuss the historical nature of the teaching of grammars as they relate to the teaching of writing. Their chapters deal with the importance of grammar in earlier educational philosophies; examine the changing face of grammar instruction in classical times, grammar instruction in medieval education, grammar instruction and the education of immigrant America, the place of grammar in early English departments in America and Britain; and the importance of past grammarians in the teaching of writing. The historian of composition along with teachers and researchers concerned with shaping a coherent pedagogy for the present will benefit from these discussions.

In the section on present concerns about grammar and writing, John Edlund, Joan Mullin, R. Baird Shuman, Byron Stay and Carl Glover, Donald Bushman and Elizabeth Ervin, Stuart C. Brown, Robert Boswell, and Kevin McIlvoy, and Wendy Bishop re-evaluate the belief that little or no grammar instruction is needed to teach writing, as they focus on grammar instruction and the teaching of writing in various sites and for various groups: college composition classrooms, writing centers, writing-across-the-curriculum projects, and creative writing classrooms.

In the section on the future places of grammar in writing instruction, David Blakesley, Irene Brosnahan and Janice Neuleib, Eric Hobson, and Neil Daniel and Christina Murphy speculate about grammar instruction and the teaching of writing in the future. Their chapters evaluate what we have already learned with a view to what we still need to learn or teach the next generation of writing teachers about the role of grammar instruction. To conclude the collection, coeditor Susan Hunter looks to the arguments of the contributors to extrapolate the position of grammar in writing classes of the future.

Addressing an issue that has been skirted for quite some time by many teachers and researchers of college writing, this collection offers the reader an opportunity not only to understand why we have arrived at this point, but also to learn what some in the profession are doing about this situation. The contributors are all specialists in college composition and pedagogy who share their insights about the place of grammar instruction from multiple perspectives: as college composition teachers, as writing center directors, as rhetoricians, as students, and as writers themselves. They are not grammarians in the conventional sense. They are, instead, voices from various college writing settings who show us how to reconnect grammar and writing.

I

Past Attitudes Toward Grammar Instruction

Presenting lessons and admonitions from the past, the five chapters in this section focus on past pedagogies, cultural attitudes, and texts that have shaped and continue to shape contemporary views about the place of grammar in writing instruction. In the first three chapters, Cheryl Glenn, Jon Olson, and Gina Claywell alert us to the ways in which the connotation and value of grammar have changed from Greek and Roman times. Focusing on past texts and pedagogies, these authors demonstrate how grammar conceived and taught as a means to literacy and stylistic fluency had served to empower writers. But as Glenn points out in "When Grammar Was a Language Art," while we may still subscribe to the goals of the ancients, we ignore their pedagogy. Using Edward P. J. Corbett's teaching methods as a model, she makes a case for adapting the pedagogy of the ancients to the contemporary composition classroom.

Moving into nineteenth-century America in "A Question of Power: Why Frederick Douglass Stole Grammar," Olson recalls the case of African–American Frederick Douglass, who was born a slave and recorded in his autobiography a program for teaching himself to read and write that mirrors the empowering pedagogy of the ancients—not the teacher-centered practices of current-traditionalists in American colleges and universities of the time. Claywell's argument for "Reasserting Grammar's Position in the Trivium in American College Composition" warns us of the danger of disassociating grammar from writing instruction simply because of the current-traditional model of composition pedagogy and the prescriptive role of grammar we have inherited from nineteenth-century American rhetoricians. Glenn, Olson, and Claywell advocate using the ancients' program of language study in today's writing classrooms, that is, following the historical precedent of the trivium where grammar, rhetoric, and logic are interconnected.

Focusing on negative lessons from the past, Richard Boyd reads nineteenth-century grammar texts and Garry Ross reads five volumes issued by the NCTE Commission on the English Curriculum from 1952 to 1965 to uncover past cultural forces that have narrowed our view of grammar in today's writing classrooms. Their chapters confirm the separation between grammar as correctness and composing as a process as well as the dichotomy between teacher-centered and student-centered pedagogies. In "'Grammatical Monstrosities' and 'Contemptible Miscreants': Sacrificial Violence in the Late Nineteenth-Century Usage Handbook," Boyd demonstrates the post-Civil War obsession with mechanical correctness in student writing. He examines William Mathews' *Words: Their Use and Abuse* to show the dangers of what theorist René Girard has called mimetic desire and scapegoating the "other." For codifiers of usage like Mathews, Boyd argues, imitation of the teacher's models becomes a class issue; that is, a student gains power by imitating the usage and grammatical correctness espoused by the teacher.

Closing this section on past attitudes toward grammar, in "The 1945 NCTE Commission on the English Curriculum and Teaching the Grammar/Writing Connection," Ross interprets the Commission's reports as a missed opportunity to reconnect grammar and writing. He argues that although these documents were issued between 1952 and 1965—between the rise of structuralism and the Chomskyan revolution—they set forth a literature-based program of language arts, ignoring the insights linguists were making into the grammar/writing connection.

1

When Grammar Was a Language Art

Cheryl Glenn

No direct relation exists between grammar instruction and writing improvement. We have known this for over thirty years. George Hillocks, Sara D'Eloia, and Patrick Hartwell have all tried to warn us away from the temptation to think otherwise. In his impressive meta-analysis *Research on Written Composition*, Hillocks reports that "none of the studies reviewed . . . provides any support for teaching grammar as a means of improving composition skills" (138). He was referring to the massive research project conducted by Richard Braddock, Richard Lloyd-Jones, and Lowell Schoer, in which they write that "in view of the widespread agreement of research studies based upon many types of students and teachers, the conclusion can be stated in strong and unqualified terms: the teaching of formal grammar has a negligible or, because it usually displaces some instruction and practice in actual composition, even a harmful effect on the improvement of writing" (37–38). In "The Uses—and Limits—of Grammar," D'Eloia writes that

> Wherever it has been seriously researched, the analytical study of grammar has failed to produce significant results in student writing across the board. . . . If there is one conclusion to be drawn which cuts across all the studies, it is this: the more time spent analyzing grammar as grammar, the less time spent writing; the less time spent writing, the less improvement in the written product. (1)

In his well-known "Grammar, Grammars, and the Teaching of Grammar," Hartwell tells us straightaway that for him, "the grammar issue was settled" (105) by the kinds of studies I have mentioned thus far. And he closes his article by encouraging teachers to formulate theories of language and literacy that can guide teaching, and by encouraging researchers to "move on to more interesting areas of inquiry" (127).

But in "Closing the Books on Alchemy," Martha Kolln takes a different tack. Although she confirms that there is no direct relation between grammar instruction and writing improvement, she admonishes us that there are other, very important reasons for teaching grammar that have to do with analyzing discourse and building shared vocabulary and conceptual frameworks. She explains her stance further in *Rhetorical Grammar*:

> Those findings that report no correlation between the formal teaching of grammar and writing ability conclude only that grammar should not be taught *in isolation*, as an end in itself. They do not conclude that it should not be taught at all. . . . Unfortunately, the result of the research has been to drive grammar instruction out of the composition classroom, rather than into it, where it belongs. (vi)

Grammar as a Language Art

Back when grammar was a language art, grammar *was* where it belongs. For centuries, grammar occupied the central position in the composition classroom and informed theories of language and literacy. The triangulation of grammar, rhetoric, and logic known as the *trivium* provided a stable, coherent, and comprehensive language-arts program that guided both teachers and students through the intricacies and proficiencies of language-learning. When grammar was a language art, it was more than punctuation and usage, more than rules of linguistic etiquette, more than isolated drills and exercises. It was a language art that enhanced—rather than displaced—instruction and practice in composition. Thus, grammar was fully realized in language itself—in fluid, flexible, lively, ever-changing, emotional, beautiful, stylish, graceful language performance. And that performance played itself out as *style*.

The ultimate goal of teaching grammar seems always to have been to help students become more efficient and effective language-users, to improve their language performance. And because grammar and style are two sides of the same linguistic coin, those programs that obviously and purposefully fuse the study of grammar with the study of style better meet the goal of improved language performance. The ancients perfected such a program of language study, a program that successfully realized their goals and produced spectacularly proficient wordsmiths such as Isocrates, Demosthenes, Aristotle, Cicero, and Quintilian. Yet we moderns have, for the most part, ignored their language-arts program while resolutely (and ironically) holding tenaciously to their goals. In this chapter, I am offering up that ancient pedagogy for translation into our modern classrooms. And I want to use Edward P. J. Corbett's pedagogy as well as his *Classical Rhetoric for the Modern Student* as the touchstone for such translation.[1]

The Greek Language-Arts Program

Since our goals and many of our beliefs are the same, why don't we share the best of that ancient pedagogy? We share with the ancient Greeks the belief that style (*elocutio*) lies somewhere between invention (*inventio*) and delivery (*pronunciatio*), somewhere between discovering the right things to say and arranging those "right" things. Style is grammar delivered, the "right" and best grammar delivered. Therefore, in establishing the core of what would become our Western educational system, the Greeks and Romans never lost sight of grammar, which was to them as organic to style as style was to content. For them, language-learning and performance was a vibrant, organic whole that was not to be disfigured either by dissection or attempts at cosmetic improvement. And their students enrolled in a continuous, standard language-learning program that evolved in complexity and difficulty as students developed in proficiency and fluency.

That program, which we can learn from and build on, flourished until the early seventeenth century, when Peter Ramus created his vision of a more logical system of education by removing invention and arrangement from stylistic studies. Without the noetic obligations to and linguistic expectations of invention and arrangement, grammar and style transformed into nothing more than the verbal dress of disembodied thought. Little wonder, then, that contemporary research continually confirms the separation between grammar (as correctness or etiquette) and purposeful composition. But for the ancients, the *two* were an inseparable, constantly interrelated *one*.

Long before Longinus argued that the concept of composition is an act of creative genius, long before he wrote his treatise *On Great Writing* (better known as *On the Sublime*, c. 40 AD), Isocrates, Plato, and Aristotle had said the same thing. They, too, felt certain that "sublimity is the echo of a noble mind" (IX.2) and that "beautiful words are in truth the mind's peculiar light" (xxx.1). They too were convinced of the crucial connection of grammar and style to effective discourse, and they too believed in a programmatic course of study, in the eurythmy of grammar and style.

Before his retirement, Corbett regularly marched his graduate students through such a demanding program.[2] No doubt the ancients would smile to watch the modern student work to develop competence and then confidence in language, for Corbett followed the ancients in his careful sequencing of assignments so that students would first develop a "variety of techniques of (1) analyzing the style of prose passages" before they began "(2) practicing various exercises designed to improve [their] own style or to help others improve their style" (syllabus). Corbett resolutely believes that "grammar is preoccupied with how a particular language works—how words are formed and how words can be put together in phrases and clauses" (383) and that "no one can begin to develop a style until he or she has a basic competence in the grammar of the language" (398). Corbett's usual beginning assignment entails close, grammatical analysis of another's prose, a stylistic analysis informed and made possible by grammatical knowledge. To follow Corbett's program, then, students must be either already fluent or undergoing intense remediation in the language of grammar.

The first Greek grammarian, Plato, debated theories of the origin of language and of the correlation between thought and language in the *Cratylus* (BCE 385). Moreover, he examined the concepts of *truth* and *falsehood* to see if they could be translated into and transmitted by any particular grammatical structure. Although he successfully and permanently separated judgments regarding grammatical structure and *truth*, no grammarian has ever been able to dislodge the specious connection between grammatical correctness and morality. Plato's most important contribution to grammar, the sentence division into nominal (*onoma*) and verbal (*rheme*) components, has remained the primary grammatical distinction underlying syntactic analysis and word classification in all linguistic description; all grammatical approaches divide sentences into two parts, subject and verb. And later, in the *Rhetoric*, Aristotle added a third grammatical category of function words (*syndesmoi*) that includes conjunction, articles, and pronouns. Plato's categories remain full parts of speech because they have meaning in isolation; Aristotle's function words, however, have only grammatical meaning.

The Greeks expected young nobles to master grammar and language in preparation for the only way of life permitted for them, the only way that would distinguish and sustain them: the life of the mind and tongue. In *Against the Sophists*, Isocrates extols the rigor of "formal training [that] makes men more skillful and resourceful in discovering the possibilities of a subject," but he is quick to add that such training "cannot fully fashion men who are without natural aptitude" (294.15). Thus, the ancients used grammatical exercises and study to provide their students ways to acquire the variety of styles appropriate for the variety of subject matter, occasion, and audience that they would be expected to address with their compositions. Early on, then, the Greeks were preparing their students to take what Wayne Booth has labeled a "rhetorical stance" (139) and were developing what Lloyd Bitzer would call an awareness of the rhetorical situation (1). And to the end of analyzing and composing effective discourse—technical excellence—the study of grammar and style was divided into three areas: *ars*, a study of precepts or principles; *exercitato*, practice in writing; and *imitatio*, imitation of the practice of others (Corbett 382). Very often, the systematic course of study (rules, principles, precepts) was recorded in the *ars* (or *techne)* itself, a term which quite simply means the textbook or handbook.

Young boys, accompanied to school by their *pedagogues,* began their studies in the grammar school, where they were drilled in the *ars* and the poets, for poets provided necessary knowledge in war, statecraft, and morality. Using poetry as the body of study, then, the teacher (or *grammaticus)* taught students not only correctness of language, the meaning of words, and correct accent and delivery, but also the interpretation and moral precepts of the historians and the poets. Language study was embedded in grammar study. And by the time the boys entered a secondary school such as Gorgias', they were accustomed to working through successive stages that integrated their language learning.

Although none of the handbooks have survived that Gorgias (fl. BCE 420) used in his famous school of rhetoric, we know that he fully realized the impact of technical excellence on persuasion. Gorgias critiqued his students' grammatical style—spoken and written—for correctness, effectiveness, and appropriateness, especially in terms of the stylistic embellishment for which his school was renowned. Thus, their compositions demonstrated their potential and power. And by means of their language expertise, Gorgias' students could "make things seem" in their compositions—a technique Gorgias taught his pupils through imitation exercises. Those specific models for imitation (*imitatio*) are now lost, but we still have access to Gorgias' grammatical technique: his attention to deliberate use of patterns to manipulate a hearer's reactions. Even today, his Gorgian figures—the grammatical categories of alliteration, assonance, antithesis, parallelism—synergize to produce persuasion. Thus, their intense program of language arts and the beauty of their persuasive abilities made Gorgias and his students prodigiously successful. However, Gorgias was not the most influential of the ancient teachers. That distinction goes to Isocrates.

A student of Gorgias and of Socrates, Isocrates (BCE 436–338) was founder of the rhetorical school at Athens, which he differentiates from other sophistic schools in *Against the Sophists*. Although he does not spell out the exact training devices that, for fifty years, he consistently used with success, he does provide us a window into his educational goals and methods, which were based on basic grammatical principles of correct, current, and effective language use. Natural ability reigns paramount in Isocrates' school; nevertheless, the natural ability of his students must be enhanced by grammatical and rhetorical practice in *ars, exercitato,* and *imitatio.* But instead of a regimen of "hard and fast rules" (12) of Gorgian language manipulation, Isocrates outlines for his pupils the general rules of successful composition or oratory (*ars*) and supervises their creative application of those rules—all within the realm of their main occupation, *Imitatio.* He directed his students toward imitation exercises emphasizing accurate diction, logical transitions, smooth sounds and rhythm, periodic sentences. The holistic aim of these grammatical calisthenics was a smooth prose style, a refinement of Gorgias' rather artificial style, which transformed a student's composition into a literary form. Unlike his predecessors, Isocrates required his students to write out their compositions rather than only deliver them orally. And because he seemed to know that he was a classic in his own age, he asked his students to take his own carefully edited, polished, and published prose as their model, for composing as well as for living:

> To obtain a knowledge of the elements out of which we make and compose
> all discourses is not so very difficult if anyone entrusts himself . . . to those
> who have some knowledge of these things. But to choose from these ele-
> ments those which should be employed for each subject, to join them
> together, to arrange them properly, and also, not to miss what the occasion
> demands but appropriately to adorn the whole speech with striking thoughts
> and to clothe it in flowing and melodious phrase—these things, I hold,
> require much study and are the task of a vigorous and imaginative mind: for
> this, the student must not only have the requisite aptitude but he must learn
> the different kinds of discourse and practise himself in their use; and the
> teacher, for his part, must so expound the principles of the art with the
> utmost possible exactness as to leave out nothing that can be taught.
> (*Against* 294.16–18)

If Gorgias had intoxicated Isocrates with the potential of grammar study
for stylistic fluency, Socrates was a sobering influence: Isocrates' school
would be known for its rigorous and scrupulous language-arts program, and
his students would be distinguished by an artistic facility with language, by
a smooth, literary prose style that refined and transcended Gorgian excess
and artificiality. Isocrates' specific contribution to grammar study was the
periodic sentence, which he and his students popularized in setting new standards in form and rhythm for prose style.

As the smallest unit of meaningful discourse, the sentence would seem
to merit our attention. And during various times since Isocrates, the sentence
has been the standard linguistic cynosure—whenever imitation exercises
have been used to strengthen, develop, and intensify sentence design. Yet
today, despite the highly regarded efforts of Noam Chomsky, Francis Christensen, Richard Coe, Frank O'Hare, and Joseph Williams to connect sentence work with syntactic fluency, teachers and students alike tend to ignore
the sentence in terms of artistry, meaning, style, and context. Instead, they
continually concentrate on isolated, acontextual issues of correctness within
sentence boundaries, surface-error issues of punctuation, capitalization,
agreement, and tense. And instead of learning from or building on the successful and systematized, sentence-level grammatical studies of the ancients,
we have somehow forgotten, never discovered, or purposefully neglected
what they perfected.

In *Classical Rhetoric for the Modern Student*, Corbett, however, engages
his students in sentence-level work, work that they must continually connect
with their writing. For instance, when students hand in an assignment, he
asks them to count the number of words in each sentence, providing information for the average sentence-length (to the first decimal point—"18.7
words per sentence, *not* 19 words per sentence"), their longest sentence, and
their shortest sentence; then he asks them to provide the same kind of information about the average number of sentences in a paragraph (to the first

decimal point again), the highest number of sentences in a paragraph, and the lowest. He regularly asks students to provide information about the "types" of sentences they use and the frequency of their use—simple, compound, complex, compound-complex. And he wants students to account for the types and frequencies of "sentence openers" they use: subject, expletive, coordinating conjunction, adverb word, conjunctive phrase, prepositional phrase, adjective phrase, absolute phrase, adverb clause, front-shift (415, 422). To respond to even the simplest of Corbett's requests, students must be able to recognize sentence boundaries, sentence types, and parts of speech. Isocrates' art of the sentence is neglected today; that is, except for those of our contemporaries who value the sentence in terms of its role in developing prose style, contemporaries whose teaching is based on classical pedagogy.

Although surely influenced by Isocrates' school, Plato was more interested in establishing the truth of any matter than in developing prose style. Even his identification of the two basic sentence elements, subject and verb, established the truth more than the style of the sentence.[3] Nevertheless, grammar studies underpinned the Greek language-arts program, for the Greeks saw its necessity in preparing young orators (both speakers and writers, seeing little distinction between the two practices). And in the *Phaedrus*, the Platonic Socrates admonishes young orators that they "will not gain" stylistic fluency "without much diligent toil" (273e). Plato's advice for diligent toil (*exercitato*) in the language arts, preparatory exercises that helped children grasp the mechanics of their mother tongue—analyses of everything from letter "sounds" and syllable duration to the eight parts of speech and their individual categories—prepared the student to move directly into rhetorical exercises and ultimately into actual practice. Plato recognized the expectations of those students. Eventually, these students would demonstrate their language abilities, for the speaker "must find out the class of speech adapted to each nature, and must arrange and adorn his discourse accordingly, offering to the complex soul elaborate and harmonious discourses, and simple talks to the simple soul" (277c). The benefit of grammar exercises, then, was in their connection with composition.

For developing prose style, Plato advised diligent toil (*exercitato*). All of us who write and teach writing know that only diligent toil polishes our style, for it is in the process of toiling itself that our style emerges with any efficiency and speed. Each time we write, each time we combine our attention to the details of sounds and sense, we exercise our style, our choice of things that language allows us to do. Corbett stresses the toil as well when he tells us that the "difficulty that everyone has, in varying degrees, in putting thoughts into language stems partly from the intertia that must be overcome at the beginning of any task, partly from the lack of something to say, partly from indecisiveness about what to say first, and *partly from the variety of possible ways to say something*" (emphasis added, 380). And he quotes Stendahl when he writes that "style is this: to add to a given thought all the circumstances fitted to produce the whole effect which the thought is intended to produce'' (381). Thus, every time we alert our students to the implications of style, tone, or delivery in response to audience, an occasion, their purpose, and their personality, we address Plato's concern for a repertoire of discourse styles.

Aristotle, too, concerned himself with varieties of discourse styles; he was, after all, the first to coin *rhetoric* as "the faculty of observing in any given case the available means of persuasion," techniques of style being important means of persuasion (*Rhetoric* I.2.1355b). In the third book of his *Rhetoric* (c. BCE 350), devoted entirely to style, Aristotle tells his pupils that even if they learn *what* to say (*res*), they still must know just *how* to say it (*verba*):

> Style to be good must be clear, as is proved by the fact that speech which fails to convey a plain meaning will fail to do just what speech has to do. It must also be appropriate, avoiding both meanness and undue elevation; poetical language is certainly free from meanness, but it is not appropriate to prose. Clearness is secured by using the words . . . that are current and ordinary. (1404b)

What else do we want for our student writers—and for ourselves as well—than clear, appropriate, stylistic communication? Although Aristotle was not so much interested in particular ways of achieving prose style as he was in the invention of arguments, he was interested in the effect of those prose styles; consequently, he lays the groundwork for future studies of *lexis*, the quality of prose style, with which we are all familiar. In the third book of his *Rhetoric*, Aristotle stresses the importance of these stylistic qualities: clarity, including diction, poetic devices (metaphor, simile); correct idiom; impressiveness, including emphasis, rhythm, sentence structure; liveliness, including antithesis, balance, elements of surprise (hyperbole); and propriety—the ideas, if not the actual terms used, in every English handbook today.

Aristotle believed that whatever teachers want their pupils to learn should be available for analysis and imitation. And to that end, he fills his treatise with model sentences that illustrate the various figures of thought and language and the periodic sentence, all grammatical techniques that students should easily recognize from their schooling—particularly in Book III. Written much later than Books I and II, after he had written the *Poetics*, and after style and delivery became concerns of rhetoric, Book III provides specific advice regarding diction (the choice of words, the composition of words into sentences), which came to be known as *synthesis*, "putting together"; that book also offers information about the faults or "frigidities" that come from violating grammatical and stylistic principles. Aristotle devotes the fifth chapter of Book III to *Hellenizein*, or grammatical correctness, writing that "the first principle of *lexis* is to speak good Greek [*to hellenizein*]." And he goes on to explain the five ways to achieve good Greek: by using the correct connectives, by calling things by their specific names, by avoiding equivocation, by observing Protagoras' classification of the gender of nouns, and by the correct naming of plural and singular.

Because good Greek supports *lexis* in terms of appropriate emotion, character, and proportion, "the proper *lexis* also makes the matter credible: the mind [of the listener] draws a false inference of the truth of what a speaker says because they [in the audience] feel the same about such things, so they think the facts to be so, even if they are not as the speaker represents them" (III.7.1408a). By way of explicit examples and clear instructions, Aristotle emphasizes his belief that students' developments in language facility and knowledgeable application, based as they are on close analysis and understanding of language workings, should be applied both to oral speech and to written prose. Hence, *hellenizein* informed delivery (*pronuntiatio*).

Although he encourages application to all compositions, Aristotle does differentiate between spoken style and written style: "The written style is the more finished: the spoken better admits of dramatic delivery—alike the kind of oratory that reflects character and the kind that reflects emotion" (III.7.1413b). Even though the educational aims were to prepare public, political *speakers*, who published their compositions in oral delivery, Aristotle was well aware of the prevalence of written publication as well. Both Gorgias and Isocrates had established a precedent for publishing written, polished versions of the speeches they had earlier delivered. By Aristotle's time, both oral and written publication were in common practice; therefore, he differentiates among the kinds of style for each discourse, concluding that "where there is most need of performance, the least exactness is present" (III.7.1414a). For perfect understanding on the part of the audience, written discourse needed to be exact.

The Roman Language-Arts Program

Building on Aristotle's work, Cicero wrote *De Oratore* (*The Making of an Orator*, c. BCE 55), a treatise devoted primarily to style, particularly in terms of composition. And building on Isocrates' notion of the citizen-orator, Cicero wrote that an orator's style, his composition, expressed the depths of his knowledge in ways mere eloquence simply could not. Because eloquence alone can never demonstrate—let alone bestow—a consequential measure of knowledge, Cicero wants to train the perfect orator in ways that will. Cicero's orator must be educated broadly by means of a liberal language-arts course that envelops eloquence. Eloquence achieved by practice alone is never enough, but when it encompasses a vast knowledge,

> Eloquence is one of the supreme virtues . . . [which] gives verbal expression
> to the thoughts and purposes of the mind in such a manner as to have the
> power of driving the hearers forward in any direction in which it has

applied its weight; and the stronger this faculty is, the more necessary it is
for it to be combined with integrity and supreme wisdom, and if we bestow
fluency of speech on persons devoid of those virtues, we shall not have
made orators of them but shall have put weapons into the hands of madmen.
(III.xiv.55)

Because *De Oratore* is written in the form of a dialogue, we can only
infer what kinds of stylistic exercises Cicero may have asked of the pupils in
his *Progymnasmata*. But we know that, in its entirety, a Roman's preliminary
education would have conducted the student through a course of liberal language arts that disciplined, practiced, prepared, and delivered him into rhetoric. We know that each grammarian disciplined his orators-to-be by means
of the *Progymnasmata*, a graded series of exercises in writing and speaking
originally designed by Aphthonius. Like any useful grammar exercise, these
drill situations moved from the relatively easy to more difficult assignments.
Each exercise depended on those that had preceded it, and also implanted
skills necessary for the future. And all the drill situations were connected
with compositions and with style. But not until the end of his grammar
school career, not until he had mastered the rudiments of style and composing, would a Roman student be assigned a thesis to argue. Thus, everything
that came before his thesis prepared and disciplined him for speaking well.
      Crassus, who is the mouthpiece for Cicero's own opinion, tells Catulus
that "the style must be in the highest possible degree pleasing and calculated
to find its way to the attention of the audience, and . . . it must have the fullest possible supply of facts" (III.xxiv.91). Only a Roman well-educated in
the precepts of a liberal language-arts program could ever hope to achieve
such style. In the face of much opposition regarding the primacy of rhetorical theory or natural ability or practice, Crassus goes on to explain the vital
connection between grammatical or stylistic studies and efficacious oratory:
"the embellishment of oratory is achieved in the first place by . . . a sort of
inherent colour and flavour; for that it shall be weighty and pleasing and
scholarly and gentlemanly and attractive and polished, and shall possess the
requisite amount of feeling and pathos" (III.xxv.96).
      As they move into a more detailed discussion of style, Cicero's charac-
ters discuss the components of a successful oration that students must study
in their language-arts program: diction, lucidity, ornamentation, the lines of
argument, and eloquence. Only a genius could risk forgoing such intense
language study. Even the naturally gifted must study the precepts as well as
the best models of language use. Cicero's Antonius tells how the young and
gifted Suplicius Rufus improved upon his oratory by imitating the style of
Crassus himself: "Assuredly Nature herself was leading him into the grand
and glorious style of Crassus, but could never have made him proficient
enough, had he not pressed forward on that same way by careful imitation,
and formed the habit of speaking with every thought and all his soul fixed in

contemplation of Crassus" (II.xxi.89). Imitation practices, then, are imperative to the development of an orator's style, and Antonius goes on to counsel that

> we show the student whom to copy, and to copy in such a way as to strive with all possible care to attain the most excellent qualities of his model. Next let practice be added, whereby in copying he may reproduce the pattern of his choice . . . . But he who is to proceed aright must first be watchful in making his choice, and afterwards extremely careful in striving to attain the most excellent qualities of the model he has approved. (II.xxii.90–92)

Antonius supports his argument by invoking all the speaking-greats who have followed that course of study: from Pericles and Alcibiades to Demosthenes, Isocrates, and Aeschines. And he warns that whoever "hopes by imitation to attain this likeness, [must] carry out his purpose by frequent and large practice, and if possible, by written composition" (II.xxiii.96), echoing Crassus's earlier pronouncement that "the pen is the best and most eminent author and teacher of eloquence" (I.xxxiii.150). This emphasis on careful and deliberate written composition continues, with Crassus saying "all the thoughts and expressions . . . must needs flow up in succession to the point of our pen; then too the actual marshalling and arrangement of words is made perfect in the course of writing, in a rhythm and measure proper to oratory . . . [for] no man will attain these [the things which in good orators produce applause and admiration] except by long and large practice in writing . . ." (I.xxxiii.151–152). Thus, according to Cicero, students of all ages depended upon these earliest of grammar exercises to underpin their stylistic fluency and their oratorical power as well as to deepen their understanding and appreciation of the inextricable link between grammar and composition.

Later in *De Oratore*, Crassus explains how he had improved his own style by doing double-translation exercises, grammatical exercises akin to imitation:

> I resolved—and this practice I followed when somewhat older,—to translate freely Greek speeches of the most eminent orators. The result of reading these was that, in rendering into Latin what I had read in Greek, I not only found myself using the best words—and yet quite familiar ones—but also coining by analogy certain words such as would be new to our people, provided only they were appropriate. (I.xxxiv.155)

As teachers, most of us will have little opportunity ourselves—let alone the opportunity to require our students—to do double translations. But if we related these exercises to the 1990s, we can reap their benefits. We can ask our students to turn prose into verse and verse back to prose, and we can ask them to paraphrase texts worthy of imitation.

In Corbett's seminar on stylistics, for instance, he regularly asked students to paraphrase, turning to Thomas Whissen's *A Way with Words* for specific assignments that include memorable examples and then new situations for paraphrasing and imitating, such as: "Can you pick out the jargon? identify the clichés? indicate the routine diction? Is the tone sober and sincere? What is the writer really thinking? Write a letter in which you handle a customer complaint of a different kind. Make your own style as bland and innocuous as you can" (Whissen 161–162). Assignments like those of Corbett's are just one way that we too can build our students' appreciation of grammar and composition in concert, just as Crassus has done for himself:

> In my daily exercises of youth, I used chiefly to set myself that task which I knew . . . my old enemy was wont to practise: this was to set myself some poetry, the most impressive to be found, or to read as much of some speech as I could keep in my memory, and then to declaim upon the actual subject-matter of my reading, choosing as far as possible different words. (I.xxxiv.154)

A later work closely associated with (but not written by) Cicero, the *Rhetorica ad Herennium* (c. BCE 84), offers its readers a dictum on the importance of imitation, theory, and practice to the development of competent orators, and the foremost of those is imitation. The *ad Herennium* (or *On the Theory of Public Speaking*) is the first rhetoric to concern itself with the kinds and orders of style as well as the first to taxonomize the stylistic figures. According to the author, imitation is paramount to achieving proficiency in both categories, and he offers the following principle: "imitation stimulates us to attain, in accordance with a studied method, the effectiveness of certain models in speaking" (I.ii.3). The orator should learn to adapt his words to the cause and occasion of the speech, and imitation exercises provide an efficient way to learn just that. In addition, he should be familiar with the three acceptable styles of discourse: the grand style, which is characterized by ornate words, impressive thoughts, and numerous figures; the middle style, which is relaxed, yet not colloquial; and the simple style, which communicates ideas in the most casual of standard language and form. Figures of diction and figures of thought embellish speech, making it more appealing to the audience and more persuasive in its intent. "To be in fullest measure suitable to the speaker's purpose," writes the pseudo-Cicero, "such a style should have three qualities: Taste, Artistic Composition, and Distinction" (IV.xii.17).

In his scanty treatment of composition, the pseudo-Cicero confines his advice to the avoidance of stylistic faults rather than to the construction of any composition theory. He defines "Taste" as a matter of "Correct Latinity and Clarity": "Correct Latinity . . . keeps the language pure, and free of any fault"; "Clarity renders language plain and intelligible" (IV.xii.17); and

"Artistic Composition consists in an arrangement of words which gives uniform finish to the discourse in every part. To ensure this virtue we shall avoid the frequent collision of vowels, which makes the style harsh and gaping . . ." (IV.xii.18). No one knows if this author ever wrote a tract on grammar, but his is the earliest mention in extant literature of a specific Latin *ars grammatica*: "How to avoid these faults I shall clearly explain in my tract on Grammar" (IV.xii.17).

Nearly one hundred years later, Quintilian, too, would emphasize the importance of careful instruction in grammar for developing one's repertoire of styles. In his *De Institutione Oratore* (or *Education of the Orator*, c. 94 AD), Quintilian writes that "only the really eloquent speaker can [say what is necessary] in ornate and appropriate language" (VIII.Pr.13). And hearkening back to Cicero's work, he writes that "Cicero long since laid down this rule in the clearest of language, that the worst fault in speaking is to adopt a style inconsistent with the idiom of ordinary speech and contrary to the common feeling of mankind" (VIII.Pr.25).

Hired by Emperor Vespasian to write and codify the comprehensive Latin statement regarding the education of the citizen-orator, Quintilian emphasized that the ultimate goal of any such training would be eloquence, but his would be a pure eloquence, one refined through a series of demanding, concentrated, and sequential grammatical exercises:

> the verb *eloqui* means the production and communication to the audience of all that the speaker has conceived in his mind . . . . Therefore it is on this that teachers . . . concentrate their attention, since it cannot possibly be acquired without the assistance of the rules of art. It is this which is the chief object of our study, the goal of our exercise and all our efforts at imitation, and it is to this that we devoted the energies of a lifetime; it is this that makes one orator surpass his rivals, this that makes one style of speaking preferable to another. (VIII.Pr.16–17)

The preferable style was clear, elegant Latin, well-adapted to produce the desired effect.

A teacher needed to begin developing stylistic purity and manliness "as soon as a boy is entrusted to him" (I.iii.1–3). Therefore, the *grammaticus* began immediately to ascertain the potential of his charge, realizing that the "surest indication in a child is his power of memory" and that "the indication of next importance is the power of imitation: for this is a sign that the child is teachable: but he must imitate merely what he is taught, and must not, for example, mimic someone's gait or bearing or defects" (I.iii.1). The *grammaticus* worked with his students on reading, writing, speaking, spelling, parts of speech (nouns, verbs, conjunctions, articles, prepositions, adjectives, pronouns, participles, interjections), conjugations, vocabulary, drilling them in the "special rules which must be observed both by speakers and writers" (I.vi.1).

Grammar study could not be separated out of the boys' liberal education like cream or whey. Grammar was a language art; there was no cream to rise to the top, no whey to fall to the bottom. Grammar was a language art, in balance with the rest. Quintilian writes that the language arts were

> so intimately and inseparably connected, that if one of them be neglected, we shall but waste the labour which we have devoted to the others. For eloquence will never attain to its full development or robust health, unless it acquires strength by frequent practice in writing, while such practice without the models supplied by reading will be like a ship drifting aimlessly without a steersman. (X.i.1–3)

Eloquence of composition and delivery was the only goal, and grammar was the only means: ''The judgment of a supreme orator is placed on the same level as reason . . . . Usage however is the surest pilot in speaking, and we should treat language as currency minted with the public stamp'' (I.vi.3).

Quintilian emphasized the investment returns of grammar exercises, especially the returns on a diversified portfolio of imitation exercise:

> I should be reluctant even to advise a student to select one particular author to follow through thick and thin. . . . We shall do well to keep a number of different excellences before our eyes, so that different qualities from different authors [among those he mentions are Euripides, Demosthenes, Cicero, Homer, Plato] may impress themselves on our minds, to be adopted for use in the place that becomes them best. (X.ii.26)

In the classical tradition, Corbett, too, regularly asks students to imitate passages of admirable prose, cautioning them not to spend too much time on any one author. Students are to read through slowly a five-hundred word passage and then copy it out by hand and word-for-word, and he guarantees that they ''will derive the maximum benefit from this copying exercise if [they] practice it over an extended period of time. Transcribing a single different passage every day for a month will prove more beneficial . . . than transcribing several different passages every day for a week. You must have time to absorb what you have been observing in this exercise . . .'' (475–476). And like Quintilian, Corbett cautions teachers and students that not all works by great authors will be of high quality; therefore, students must be sure to choose models judiciously and to imitate the strengths—rather than the flaws—of their speeches.

These grammatical exercises are vital to the education of the ''perfect orator,'' inextricable from the art of composition. When Corbett quotes George Campbell as saying that ''the grammatical art bears much the same relation to the rhetorical which the art of the mason bears to that of the architect'' (389), he again echoes the ancients. Quintilian realized that those external exercises of paraphrasing and imitating must be linked with composition, an internal exercise ''which we must supply for ourselves'': ''it is the pen which brings at once the most labour and most profit. . . . We must therefore write as much as possible and with the utmost care. . . . It is in writing that eloquence has its roots and foundations, it is writing that provides that holy of holies where the wealth of oratory is stored . . .'' (X.i.1–3).

For this court-appointed rhetorician, then, grammar and composition were an indivisible continuum of language growth and proficiency. Thus, it comes as no surprise that he would engage his students in revision of their written compositions, revisions that incorporated their storehouse of grammatical, stylistic, and oratorical knowledge. He writes that

> our pen must be slow yet sure: we must search for what is best and refuse to give a joyful welcome to every thought the moment that it presents itself; we must first criticise the fruits of our imagination, and then, once approved, arrange them with care. . . . In order to do this with the utmost care, we must frequently revise what we have just written. For beside the fact that thus we secure a better connexion between what follows and what precedes, the warmth of thought which has cooled down while we were writing is revived anew, and gathers fresh impetus from going over the ground again. . . . [W]e love all the offspring of our thought at the moment of their birth; were that not so, we should never commit them to writing. But we must give them a critical revision, and go carefully over any passage where we have reason to regard our fluency with suspicion.''
> (X.iii.5–7)

And for the most practical of reasons, Quintilian advises students to write on wax, to facilitate fast and easy-to-erase writing; to leave wide margins for additions, deletions, emendations, notes, and corrections; and to leave plenty of space for other jottings, "for sometimes the most admirable thoughts break in upon us which cannot be inserted in what we are writing, but which, on the other hand, it is unsafe to put by, since they are at times forgotten, and at times cling to the memory so persistently as to divert us from some other line of thought'' (X.iii.31–3).

Convinced that a liberal language-arts curriculum would produce citizen-orators of the highest quality, Quintilian laid out the consummate program for doing just that. A thousand years later, his program would be revived to educate the very best of Renaissance writers and speakers who would be trained in neoclassical precepts.

Renaissance Grammar, Style, and Composition

During the Renaissance, the Golden Age of literature, all the European *literati* acquainted themselves with Greek and Latin classical texts. And their eyes were watching both Italy, the cradle of Renaissance neoclassicism, and Greece, the birthplace of classical learning. The *literati* soon discovered that the medieval perception of the ancients had been badly flawed; for the medieval fashion had been to extract from and modify the classics and classical educational practices in order to substantiate Christian tenets. During the Middle Ages, grammar was the foundation discipline, the gateway to all language study, the supreme language art. Jeffrey Huntsman writes that

> Grammar was thought to discipline the mind and the soul at the same time, honing the intellectual and spiritual abilities that the future cleric would need to read and speak [and write] with discernment. Of course, for all the prominence given grammar in the curriculum, it was but one part of the total sequence of study necessary to prepare a young man for a successful career . . . [for] the properly educated man needed the knowledge slowly accumulated by humankind to thrive in this world and to prepare himself for the next. (59)

Unlike the medieval scholastics and like the ancients themselves, the Renaissance *cognoscenti* regarded education as bound up with politics and society—not with religion—and those politics played themselves out in the written and oral compositions of the day. But whether preparing the boy for his life's career or for his afterlife, grammar was essential for him.

When Virginia Woolf asked "why no woman wrote a word of that extraordinary literature when every other man, it seemed, was capable of song or sonnet" (43), she knew the answer lay in the Renaissance educational practices, the ancient *trivium*, that were available only to young boys, not to young girls. The Renaissance schoolboys who became the greatest wordsmiths in the English language were the products of a language-arts pedagogy underpinned by the grammars of languages. Theirs was a pedagogy conducted in and based on Latin and Greek grammar, grammar studies that kept them focused on individual words and attentive to words in a continuum, to literature. Thus, in the process of studying grammar, Renaissance schoolboys learned classical languages and literature, fundamental language arts that enabled them to translate the King James version of the Bible and to write *In Praise of Folly*, *Utopia*, *Euphues*, *The Faerie Queene*, the *Holy Sonnets*, *Dr. Faustus*, *Hamlet*, *King Lear*, and *Paradise Lost*. Their literary accomplishments grew out of their understanding of the ways language works, their understanding of grammar.

In *Shakespeare's Use of the Language Arts*, Sister Miriam Joseph tells us that the grammar school curriculum prescribed unremitting exercise in grammar, rhetoric, and logic, with grammar dominating the lower forms. In every form, students were to learn the grammatical precepts so they could employ them as a tool of analysis in reading as well as a guide in composition (8–9). By learning to analyze the structure of classical writings—writings by Cicero, Aristotle, Longolius, and Demosthenes—and by performing exercise after grammatical exercise, the students were to be able to generate compositions of their own in *any* of the tongues, original and inventive compositions that demonstrated their language felicity. The essential feature of grammar study, then, lay in its value as a linguistic and a literary discipline that would enhance eloquence in any language.

Renowned Renaissance schoolmaster Roger Ascham, one of the first great masters of a distinctly native English prose style, writes that "because the providence of God hath left us the true precepts in no other tongue except Greek and Latin, we must seek in the authors, only of those two tongues, the true pattern of eloquence, if in any other mother tongue we look to attain, either to perfect utterance of it ourselves, or skillful judgment of it in others" (275). If English were to become as expressive as the ancient tongues, learners would be best served by imitating wisely the practice—speech or writing—of the eloquent ancients.

The didactic curriculum sustaining this pursuit of eloquence was outlined in the aforementioned *Rhetorica ad Herennium*, which Erasmus translated and then reworked into his own *De Copia*. His own text helped maintain the Renaissance enthusiasm for classical literature and the concomitant pedagogy of imitation, and it set the pattern for the English grammar school curriculum. Supporting Erasmus, Ascham wrote that the core of the language-arts curriculum should be the grammatical technique of *imitatio*, "a faculty to express with liveliness and perfection that example that you go about to follow" (234). Students who want to write well in any language, according to Ascham, need to imitate passages of the best writers ("Gods holie Bible," Plato, Aristotle, Xenophon, Isocrates, and Demosthenes), analyzing the use of words, forms of sentences, and handling of material in each selection. For grammar-boys, the rewards of imitation practices would be threefold: a sensitivity to diction, an awareness of form, and an exposure to the finest of ideas.

At St. Paul's school, *alma mater* of Samuel Pepys and John Milton, the schoolmasters were interested in the imitation necessary for their charges to speak and write "clean and chaste Latin." The line was fine between imitation and plagiarism: boys were to demonstrate an ability to imitate, yet nothing should appear borrowed or stolen. Their constant task was taking words, phrases, figures of speech and figures of thought, and turns of ideas as well as turns of expression, from the models they were imitating. And although there was some controversy over the authors to be imitated, Cicero—"not the name of a man but the name of eloquence itself"—was on every list for students at every level. Imitation was a two-step process. After the students analyzed the matter and manner (the precepts) of the literary model, they began the imitative exercises: memorizing, to impress the model in their minds; translating, to improve their command of the mother tongue; and paraphrasing, to improve copiousness.

Those imitative exercises of *analysis* were considered the basis for the imitative exercises of *genesis*. These more advanced exercises introduced the student to the problems of discovering something to say, *invention*, and the problems of giving form to what was being said, *dispositio*. Students could learn either by imitating the best models (Erasmus, Vives, Cicero, Demosthenes) or by following grammar book rules. They began by writing Latin epistles, adjusting their style to the writer, the receiver, and the circumstances. Next, they worked on writing verses, from elegy to eclogue, applying their study of prosody and their imitative skills. The precedents and patterns for their themes came from the "sweetest Latin" and the "choicest matter," and their themes were amplified and adorned with gleanings from the commonplace books they were taught to keep. Students learned how to classify and find arguments and how to write themes according to the *Progymnasmata*, which provided a formulaic sequence of grammatical exercises for analyzing, imitating, or generating language.

In his 1612 *Ludus Literarius*, schoolmaster John Brinsley also supports the grammar-school emphasis on imitation, "For what can a child have in his understanding to be able to conceive or write of, which he has not read or someway known before?" (167). After reading, construing, and parsing Cicero's letters, for example, Brinsley's students were to write a letter in imitation of Tully (Cicero), "using all the phrases and matter of that Epistle; only applying and turning it to some friend, as if they had the very same occasion" (168). On the following day, the students are to write a letter *from* that friend, answering each point and retaining the same phrases. These grammar exercises developed important language skills: the ability to précis, to amplify, and to alter according to occasion and circumstance.

And just as epistles must follow the course set down by Tully, themes must follow the sequential, formulaic course of the *Progymnasmata*. Brinsley goes on to write that by composing imitative themes, students would internalize the forms, frames, and judgments of the best and wisest writers. Students must start with easy themes (in Greek or Latin), using prelection (reading aloud) to understand the meaning, form, and force of each argument. After doing double translation of the theme, students try to gather a short theme of their own, based on the principal sentences, reasons, and order of the original. Students might also examine the arguments in a theme and amplify, find fault with, or mend those arguments, thereby developing a theme that follows the basic pattern and substance of the original. And since the ancients (especially Cicero) provide the best models for patterning themes, students should indicate, in the margins of their translations, the parts of the theme, the important arguments, and the figures and tropes. To be able to express the persuasive arguments, the witty and pithy sayings, or the stylistic flourishes of these "first authors" required much practice in imitation. Thus, when grammar was a language art, then, grammar and composition were so closely aligned, both in study and practice, as to be indivisible, often indistinguishable.

The Art of Grammar

When grammar was a language art, writing was one too, for the "right and proper" use of language was requisite for participating in the intellectual, economic, and political life of the day. And instruction in grammar was the most powerful means of immersing students in the skillful use of language, whether Greek or Latin or English. Students received help in acquiring these language arts and encouragement for practicing them as well.

When students study grammar intensely and purposefully, they learn to analyze, internalize, generalize, and generate structures that stretch beyond their own natural abilities and tendencies. Corbett writes that if students are to improve their style, "they must know the grammar of the language, and they must have an adequate vocabulary" (389). But he also stresses hard work, writing that "precepts [*ars*] and imitation [*imitatio*] can *teach* the student how to write, but it is only by writing [*exercitato*] that the student will *learn* how to write. *One learns to write by writing*. Once is enough to enunciate that truism; but its truth cannot be recalled often enough" (original emphasis, 382). As far back as Quintilian and as far forward as Corbett, then, teachers have realized that intensity pays off.

Yet Quintilian is careful to write that students should not wish to compose better than their nature will permit: "For to make any real advance we need study . . . . [I]t is not merely practice that will enable us to write at greater length and with increased fluency, although doubtless practice is most important. We need judgement as well" (X.iii.15). When teachers believe that grammar, style, and composition are language arts, they believe that those arts are organic entities. As such, the arts not only develop and grow naturally, but they can be improved and beautified with practice.

For the best of language artisans, then, writing well is not an art but a craft, and the tools of this craft are the individual words, taken apart and put together. Thus, for them, the course of grammar studies is a systematic, evolutionary one that ensures students stay on track in the process of learning to write and speak well. Naturally, some teachers have been disappointed in the judgment and sophistication evidenced in the writing of some students, but there is much more evidence for student success.

When grammar was a language art, those educated took care with their language, wrote and spoke in the style of the masters, and realized the importance of close language study. When grammar was a language art, it was presented in a complex, step-wise progression that demanded students analyze, understand, imitate, and generate. Such students were nourished and supported by the conventions of language use and could develop their language arts, for in the process of submitting to the most servile of grammatical exercises, they stopped to savor the language, the wisdom, and the eloquence of the masters. As a result of their painstaking work, language was

de-mystified, and students could develop a range of styles that complemented as well as reinforced the substance of their compositions. Since those
results are the dream of nearly every twentieth-century English teacher, the
age-old study of grammar has implications and applications for us today.

When Corbett asks his students to analyze their own prose in terms of
average sentence-length, average paragraph-length, number of monosyllabic
and multisyllabic words, Anglo-Saxon and Latinate vocabulary, nouns and
pronouns, finite and linking verbs, active and passive verbs, transitive and
intransitive verbs, sentence types, and repeated terms and phrases, he's asking his students to pay careful and informed attention to their individual
words, taken apart and put together.[4] On the surface, such grammar study
might appear to be little more than mindless mechanical activity. But if we
peel away the layers, we find that the process becomes increasingly sophisticated, for to gain any measure of language proficiency, Corbett's students
must possess the means of stepping from something they already know to
something they do not yet know how to do. With *ars, imitatio,* and lots of
exercitato, students can perform much better and improve more quickly than
they would have if left to their own natural development.

When grammar is a language art, then, it marches ahead of the students'
development, assisting them. Grammar study leads them forward, orienting
them toward what they can learn to do well rather than focusing on what they
do wrong (the focus of too much contemporary grammar work). As a language art, grammar study does not guarantee that students will automatically
acquire new grammatical or syntactic forms; however, students do become
aware of what they are doing and learn to apply their skills consciously.
When grammar is a language art, writing is one too. Not surprisingly, the
steps in such a program of grammar-study are closely related to those we
currently stress in our writing classes: following conventions of Edited
American English, using appropriate language, establishing *ethos* and a
voice, attending to the rhetorical situation, building persuasive arguments.
When grammar and writing are language arts, they are sister arts. And in
concert, these sister arts dutifully prepare their young charges for a lifetime
of always competent and often brilliant language performance.

Notes

1. Winifred Bryan Horner's *Rhetoric in the Classical Tradition* and Sharon
Crowley's recent *Ancient Rhetorics for Contemporary Students* also translate the
ancient pedagogy into purposeful plans and sensible exercises that, like Corbett's
book, wisely connect grammar with writing in terms of style and delivery rather than
in terms of "correctness."

2. Corbett's reputation as a task-master never wavered, and yet his seminars
were always full. He always laid out his objectives and requirements on the first day

of class–and made no exceptions. For his ten-week course in stylistics, for instance, he writes:

> This seminar will introduce [students] to a variety of [mostly classical] techniques of (1) analyzing the style of prose passages and (2) practicing various exercises designed to improve one's own style or to help others improve their style. We will start out by analyzing the style of a number of passages of professional prose, primarily to get some idea of what style is and of what to look for when we are studying style. After we acquire a certain adeptness in analyzing the style of other writers, we will do similar analyses of our own prose style. The rest of the seminar will be occupied in doing various kinds of imitative exercises that we can indulge in to improve our own style or that we can engage our students in to help them improve their styles.
>
> There will be three or four short papers (4–6 pages) in which students will analyze the style of some author of their choosing or their own style or will present their response to some of the reading in our texts. The final paper will be a slightly longer paper (6–8 pages) in which the students will present the result of some research they have done in articles and books on some aspect of style that they have chosen to pursue. The page limits on these papers will be strictly enforced. Students who anticipate some difficulty in getting to school in time for an 8:00 [a.m.] class during Winter Quarter are advised not to enroll in this seminar, because I expect enrollees to attend every meeting of the twice-a-week class and to be in their seat, ready to go, when the 8:00 bell rings. Students should also be advised that I do not give Incomplete grades.

In this chapter, I will occasionally refer back to these requirements, requirements that Corbett posted during the harshest Ohio winter of the 1980s. In good weather, my commute took an hour, so that winter, I had to leave home at 5:30 a.m. Nearly all of us were doctoral students in our thirties, "ready to go" by the bell—all but one woman. Corbett asked her to drop the class.

3. The Greeks were simply not as successful in analyzing the structure of language as they were in developing Euclid's geometry and Pythagoras' acoustics; therefore, they didn't come close to establishing anything comparable to Sanskrit grammar studies.

4. A typical assignment in his stylistics seminar.

2

A Question of Power: Why Frederick Douglass Stole Grammar

Jon Olson

Grammar class has long been a site for displaying power. The power differential has usually favored the teachers as they've demonstrated how language should and should not work. The power of grammar teachers over their students was never more evident than in the first century AD when the *paedagogus* would often resort to flogging to help his students learn difficult grammar lessons, a practice that caused Quintilian to write, "I disapprove of flogging, although it is the regular custom" (I.iii.13), for "when children are beaten, pain or fear frequently have results of which it is not pleasant to speak" (I.iii.16). While grammar teachers' methods have varied widely from the Sophistic teachers of the fifth century BC to teachers of the present, it is no exaggeration to say that students of grammar throughout the last twenty-five centuries have not always had an easy time of it, nor have they always enjoyed the experience.

During the Middle Ages and the Renaissance, Grammar was allegorized as a feminine power: "as a nurse giving suck to infants, as a schoolmistress threatening little children with a birch, or as a teacher opening with a key the narrow gate to the tower of knowledge so that little children may enter" (D. Clark 5). Of the three, the threatening schoolmistress is, no doubt, the Grammatica best known to students. She is "the squinting figure" Mike Rose describes "who breathes up to" the sides of students whenever they sit down to write, the one with pincers and scalpel ready to cut out their errors and then grasp them by their necks, leaving these student writers strangled, mouths "open but silent, muted" (1–2).

In many of our classrooms, there seem to be two reasons why grammar cannot be personified as a teacher giving nourishment and the keys to power.

(1) We have moved far from the broad view of grammar taken by the Greeks of antiquity. Even if we view grammar in all five ways Patrick Hartwell defines—as the internalized rules shared by native speakers of a language, as the scientific study of those rules, as the school-book reduction of those scientific rules, as usage, and as style (109–125)—the view is too narrow. The Ancients saw grammar as the study of poetry, history, oratory, and philosophy *in addition to* the aspects of language noted by Hartwell. (2) Even if we support a broad view of grammar which focuses on the ends of language rather than the particulars, we cannot really empower students by opening the tower of language if we keep the key and remain the gatekeepers.

Because our view of grammar remains so narrow, our students continue to see us as "squinting." But Frederick Douglass saw grammar broadly as the Greeks did; therefore, he stole the key of language, let himself into the tower of knowledge, and broke the tower gate wide open. In a sense, *he* flogged Grammatica and broke her birch whip.

He learned to read and write as a self-defining act of aggression. Through force of will and sleight of hand, Douglass literally stole grammar from those who had power to keep him enslaved. Stealing grammar was for Douglass an act of rebellion designed to gain the power with which he could overthrow his oppressors, gain his freedom, and, in the process, sustain his own humanity. By stealing grammar from his masters and from white schoolchildren, he was able to change himself from a slave/animal eating food out of a pig trough to a man who dined with and counseled the President of the United States.

In Douglass's three autobiographies (1845, 1855, 1892), we can see a dramatic example of empowerment gained through autodidactic grammar acquisition. His education can inform the way we see the place of grammar in our own writing classrooms. His experience can validate instruction which has the empowerment of students as its purpose. His example can prompt us to see grammar as it was defined by the grammar teachers of ancient Greece. Douglass's view seems consistent with that found in the Greeks' educational culture, their *paideia*. This view of grammar can help students keep the rhetorical ends of language in focus, keep them from losing sight of the whole while looking too closely at the parts.

Grammar in Ancient Greece

With the Sophists, grammar (as well as rhetoric, dialectic, poetry, and music) had *areté* as its goal—what Werner Jaeger has defined as "intellectual power and oratorical ability" (291). It seems to have been a strikingly different view of grammar than the particularized views we have today. The Greek system of teaching grammar, which by the first century BC had developed from the groundwork of the Sophists, was as arduous as any system students might loathe today. Seven-year-olds who went to a *grammatistes* for grammar instruction in, say, 100 BC Greece were taught to read, write, and count through laborious copying and rote memorization (Kennedy 268), an ordeal more strenuous than the copying and filling in blanks on dittoed sheets that many school children experience today. And after Greek children learned to read and write, they were advanced to the school of the *grammatikos*, a grammarian who taught them Greek language and literature. Grammarians often started their students on rhetorical composition as well, though that was mostly left for the rhetorician to whom the children came for instruction in their mid-teens (Kennedy 268–269).

The methods of teaching grammar in antiquity will not likely inspire us to pedagogical imitation today, for those methods depended on lists, lectures, exercises, and handbooks such as the *Art of Grammar* written by Dionysius Thrax (100 BC), to say nothing of the corporal punishment so common in Roman schools. But the inspiring difference between then and now is curricular. Then, learning grammar meant learning literacy, literary history, and critical thinking about literature (Kennedy 269). Now, learning grammar for most students means learning "how the structural system of a language combines with a vocabulary to convey meaning" (Corbett, *Little English Handbook* 5), which generally involves studying phoneme, syllable, word, phrase, and clause; it does not usually involve studying paragraph, division, and whole composition, which are exclusive to the province of rhetoric (Corbett, *Classical Rhetoric* 383).

For the Sophists in the fifth century BC, learning grammar (and all other subjects) meant increasing political awareness. As Jaeger points out, the Sophists transformed formal and encyclopaedic teaching with a type of education that was political and ethical: "It differed from both the formal and the encyclopaedic methods by treating man not abstractly, as a lone individual, but as a member of the community; and thereby it gave him a firm position in the world of values" (293). The one thing all the Sophists had in common, according to Jaeger, is that they taught "political areté," and they "all wished to instill it by increasing the powers of the mind through training—*whatever they took the training to be*" (293, emphasis added). In this pedagogy, the means—be they encyclopaedic or holistic—seemed entirely subordinate to the end. The end not only justified the means, the means seemed to have been fairly unimportant so long as the powers of the soul were strengthened and humanity was empowered. Such was the case with Frederick Douglass's self-education, starting with grammar.

Grammar and the Education of Frederick Douglass

The *persona* Douglass creates in his three autobiographies represents a pedogogical ideal: a man who gained results from his education. Central to that education was grammar broadly defined—defined in the terms we find as we study classical rhetoric. And Douglass is not an isolated case. Similar educational goals and methods are apparent in the autobiographies of Booker T. Washington (who was born a slave and taught himself to read and write) and Malcolm X (who taught himself to write in prison). By looking closely at the case of Douglass, and then briefly at the complementary cases of Washington and Malcolm X, we can find reason to teach writing with a wide view of grammar that includes the whole apparatus of literary study: critical, historical, and political, as well as linguistic. This view focuses less on methods of instruction and more on goals of realized student empowerment.

In 1827 when Douglass was a nine-year-old slave, he was loaned to his overseer's brother, Hugh Auld, who lived in Baltimore. Mrs. Auld would often read her Bible aloud in her husband's absence. Frederick lived in the house with the Aulds and would creep into hearing distance during those readings. Hearing the poetry of The Book of Job made him wish he could read, and Sophia Auld readily consented to teach him. Having gotten past the alphabet and into spelling three-syllable words, she "exultingly" praised "Freddy's aptness" to her husband and confided her plans to teach the boy to read the Bible. Douglass writes, "Master Hugh was astounded beyond measure and, probably for the first time, proceeded to unfold to his wife the true philosophy of the slave system, and the peculiar rules necessary in the nature of the case to be observed in the management of human chattels" (*Life* 78). He forbade his wife from giving further instruction, telling her it was not only unlawful to teach a slave to read but it was also unsafe. Douglass heard him say,

> "[I]f you give a nigger an inch he will take an ell. Learning will spoil the best nigger in the world. If he learns to read the Bible it will forever unfit him to be a slave. He should know nothing but the will of his master, and learn to obey it. As to himself, learning will do him no good, but a great deal of harm, making him disconsolate and unhappy. If you teach him how to read, he'll want to know how to write, and this accomplished, he'll be running away with himself." (*Life* 79)

His master gave Douglass his most important lesson in grammar, teaching him how language works politically.

Douglass describes how Hugh Auld's words "sank deep into my heart, stirred up sentiments within that lay slumbering, and called into existence an entirely new train of thought." Those words explained some of the perplexing things he'd struggled in vain to understand—"to wit, the white man's power to enslave the black man" (*Narrative* 78). "'Very well,'" he thought. "'Knowledge unfits a child to be a slave'" (*Narrative* 79). "From that moment," he writes, "I understood the pathway from slavery to freedom. . . . Though conscious of the difficulty of learning without a teacher, I set out with high hope, and a fixed purpose, at whatever cost of trouble, to learn how to read" (*Narrative* 78-79). However, Sophia Auld then "set her face as flint against my learning to read by any means" (*Bondage* 96).

His master's wife "became even more violent in her opposition than her husband himself. Nothing seemed to make her more angry than to see me with a newspaper," Douglass writes (*Narrative* 82). She watched him closely:

> If I was in a separate room any considerable length of time, I was sure to be suspected of having a book, and was at once called to give an account of myself. All this, however, was too late. The first step had been taken. Mistress, in teaching me the alphabet, had given me the *inch*, and no precaution could prevent me from taking the *ell*. (*Narrative* 82, *Bondage* 98, *Life* 82–83)

In order to take the ell, he was "compelled to resort to indirections" (*Bondage* 96, *Life* 81).

Douglass describes one plan he adopted—"that of using my young white playmates, with whom I met in the streets, as teachers" (*Bondage* 98). He explains, "I used to carry, almost constantly, a copy of Webster's spelling book in my pocket; and, when sent of errands, or when play time was allowed me, I would step, with my young friends, aside, and take a lesson in spelling" (*Bondage* 98). The book was Noah Webster's *American Spelling Book*, first published in Hartford, Connecticut, in 1783, under the title *A Grammatical Institute of the English Language*. It was the standard nineteenth-century text of its kind. In another pocket, he carried bread taken from his master's table to pay his "tuition fee" to the boys: "For a single biscuit, any of my hungry little comrades would give me a lesson more valuable to me than bread" (*Bondage* 98). "When I was sent of errands, I always took my book with me, and by going one part of my errand quickly, I found time to get a lesson before my return" (*Narrative* 82). By trading bread to white boys in exchange for lessons from Webster's book, Douglass learned to read.

A growing awareness of social politics seemed to accompany his growing skill in reading. During the lessons in grammar and spelling, which he furtively took from "hungry little urchins" in the street "at different times and in different places," he would often bring up the subject of slavery. "I would, sometimes, say to them, while seated on a curb stone or a cellar door, . . . 'You will be free, you know, as soon as you are twenty-one, and can go where you like, but I am a slave for life. Have I not as good a right to be free as you have?'" Such words seemed to genuinely trouble the boys. Douglass observes, "I do not remember ever to have met with a *boy*, while I was in slavery, who defended the slave system; but I have often had boys to console me, with the hope that something would yet occur, by which I might be made free." His grammar teachers identified with him and told him they believed he had "as good a right to be free as *they* had." They hoped for his empowerment—which was indeed developing as their discussions of spelling and grammar blended with issues of social equality: "The reader will easily see, that such little conversations with my play fellows, had no tendency to weaken my love of liberty, nor to render me contented with my condition as a slave" (*Bondage* 98–99).

By the time Douglass was thirteen years of age (the age of the book's character; the author was actually twelve), and having learned to read, he was searching for anything he could find to read about the free states. He acquired a book the white boys in the street were using at school which gave him hope of freedom. The book was an anthology of speeches and a grammar of eloquence combined, compiled by Caleb Bingham, under the full title of *The Columbian Orator: Containing a Variety of Original and Selected Pieces, Together with Rules; Calculated to Improve Youth and Others in the Ornamental and Useful Art of Eloquence*. First published in Boston in 1797, it became the standard work of its kind during the next few decades as it went through numerous editions. The young slave who fourteen years later would become the consummate stylist of the *Narrative of the Life of Frederick Douglass, an American Slave, Written by Himself* now began learning his argumentative essayist craft as he read the book, which included selections such as "one of [Richard Brinsely] Sheridan's mighty speeches, on the subject of Catholic Emancipation [a speech which actually may have been "Part of Mr. O'Connor's Speech in the Irish House of Commons, in Favour of the Bill for Emancipating the Roman Catholics, 1795"], Lord Chatham's speech on the American war, and speeches by the great William Pitt and by [Charles James] Fox" (*Bondage* 100, *Life* 85). As stirring as those speeches were, what affected Douglass most profoundly seems to have been a brief, three-page dialogue between a master and a runaway slave. The slave argues triumphantly against slavery. At the end of the dialogue, the master admits the errors of his own logic and emancipates the slave.

Douglass writes that he read the speeches, dialogues, poems, and essays of *The Columbian Orator* over and over "with unabated interest," and they "added much to my limited stock of language"—especially the abolitionist entries which "gave tongue to interesting thoughts of my own soul, which had frequently flashed through my mind, and died away for want of utterance. . . . The more I read, the more I was led to abhor and detest my enslavers" (*Narrative* 84). He not only let the words he read give expression to his own thoughts, he took Caleb Bingham's stylistic advice to heart, especially regarding antitheses and apotheses, as he later showed in his own writing (Gates 232, n. 18). At the time he overheard Hugh Auld scolding his wife for teaching a slave how to read, Douglass discovered that control of language—the goal of grammar study—meant control of power. Bingham's introduction to the book reinforced that lesson. A good man speaking well equaled power, and Bingham invoked Cicero to make the point. Bingham describes what happened when Caesar, having won through battle "the empire of the world," heard Cicero speak. The power of Cicero's words sent Caesar into "such a fit of shivering, that he dropped the papers which he

held in his hand'' (9). Bingham equated language power with language correctness: ''The best judges among the ancients have represented Pronunciation, which they likewise called Action, as the principal part of an orator's
province'' (7). The lesson was clear. If Douglass could say the words correctly, he could act. He could make slaveholders shiver and drop the deeds
of human ownership they held in their hands.

For Douglass, the mechanics of correct pronunciation went together with
the ''mighty power and heart-searching directness of truth'' (*Bondage* 100,
Life 85). But while reading freed his mind, his body remained enslaved. The
discontentment Hugh Auld had predicted arrived with ''unutterable anguish'':
''I would at times feel that learning to read had been a curse rather than a
blessing. It had given me a view of my wretched condition, without the
remedy. . . . In moments of agony, I envied my fellow-slaves for their stupid-
ity'' and ''often wished myself a beast. . . . Any thing, no matter what, to get
rid of thinking'' (*Narrative* 84). The agony of critical awareness without
freedom was so intense that he found himself ''wishing myself dead; and but
for the hope of being free, I have no doubt but that I should have killed myself,
or done something for which I should have been killed'' (*Narrative* 85).

In this ''wretched'' and ''unhappy state of mind,'' he was ''keenly sen-
sitive to know any and everything possible that had any relation to the subject of slavery.'' He was ''all ears, all eyes'' when white people discussed
slavery. During such discussions, the word *abolitionists* frequently came up,
but Douglass had no idea who or what abolitionists were—except that they
were ''cordially hated and abused by slaveholders of every grade'' and were
blamed for every act of violence or crime committed by a slave. Recognizing from the socio-linguistic context that *abolition* ''was not unfriendly to
the slave, nor very friendly to the slaveholder,'' Douglass set out to define
this new item of vocabulary. The dictionary offered little help: ''It taught me
that abolition was 'the act of abolishing,' but it left me in ignorance at the
very point where I most wanted information, and that was, as to the thing to
be abolished'' (*Bondage* 103, *Life* 88). ''After a patient waiting,'' however,
he ''got one of our city papers [*The Baltimore American*], containing an
account of the number of petitions from the north, praying for the abolition
of slavery in the District of Columbia, and of the slave trade between the
States.'' Having an understanding now of what *abolition* and *abolitionist*
meant, he ''always drew near when that word was spoken, expecting to hear
something of importance to myself and fellow-slaves'' (*Narrative* 85).

Thus he continued to strengthen a basic grammatical category—his
vocabulary—by stealing words and meanings from white people. He never
disclosed his purpose even when white people seemed friendly. One day at
the wharf, he helped two Irishmen unload some ballast from a boat. When
the men learned he was ''a slave for life,'' they seemed ''deeply affected''
and advised him to run away to the north where he would find abolitionist
friends and would ''be as free as anybody'' (*Bondage* 107, *Life* 92). He

"pretended not to be interested" fearing they "might be treacherous. White men have been known to encourage slaves to escape, and then, to get the reward, catch them again and return them to their masters" (*Narrative* 86). But he nevertheless remembered their advice and resolved to run away. Before doing so, however, he "wished to learn how to write, as I might have occasion to write my own pass" (*Narrative* 86, *Bondage* 107, *Life* 92). He now not only had the "hope of freedom" but also "a foreshadowing of the means" by which he could attain it (*Bondage* 107, *Life* 92). Having learned to read, he set about "taking an *ell*" and "running away with himself" as his master, Hugh Auld, had predicted.

He discovered how he might learn to write while he was doing odd jobs in the shipyard where Auld worked. Douglass noticed that when the ship carpenters were getting a piece of lumber ready for use, they would mark it for whichever side of the ship it was intended: *S* for starboard, *L* for larboard, *L.F.* for larboard forward, *L.A.* for larboard aft, *S.A.* for starboard aft, and *S.F.* for starboard forward. He would copy those four letters when the carpenters would go to dinner and leave him to keep the fire burning under the steam box. When he could easily make those letters, he then "entered the lists . . . in the art of writing" (*Bondage* 107) with the white boys around the churchyard, in the street, or on the playgrounds:

> When I met with any boy who I knew could write, I would tell him I could write as well as he. The next word would be, "I don't believe you. Let me see you try it." I would then make the letters which I had been so fortunate as to learn, and ask him to beat that. In this way I got a good many lessons in writing, which it is quite possible I should never have gotten in any other way. (*Narrative* 87)

By tricking white boys into becoming teachers, and by using "fences and pavements for . . . copybooks" and "chalk for . . . pen and ink," Douglass "learned the art of writing" (*Bondage* 107).

Forming letters and spelling words correctly were a part of grammar exercises then as they are today, and he therefore used a spelling book to help him adopt "various methods for improving my hand. The most successful was copying the italics in *Webster's Spelling-Book* until I could make them all without looking on the book" (*Life* 93). His handwriting as an adult, which had a marked italic slant to the right, evinced this early method of improving his penmanship. By the time Frederick had accomplished italics writing, Master Tommy was old enough to be bringing home copybooks from school. Tommy's proud parents would show the books to the neighbors, then would put them away and forget about them. On Monday afternoons when Mrs. Auld would go to the meetinghouse, leaving Frederick to take care of the house, he would get out the books and with pen and ink copy Tommy's writing between the lines. From Tommy's copybooks, he graduated to copying passages from the Bible, the Methodist hymnal, and other books he could get hold of late at night when everyone else in the house was asleep. "Thus," he writes, "after a long, tedious effort for years, I finally succeeded in learning how to write" (*Narrative* 87). True to his resolve, he did write himself a pass, and he escaped to the north by ship.

Douglass's Spartan methods of self-education were, of course, not exceptional. The grim stories of two other self-taught African-American leaders—Booker T. Washington and Malcolm X—are well known. Washington describes how he began learning to read by noticing numbers placed on barrels in the salt factory where he worked as a child. Later, he taught himself more by means of an edition of the same spelling and grammar book Douglass had used:

> Webster's "blue-back" spelling-book, which contained the alphabet, fol-
> lowed by such meaningless words as "ab," "ba," "ca," "da." I began at
> once to devour this book, and I think that it was the first one I ever had in
> my hands. I had learned from somebody that the way to begin to read was
> to learn the alphabet, so I tried in all the ways I could think of to learn
> it,–all of course without a teacher, for I could find no one to teach me. At
> that time there was not a single member of my race anywhere near us who
> could read . . . . (43)

Perhaps the most famous exemplar of this tiresome autogogy in the twentieth century is Malcolm X, who copied a dictionary while in prison. Although the scope of his copying seems more daunting than that of Douglass's, Malcolm X didn't risk getting a flogging as Douglass did. The lack of danger might have made the enterprise more dull, but the lack of alternatives could have made it more challenging. Be that as it may, it is hard to imagine a more demanding method of learning grammar than to copy, with pencil and tablet, every page of a dictionary. How could *aardvark* possibly spring to life for this man in prison as he copied that word and its etymology in order "to improve my penmanship" (172), and then kept copying day after day until he'd worked his way through the *Z* section and on into the "new world" opened up by the books he could now for the first time read? How could that slavish copying achieve a facility with language—the grammar of power— which enabled him to say of those prison days, "I never had been so truly free in my life" (173)? Not because Malcolm X—or Washington or Douglass— wisely adopted the method of laborious copying advocated by the *gramma-tistes* and the *grammatikos*. Rather, the answer would seem to be that these men, who were hungry for language learning, took a large view of grammar, a view shared by grammarians of antiquity, such as Dionysius Thrax, who defined grammar as an acquaintance with the ideas communicated by writers of poetry and prose, a process of learning which not only involved exegesis of tropes, explanations of historical references, and practice of inflexions, but which also emphasized reading in order to analyze meaning, judge value, and define self (Kennedy 269; Sextus Empiricus 1.248–252).

Like Dionysius Thrax before him, Booker T. Washington during his lifetime, and Malcolm X after him, Frederick Douglass saw grammar not as a specialized study of language structure from phoneme to clause, an activity which for many students inevitably seems to kill language; he saw grammar as the way to gain freedom and sustain himself as a human being. His autodidactic experience reminds us how important it can be to keep the ends of language in view when we consider the place of grammar within our writing instruction.

Grammar and the Empowerment of Students

Patrick Hartwell's seminal essay on the place of grammar in writing instruction is generally remembered for its definitions of grammar and for its survey of research. Its conclusion is easy to overlook, especially with the relatively limp final sentence about how it is time teachers formulate theories of language, let those theories guide their teaching, and then move on to more interesting areas of inquiry. The penultimate sentence, however, flexes: "At no point in the English curriculum is the question of power more blatantly posed than in the issue of formal grammar instruction" (127). The consensus he detects from within the field of composition is that "the thrust of current research and theory is to take power from the teacher and to give that power to the learner" (127). That is a lesson we can learn from the education of Frederick Douglass.

Grammar may have a place in writing instruction insofar as it can help transfer power from teachers to students. The power will not be freedom from rules of usage; rather, the rules will be contextualized, subordinated to the ends of political areté, i.e., language used as an act of intellectual and ethical power to sustain freedom within a community. Hartwell's seemingly exhaustive survey of myriad empirical studies shows that grammar instruction has no positive effect on writing and can have a significant negative effect if it leads writers to become too concerned, too soon, with grammatical accuracy. Owning and using language improves writing more than instruction in grammar.

One hardly needs to review all the research and scholarship Hartwell surveys in order, say, to see the difference between Walter and Rita, the cases studied by Nancy Sommers. As you'll remember, Walter was an experienced writer who could restart the plan-write-revise cycle at any time during his writing process, and many of the ideas in his final draft were not present in his first draft; Rita was a less experienced writer who was unable to do what Walter could do because she thought she needed to follow certain school-taught rules. Rita was like the "unskilled" college writers Sondra Perl studied who seemed to think that revising was essentially editing—the application of conscious rules to small points of grammar. As Perl notes, their editing–what Stephen D. Krashen calls "monitoring" language output

(15–20)—broke "the rhythm generated by thinking and writing," causing them to "lose track of their ideas" (333).

The only thing Hartwell claims to *prove* is that empirical research won't resolve the debate over whether grammar instruction improves writing. Updating the essay Hartwell wrote ten years ago won't alter the view of teachers who are convinced that the writing skills of today's youth are in steady decline and the only remedy is a red pen deftly wielded. The issue, however, may not have much to do with the red pen, which is merely an instrument of a certain methodology. Discussions of teaching methods surely have much value, but the case of Frederick Douglass, and the example of the Sophists, give us reason to think that the issue of language power transcends the particularities of methodology.

I remember a particular seminar I conducted at my university for faculty who were going to teach writing-intensive courses in their various disciplines. One professor in the field of management and marketing told us about his experience with writing when he came out of college and entered industry. His supervisor took him aside and said, "You can't write worth a damn." The supervisor proceeded to cut the worthless writing to pieces with a red pen until his employee "learned to write." The professor told the story with a modest degree of pride, noting that the method had worked on him and ought to work on university students as well. If we take the view of literacy theorist Frank Smith, however, what seems to have led to improved writing wasn't due to the method of instruction so much as it was due to the ritual of initiation into the club of writers within that particular industry. The young man wanted to join the club of industry professionals, and one of the club members showed him a way to gain fully empowered membership. As Smith writes, teachers need to "show the advantages that membership of the club of writers offers and help students join" (564)—not just open the narrow gate to the tower but hand over the key and open up windows.

Douglass (and Malcolm X and Booker T. Washington) wanted to join the writers' club because membership in that club would supply the means to join another club, a social one of members with equal opportunities to pursue freedom and other liberties. It was a club which theretofore had excluded members of Douglass's race. He needed a membership which empowered him with the opportunity to change the club's policies.

How do we teachers help students *want* to join the club of writers? There is no easy answer to that question, but a focus on errors in form seems inherently more *ex*clusive than *in*clusive. Simply inviting students to join the status quo may not work, either. Such an invitation preserves our own power, seeks to make students like us, doesn't cause *us* to change. Empowering students might mean taking a risk ourselves, perhaps risking language usage as we know it and thereby destabilizing our own power base. We can hardly complain about how Johnny can no longer write like we do, and we can hardly belittle him for being amongst the two thirds of culturally illiterate

American seventeen-year-olds who don't know the Civil War occurred between 1850 and 1900 (Hirsch 8), then expect him to *want* to learn to write like we do. As Hartwell implies, writing teachers may be teaching grammar for the purpose of keeping their power structure efficiently in place.

Douglass's case would suggest that students will pursue whatever gives them genuine access to power within the community they want to join. But Robert Pattison observes, in an often quoted passage, that they are impatient with the minutia:

> The same students who resolutely remain in darkness about the niceties of correct English grammar are as capable of intelligence as any previous generation. They are only selective about what niceties they choose to observe. Months of exercises will not shake their nonchalance about commas, but few are likely to misspell the name Led Zeppelin. (202)

The concerns of methodology are not the most important issues here.

Jon Katz more recently describes how and why youth are "abandoning conventional journalism in stunning and accelerating numbers": "from rock to rap, TV to computers—and now especially cable—the young are fighting for and building their own powerful media. And the grown-ups—and their media—hate it" (47). The trend he describes parallels the one E. D. Hirsch decries where youth seem to have abandoned the conventional values which support a literate culture. Katz could be writing about English teachers' customary attitude toward their students' language values when he says that the traditional media should not be surprised that it can no longer reach the young. After all, he writes,

> It's hard to think of anything the industry could have done to ignore or alienate younger consumers that it didn't do—or isn't doing still. It has resisted innovative design, clung to its deadly monolithic voice, refused to broaden or alter its definitions of news and—most importantly—trashed the culture of the young at every opportunity. (48)

According to Katz, journalism's attitude has been, "Whatever we publish and broadcast, kids should read and watch. If they don't, they're dumb" (48). But now, this "dumb" generation is revolutionizing the media through cable and by computer networks, through their own power. It doesn't seem incidental that electronic mail is a discourse medium which allows writers, both in academic and in nonacademic contexts, to privilege speed in communicating ideas over mechanical accuracy of form. Nonconventional media such as rock, rap, cable, and electronic networks allow young people who are marginalized by the culture in power to shape language toward powerfully persuasive ends while sidestepping the traditional language conventions controlled by fogies.

Research would seem to indicate that we will be more likely to motivate students to write if we emphasize the ends of language instead of its parts.

James Thurber portrays a writing teacher—Grammatica with a scalpel—who was most interested in the parts of language:

> Miss Groby taught me English composition . . . . It wasn't what prose said that interested Miss Groby; it was the way prose said it. The shape of a sentence crucified on a blackboard (parsed, she called it) brought a light to her eye. . . . You remember her. You must have had her, too. Her influence will never die out of the land. (167)

Frederick Douglass was motivated by the ends of language, and he found a way to acquire the skills that would help him gain those ends. It was, after all, a question of power (Hartwell 127). By stealing grammar, Douglass stole power.

Many of our students are modern slaves of ignorance—ignorance of minute language conventions guarded, for the most part, by an exclusive club of writers. If we, like the Greeks, emphasize the ends of language, we might inspire these students to believe that writing is a key to empowerment just as it was for Frederick Douglass.

3

Reasserting Grammar's Position in the Trivium in American College Composition

Gina Claywell

College composition instruction in America is increasingly focusing on rhetoric and logic (dialectic), two of the medieval liberal arts codified in the trivium by writers such as Martianus. The third art, grammar, is a subject no longer considered by many theorists or practitioners to be an "art" that should be taught at the university level. Throughout the history of rhetoric, the three elements of the classical trivium have either congenially and effectively overlapped or completely and disastrously digressed; when one dominated, the others traditionally suffered. While such an elevation of one of the trivium components at the expense of another is not new, why such developments occur—and more specifically why grammar has been all but discarded in composition/rhetoric courses as well as what the ramifications of such actions are needs to be questioned. As Patricia Moody suggests in her reassessment of the legacy of Charles C. Fries, ". . . it is altogether appropriate to take stock to see if grammatical history can provide any insights into where we have been, where we went wrong, and why" (v). Moody's work states that Fries may have negatively affected contemporary views of grammar with his approach: ". . . the unfavorable attitude toward previous English grammatical study which Fries' work encouraged is an unfortunate heritage with serious implications for the historical study of English grammar, for pedagogy, and not the less for the history of ideas" (190).

Today, composition instructors are in danger of repeating past mistakes on two fronts: first, we run the risk of being open to historical fallacies if we fail to question (and, indeed, to be knowledgeable about) the histories of our field, and second, we may be shortchanging our students if we continue to disassociate grammatical concerns from the instruction of writing. Composition instruction stands to benefit the most when the three elements of the trivium are reunited into a coherent strategy for teaching effective written communication. This chapter (with much indebtedness to Patricia Bizzell and Bruce Herzberg's *The Rhetorical Tradition: Readings from Classical Times to the Present*) briefly traces the placement of grammar within the history of rhetoric and composition, especially American college composition courses, and it asserts the need for reinserting grammar instruction into the rhetorical trivium.

In the classical period, students studied under grammarians before learning rhetoric, and Bizzell and Herzberg suggest that Isocrates' very successful methods were crucial in establishing what later became the trivium (298, 43). Varro, a contemporary of Cicero, developed a list of liberal arts necessary to education comparable to that which Martianus later produced (Bizzell and Herzberg 370). Sue Carter Simmons notes that it is significant that James J. Murphy claims for the classical period many of the curricular inventions often claimed by twentieth-century scholars: ". . . the Roman writing classroom was interactive, integrating all the language arts and using peer response and criticism" (516–517). Furthermore, it was not unusual, according to Bizzell and Herzberg, to find grammar students analyzing poetry for examples of both correct grammar and tropes and figures (374).

The development of *ars poetriae* in the medieval period saw the introduction of prescriptive handbooks alongside descriptive formulas so that rhetoric and grammar seemed to be merged (Bizzell and Herzberg 374). In the rhetoric courses of both the classical period and the medieval period, several similarities existed: both were ". . . taught in the classroom, based on the memorization and imitation of texts, and expressed in giving voice as much to those who could not persuade as to those who did prevail" (Woods 94).

The medieval period brought the reorganization of Martianus' liberal arts list by Cassiodorus during the 6th century C E, so that rhetoric came between grammar and dialectic (logic), ". . . thus suggesting that the study of rhetoric is preliminary to the study of dialectic" (Bizzell and Herzberg 371). The seven branches of arts were further outlined in the seventh-century work of Isidore (Bizzell and Herzberg 371). In the twelfth century, Bernard of Chartres taught grammar and rhetoric according to his student, John of Salisbury; Bernard's students daily memorized passages and wrote short compositions about those readings, and, according to Marjorie Curry Woods, Bernard conscientiously explained rhetorical choice to his students (80–81). Such techniques continued to be used throughout the Renaissance period.

Ramus reiterates the significance of the trivium but also the necessity for each to have its own areas of study (although he relegates grammar and rhetoric to subservient roles):

The whole of dialectic concerns the mind and reason, whereas rhetoric and grammar concern language and speech. Therefore dialectic comprises, as proper to it, the arts of invention, arrangement, and memory ... To grammar for the purposes of speaking and writing well belong etymology in interpretation, syntax in connection, prosody in the pronunciation of short and long syllables, and orthography in the correct rules for writing. From the development of language and speech only two proper parts will be left for rhetoric, style, and delivery. (quoted in Bizzell and Herzberg 570)

For Ramus, logic gets the upper hand while grammar and rhetoric serve logic.

In many ways, this distribution of emphasis shifted during the Enlightenment period so that grammar eventually enjoyed one of its heydays. Nevertheless, despite the "new grammar books [which] were full of rules, proper models, and errors to be corrected," certain scholars, such as Joseph Priestley, denounced the prescriptive role grammar was taking: "The prevailing custom ... can be the only standard for the time it prevails" (quoted in Bizzell and Herzberg 648). Rhetoricians began including "the study of grammar, speculation about the history of language, investigation into the relationship between language and knowledge, and a practical and influential interest in dialectical differences" into their studies (Bizzell and Herzberg 648).

One of the passages from George Campbell's influential *The Philosophy of Rhetoric* published in 1776, "where grammar ends eloquence begins," was often misinterpreted and misapplied by subsequent generations of composition instructors to suggest that grammar must be learned before one can become eloquent (quoted in Bizzell and Herzberg 755). Rather, an examination of Campbell's preceding passage shows that his position is more closely allied with that of Ramus:

the grammarian, with respect to what the two arts have in common, the structure of sentences, requires only purity; that is, that the words employed belong to the language, and that they be construed in the manner, and used in the signification, which custom hath rendered necessary for conveying the sense. The orator requires *also* beauty and strength. The highest aim of the former is the lowest aim of the latter; where grammar ends eloquence begins. (quoted in Bizzell and Herzberg 754–755, emphasis added)

Thus, Campbell, as Ramus had before him, merely sets up the boundaries of the two disciplines, rhetoric and grammar. The successful orator (or rhetorician or writer) must "be master of the language he speaks or writes, and must be capable of adding to grammatic purity those higher qualities of elocution which will render his discourse graceful and energetic" (quoted in Bizzell and Herzberg 755). It is not enough, Campbell suggests, to be correct, nor is it possible to achieve eloquence without correctness. And while eloquence (rhetoric) involves "higher qualities of elocution," this does not suggest that those qualities must not be taught until accuracy is achieved, because as both Campbell and Priestley had recognized, grammar is arbitrary: ". . . proper usage is 'national and reputable and present'" (quoted in Bizzell and Herzberg 748).

By 1801, notions of the possibility of a universal grammar were beginning to take shape in the work of Destutt de Tracy, who continues the trivium divisions within his definition of philosophy; universal grammar, logic, and ideology combine to form philosophy. Such notions had allowed grammar briefly to take precedence over logic in French universities in 1795 (Bizzell and Herzberg 646).

In 1828, Richard Whately reiterates the notion that grammar followed current use, not the opposite: "No one complains of the rules of Grammar as fettering Language; because it is understood that correct use is not founded on Grammar, but Grammar on correct use. A just system of Logic or of Rhetoric is analogous, in this respect, to Grammar" (quoted in Bizzell and Herzberg 838).

The relative importance of the three trivium elements continued to be of concern in America in 1867 with Henry N. Day's *The Art of Discourse*, but under Day the role of grammar seems almost contradictory. He acknowledges the goal of grammar is not to study it for itself: "Grammar should be studied as an art rather than as a science, since the more important object, by far, to be attained by the study, especially if the grammar be that of one's vernacular tongue, is skill in speaking and writing the language, not skill in interpreting discourse" (quoted in Bizzell and Herzberg 869). Nevertheless, he makes more of a case than Campbell for learning grammar before one can acquire rhetorical skill:

> Grammar, thus, is conditional to rhetoric; but not, like logic, aesthetics, and ethics, conditional as a science, but as an art elementary and constitutive. It stands much in the relation to rhetoric in which arithmetic stands to mensuration. It is rudimental, preliminary, and introductory to the proper art of discourse. It should be familiarly understood by the student of discourse before he commences this art. (quoted in Bizzell and Herzberg 869)

Despite this emphasis on grammar as the basic knowledge needed for discourse, "The college-level rhetoric texts before about 1875 paid almost no attention to grammar" (Kitzhaber 191). The task of teaching grammar was assumed to have been accomplished in the earlier grades. For A. S. Hill, who wrote *The Principles of Rhetoric* in 1878 and revised it in 1895, "getting it right" becomes a necessity; grammar and usage take precedence in the front of the book, and rhetoric becomes "the art of efficient communication" (Bizzell and Herzberg 664). Bizzell and Herzberg point out that such concern for accuracy—mirrored, perhaps, in today's business writing environment—led to the prescriptive teaching styles so often associated with college composition:

> The "current-traditional" model of composition teaching that was thus created in the last years of the nineteenth century combines Bain's modes of discourse and paragraph unity with Hill's prescriptiveness in grammar, usage, and style. This stripped-down rhetoric was a necessity because of the large number of students and the constant turnover of new instructors who needed clear guidelines on how to teach a subject that they generally hoped to leave behind as soon as possible. (664–665)

Hill's grammar is one of several sciences closely associated with rhetoric: "Rhetoric is distinct from every form of grammar, and everywhere presupposes grammatical accuracy" (quoted in Bizzell and Herzberg 880).

By the last quarter of the nineteenth century, dissonant voices could be heard, voices such as William Dwight Whitney's, whose *Essentials of English Grammar* of 1877 suggests that we should not study grammar in order to learn correct usage; rather, grammar should be "the reflective study of language, for a variety of purposes, of which correctness of writing is only one, and a secondary or subordinate one—by no means unimportant, but best attained when sought indirectly" (quoted in Kitzhaber 198).

The Enlightenment period, then, saw very different distinctions drawn between grammar, logic, and rhetoric, with an overall emphasis heretofore unseen on grammar and accuracy, despite occasional discordant opinions. During the early years of the twentieth century, grammar instruction became a central concern of the composition classroom, drawing from both the instructors' interpretation of the faculty psychology of Scottish Common Sense philosophy (Berlin 1984) and their interpretation of previous generations of rhetoric scholars about the relative importance of grammar and accuracy. Traditional composition histories tell us that the prevailing attitude that students learned best via drill and rote delivery dominated composition instruction; grammar, more specifically, usage, would be a necessary prerequisite to writing. While we today feel such tactics to be inefficient and often useless, we perhaps need to lay less blame on the instructors than on the interpretations they and the scholars who informed them made of the materials available. For instance, Moody's study of Fries' 1925 dissertation claims that ". . . Fries skewed his assessment of nineteenth-century scholarship . . ." (viii). In so doing, Moody says, Fries encouraged "a general image of traditional grammars as uniformly arbitrary, Latinate, and prescriptive" (viii). Too often, we and our predecessors have also been guilty of assuming that what was most often taught was what was always taught, and we do not allow for individual differences among instructors and schools. For instance, many instructors were beginning to require additional hands-on writing practice, including the writing of business and social letters in the 1880s (Kitzhaber 212).

Furthermore, Heidemarie Weidner reveals that individual instructors at Butler in the nineteenth century encouraged writing across the curriculum, daily writings, teacher-student conferences, and peer evaluation (299).

Weidner claims that activities such as "declamations, orations, disputations, written exercises and compositions" kept Notre Dame "students from sitting passively in class, merely regurgitating memorized information, a method of learning used in contemporary colleges subscribing to instruction by recitation" (300). Additionally, Simmons points to Michael Halloran's discovery of peer criticism at eighteenth- and nineteenth-century American colleges, including Princeton (160). And rule numbers and sets of correction symbols for themes were being developed, not perhaps as methods to ensure prescriptive approaches to the teaching of writing as much as to help instructors handle the increasing workload from "the growing size of classes, and of more frequent composition assignments" (Kitzhaber 212). College enrollments were increasing, and longer assignments revealed the necessity to begin incorporating grammar into the curriculum of the college composition course, therein further increasing the workload: "It soon became obvious that college English teachers could not, after all, resign the job of grammar instruction exclusively to the lower level schools" (Kitzhaber 187, 196). Thus, grammar began appearing in college textbooks in the 1880s.

But in the 1890s ". . . nearly all the college-level rhetoric texts temporarily abandoned grammar" (Kitzhaber 196). Indeed, the 1890s became a period of diminished emphasis on grammar and accuracy as ". . . the paragraph and the whole composition took precedence over the sentence and smaller unit . . ." (Kitzhaber 199). Again, voices arose decrying the inordinate amount of attention grammar had traditionally received. Gertrude Buck and O. F. Emerson claimed that grammar was almost universally disfavored (Kitzhaber 195–196), with Emerson stressing the arbitrary nature of grammar and the importance of that knowledge for the classroom:

> The teacher should know and emphasize the fact that grammar is the description of a more or less unstable and changing medium of expression; that language is not hedged about by any divinity, but is merely a human institution, subject to human infirmity and human caprice; that what is grammatically correct in one age may not be in the next; that changes in language proceed along certain lines and under certain influences, a full understanding of which could not fail to make the study of grammatical relations more interesting and effective. (quoted in Kitzhaber 197)

The tide soon turned, however, and grammar again renewed its prominence in the classroom, due in part, according to Kitzhaber, to the Harvard English entrance examination: ". . . there was an increased insistence on rhetorical and grammatical correctness as the most important qualities in student writing," so that "grammar and mechanics usurped nearly the whole field" of rhetoric (199, 200).

Weidner, however, questions Kitzhaber's conclusions about the instruction of the period: "The Kitzhaber narrative concluded that during the late nineteenth century writing instruction bowed to business and industry and in

doing so lost much of its integrity, substituting demands for superficial correctness for the art of true communication,'' yet

> material examined at Butler and Notre Dame does not allow conclusive
> generalizations about the shift to mechanical correctness that so many com-
> position historians observe. Although the term ''correct expression'' occurs
> frequently throughout the time period studied, it denotes accuracy of
> expression resulting from clear thinking rather than felicitous grammar,
> spelling, or punctuation. (Weidner 305–306)

Weidner examined actual student papers and diaries and discovered that correction marks were rare, if they existed at all (306).

Conflicting responses and alternative pedagogies were being seen elsewhere, as we are increasingly discovering through revisionist composition
histories. For instance, Scott and Buck's *A Brief English Grammar* (1905)
presents ''descriptive rather than prescriptive'' grammatical ''rules,'' and is
quite contemporary in its approach, according to Kitzhaber (199). Unfortunately, its sales were not extraordinary; hence, its influence may have been
limited (Kitzhaber 199). A more typical text, according to Kitzhaber, is
Wooley's *Handbook of Composition* of 1907, with its ''negative and dog-
matic'' tone (224). That book, Kitzhaber says, encouraged an ''exalting to
the highest place'' of ''correctness in details'' (225).

James Kinneavy suggests that by 1910, the ''current-traditional'' approach was established: English teachers ''adopted without question the
modified approach to the modes of discourse'' encouraged by Bain as well
as Barrett Wendell's paragraph approach, while they also taught logic and
persuasion with little to no training in those areas themselves (169). The
trivium was resurrected early in the twentieth century by C. S. Pierce with a
theory of semiotics that claimed that ''Grammar, in semiotics, becomes the
study of the conditions of meaning; logic becomes the study of the conditions of truth; and rhetoric becomes the study of the relations among signs''
(Bizzell and Herzberg 908).

One of the problems related to the trivium and nineteenth- and early
twentieth-century composition instruction is that the modal method of
instruction so often ignored aspects of logic and rhetoric, especially the considerations of audience and purpose, in the privileging of superficial form
and correctness. Nevertheless, as David Russell points out, ''Despite periodic
alarms about the pernicious effects of American's poor writing . . . enough
Americans learned to write in the ways they needed to in order to carry on,
and rather well at that'' (18–19). This in itself creates a problem of logic;
students were taught by rote, and perhaps their writing did suffer from boring, mode-dominated prescription. Still, they apparently succeeded in writing
in the real world, in writing appropriately for various contexts. This may
have been possible, Russell suggests, because freshman composition served
to weed out weak students: ''Through this gate keeping function, general-

composition courses have offered the mass-education system a means of dealing with the successive waves of previously excluded students who have continually flocked into the higher-education system since the late nineteenth century'' (27).

As early as 1954, Jon Huston reports, grammar's reign was becoming shaky: "Today, although grammar is taught in connection with composition, it is unusual to find a high school course labeled English grammar, the study having fallen into a disrepute which may not be entirely undeserved'' (10). Georgia Clifton says that concepts often considered to be recent developments in composition were being considered by 1951: "Whatever form the written composition takes, it should come through the experience of the student and for the purpose of communication. Drill work on correct punctuation and grammar should come only when the need arises out of the pupil's work'' (132).

The process movement of the 1960s and 1970s led to the general neglect of grammar in American college composition. Statements by researchers such as Richard Braddock, Richard Lloyd-Jones, and Lowell Schoer (and studies conducted with groups other than college students) were taken out of context and wrongly interpreted by those who may have stood to gain much by such a reading—they no longer had to instruct students in any of the increasingly complex and sometimes boring grammars. Other factors leading to a deemphasis on grammar include the students' right to their own language (and the subsequent elitist, prescriptive connotation grammar studies in general developed), the open-door policy among colleges and universities and the resulting influx of students, and an increasing reliance on using the revision stage (and word processing programs) to "catch" any grammatical problems.

Rei Noguchi suggests that the deemphasis on grammar is due in part to "a growing number of equally staunch anti-grammar teachers who view mechanical errors as unimportant low-level surface features which detract little from writing quality and which students can easily edit out during the writing process'' (13). Another reason this has happened, Noguchi says, is that style has been viewed primarily as a matter of mechanics: "If classroom instruction has given too little attention to the interaction of style with content and organization, it also has probably given too much emphasis to just one aspect of style, namely, sentence mechanics'' (13). Neither approach, Noguchi warns, seems adequate: "I believe the hard-line anti-grammar teachers with their reluctance to address such errors in a systematic way are just as misguided and self-defeating as the hard-line pro-grammar teachers who address them with over exuberance. What seems lost in these internecine battles is the middle ground'' (14). Increasingly, over the last few decades, rhetoricians have begun fusing logic with rhetoric as knowledge has come to be seen as epistemic. Still, as Noguchi warns, such subjects may, like grammar, suffer from transferabililty to actual student writing:

Writing teachers, for example, often offer explicit instruction in content, organization, tone, and many other things which presumably enhance writing quality, but this instruction, too, as witnessed by the many imperfect essays turned in by students, is often not transferred to actual writing. If the problem of transfer is a general one and not restricted to grammar alone, it seems unfair in principle to castigate, not to mention, banish, one realm of knowledge and not all the others. (8)

The historical precedent of the trivium is only one reason to incorporate grammar studies with logic and rhetoric according to Noguchi; other "more immediate and practical matters, specifically, the improvement of language skills, particularly writing skills" are involved (1). The modern refusal to include grammar in writing pedagogy is best seen as a 180-degree reaction against its prominence in early composition history. Admittedly, following a pedagogy simply because it has historically been taught is anything but progressive, but reapplying essential material in an innovative and *effective* manner certainly is. The third component of the trivium, grammar—construed in its broadest sense as the description of the patterns of language as we use them in given contexts and not as a course replete with prescriptive usage rules—needs to be readmitted as a part of composition instruction because of its potential to help students gain control of their own writing and to help them complete rhetorical choices on the sentence level. We run the risk of again misreading the evidence of our own experience; rather than divorce grammar from the logical and persuasive powers of the language, we need, more than ever perhaps, to help college students learn how to fully manipulate its power. If the "failure" of nineteenth- and early twentieth-century modal composition was to deemphasize purpose and audience in the quest for superficial correctness and appropriate form, we may be succumbing to the opposite trend of emphasizing to whom and why students are writing but ignoring the fact that those same readers may be highly critical of flawed writing, readers including ". . .most of the educated reading public, which, fairly or unfairly, perceives such features as major improprieties" (Noguchi 14).

Ignoring grammar can result in the denial of some pressing demands within the rhetorical situation of the classroom. The systems underlying academic and business writing need to be available to and understood by the students; the stylistic concerns associated with particular sentence patterns, word choice, and word order need to be addressed, whether by modeling or simply by pointing out options in the students' writings. As Elizabeth Koehler Larsen points out, we do not all write the same: ". . . we are in error when we validate one single composing process. All people do not compose similarly. Rather, writers' own accounts about how they compose indicate they have used a variety of processes" (abstract). So we can neither assume that all teaching methods help students write the same, nor that because all students do not need a particular lesson, then some will not benefit from it. And, especially in the case of non-traditional students, many will actually expect, even desire, grammatical instruction because of their perceived need for it in the "real world." Avoiding grammar because it is boring or because past studies suggest its inefficacy in certain situations seems biased; if a particular student or a section of a class needs instruction, it is irresponsible not to provide it. Also, we often operate under the assumption that students are being stuffed with grammatical knowledge in their pre-college existence. Increasingly, my experience is that junior- and senior-level English majors are uncomfortable with grammar and usage. If they who love the language are so ill-informed, how can we expect students who hate Composition I and II and all things English to understand the language they are using in their essays as well as their exam responses, research papers, and projects in other classes?

If we fail to emphasize, at some point in the composition curriculum, that future employees and, indeed, some professors in the students' very near future will demand an understanding of the language elements underlying writing (as well as the accurate usage of those elements), we may be doing our students a grave disservice. Russell argues that, "To teach students the discourse of a professional elite is often a crucial part of initiating them into the profession; to exclude them is to make that initiation more difficult, if not impossible" (26-27). Finally, Noguchi suggests that, not only are readers in today's "reader-based perspective" both editorial and censorial, but that ". . . features are not so easily edited out during the rewriting process as the anti-grammar teachers claim. The problem here is that, if students do not recognize the unconventional features as unconventional, they cannot edit them out" (14).

Lessons from the past are invaluable learning tools. We have seen what does not work in grammar instruction, yet students still seem to lack control of grammatical considerations. It is time to find out what will work and to reunite the elements of rhetoric so unfortunately separated over the years. I agree with Noguchi who asserts that ". . . teachers need to be more selective in what they teach" and teach grammar not "as an academic subject" but as "a tool for writing improvement" (17). This can best be done by

> limiting the scope of grammar instruction to only those categories and principles which elucidate the most frequent and serious writing problems but also exploiting as much as possible students' already-acquired knowledge of the language. Just as important, teachers will need to integrate this minimal set of categories and principles, or "writer's grammar," with content and organization, two crucial areas that syntax-based grammars leave virtually untouched. (Noguchi 120)

Such an approach allows students to better understand their own writing, something instructors have been trying to achieve for far longer than many of us perhaps realize; Kitzhaber says of Whitney, who taught in 1877, "The reason he gave for teaching grammar (in his sense of the term) to persons who are already users of the language concerned was that it is the best way to turn the student's attention to the basic principles and relations of language as they are illustrated in his own speech and writing'' (198). We should reunite grammar with the rhetorical and logical elements of writing because to do so admits the reality of students' everyday world, and because, as Newton Garver claims, ''. . . the medieval trivium is a much sounder approach to the study of language and gives a much more adequate framework for understanding the philosophy of language than its all too fashionable neglect might lead one to suppose'' (quoted in Bizzell and Herzberg 907).

4

"Grammatical Monstrosities" and "Contemptible Miscreants": Sacrificial Violence in the Late Nineteenth-Century Usage Handbook

Richard Boyd

The Accusatory Rhetoric of Cultural Strife

In March of 1886, Josiah Strong, Congregationalist minister and regional secretary for the Home Missionary Society, offered his vision of an America beseiged by manifold "perils" to an anxious Protestant readership that would quickly make *Our Country* into a national best-seller.[1] Lamenting the waves of immigrants and offspring of "foreign parentage" (54) now inhabiting the nation's burgeoning cities, Strong warned of the "contagious . . . disease" and the "debauching [of] popular morals" carried forth by "these corrupters of youth, these western Arabs," who "menace . . . our civilization" (54–55). No stranger to the accusatory rhetoric of class warfare, Strong described for his readers a "civilization multiplying and focalizing the elements of anarchy and destruction" (182), brought down through the combined agencies of "Immigration," "Romanism," "Intemperance," and "Socialism."[2] His jeremiad, said by one modern historian to "mirror the thoughts and aspirations of [the] dominant segment of American society towards the close of the nineteenth century, and [to be] therefore a historical

54

document of major importance" (Herbst ix), moves relentlessly and with fervor to condemn the "evil conjunction" of "dangerous elements" in the culture, and it culminates in a starkly apocalyptic prophecy of social chaos: "We are preparing [Strong grimly informs his readers] conditions which make possible a Reign of Terror that would beggar the scenes of the French Revolution" (152).

Universal conversion, under the aegis of the Home Missionary Society, would seem to be all that stands between America and Armageddon. True enough, Strong might reply, but that is not quite the whole story. For Josiah Strong has not fallen into an utter pessimism toward all American institutions, and he looks hopefully—if somewhat surprisingly—to public education (and specifically the common school) as a bulwark against the rising tides of foreign "perils": "The public school is the principal digestive organ of the body politic. By means of it the children of strange and dissimilar races which come to us are, in one generation, assimilated and made Americans" (89).

Strong's alimentary trope, so richly suggestive of devourment and destruction concealed under the guise of assimilation, represents a conservative impulse in late nineteenth-century American pedagogical theory that was by no means exclusive to the annals of evangelical Protestant social commentary. Indeed, it is most interesting to note that eighteen years prior to the publication of *Our Country*, a remarkably similar excoriation of the "vulgar" (vi) appeared under the title *Vulgarisms and Other Errors of Speech*. Written by the part-time novelist and full-time verbal critic Richard Meade Bache, this text offered lessons in language "proficiency" to those not wishing to be seen in "unfavorable light" by their social superiors, those "more favored children of fortune" (iii). And while Bache's self-help book in grammatical correctness and the niceties of verbal etiquette was clearly aimed at a relatively cultivated audience who could readily imagine themselves members of the cultural elite, such a linguistic identity could not be constructed without a fierce attack on those said to endanger the "purity" (x) of the English language.

Like Strong's immigrant hordes, Bache's "vulgar" threaten the essential sanctity of rudimentary forms of cultural life, aligned as they are with the forces of "corruption" (x): "a mistake [in grammar] cannot be properly termed a vulgarism, unless it is one that is habitually made by the illiterate" (v). Even if their use of the "vulgarism" be grammatically correct, Bache argues that its exclusive use by the "illiterate" necessitates its "fall" from its prior "high estate" and thus "its degradation cannot be in any way redeemed" (v). Judging deviations from the sanctioned grammatical conventions and rules to be incontestable signs "mark[ing] the speaker as ill-educated and underbred" (39), Bache repeatedly links "errors" of speech to the criminal and morally dangerous. The "indiscriminate use of the terms gentleman and lady" by individuals "who have no right to them" is declared to have "so prostituted them [these words], that even in cases where they might with propriety be used, they are often shunned by the refined" (47). Similarly, slang should be viewed by the "refined" as deviant, as in no way an "acceptable addition to the language of the educated" (19). Rather, it must be "scorn[ed]" by the "higher general civilization" and made "separate and apart, as is the cant of thieves and gypsies" (20).

Again, as was the case with *Our Country*, it would be naive to dismiss Bache's virulent castigation of the linguistic Other as merely the rhetorical excesses of an idiosyncratic curmudgeon. In point of fact, *Vulgarisms and Other Errors of Speech* is part of a quite broadly-based attack on the grammatical "improprieties" (Mathews 326) of the American public (or at least a significant portion of it). Books such as L. P. Meredith's *Everyday Errors of Speech* (1872), Harlan Ballard's *Handbook of Blunders* (1880), and C. W. Bardeen's *Verbal Pitfalls: A Manual of 1500 Words Commonly Misused* (1883), along with frequent essays and editorials in periodicals like *Good Housekeeping*, *The Atlantic Monthly*, and *Godey's Lady's Book* and many of the major news dailies found a large and ready audience for their robust dosage of prescriptive advice on all manners of linguistic behavior (Cmiel 195). The social historian Kenneth Cmiel has compared the "thriving industry" of verbal criticism arising in the post-Civil War years to a crusade devoted to the goal of rendering "bad English exposed"[3] to universal condemnation and ridicule (123). Although Cmiel has found the number of conservative verbal critics to be relatively small, he concludes that their influence on wide sectors of American culture was nonetheless quite considerable. And among those social institutions most powerfully impacted by this campaign to "purify" linguistic behavior, secondary and post-secondary schools seem to have been particularly susceptible to the message. The academic community was quite receptive to the call for a vigorous policing of grammatical errors, and, as Cmiel notes, "[t]eachers at all levels incorporated their [the verbal critics'] ideas into the English curriculum" (124).

The Vogue of Mechanical Correctness in Writing Pedagogy

Cmiel's work is significant to our discussion because it provides an important historical context for understanding the wholesale adoption by late nineteenth-century American higher education of a composition pedagogy driven chiefly by its obsession with mechanical correctness in student writing. The years after the Civil War were marked by considerable innovation in rhetoric courses designed for the undergraduate, as most colleges and universities moved away from the traditional—and classically-based—emphasis on oral recitation to one requiring large amounts of student writing in the vernacular. According to Robert Connors' authoritative account of composition instruction in the nineteenth century, this post-war period came to be defined particularly by its singular attention to matters of superficial correctness and student proficiency in the production of grammatically clean essays:

> Between 1865 and 1895, such elements of mechanical correctness as grammar, punctuation, spelling, and capitalization, which would never have been found in textbooks before 1850, came to usurp much of the time devoted in class to rhetorical instruction and most of the marking of student writing. (65)

Such a pedagogy made "'error-free' writing the central definition of 'good' writing in many teachers' minds," and it dictated that "the goal of the freshman writing course [would] . . . be teaching the avoidance of error rather than teaching genuine communicative competence" (65).

A variety of explanations have been offered for this dramatic re-making of the undergraduate rhetoric class that rapidly gained ascendancy throughout the nation's institutions of higher learning. Connors himself has argued that much of the appeal of a mechanistic conception of writing and writing instruction was found in its perceived capacity to assist instructors overburdened by the crushing paper loads which accompanied the new writing intensive courses. Given the disinclination of college administrators to provide significant relief to overworked composition instructors,[4] those responsible for these classes turned not unreasonably to a model of instruction that promoted a streamlined response to student writing. As Connors concludes: "Faced with killing work levels, teachers had to give something up; what went, unfortunately, was rhetoric. The new emphasis on mechanical correctness [in part] grew out of . . . the understandable need of teachers to somehow deal with their huge stacks of student themes" (67).

Connors' invaluable report on the vogue of superficial correctness also looks beyond the immediate pedagogical needs of composition's overworked instructors to explain the phenomenon, and he links the passionate attack upon grammatical errors to a "furor over 'illiteracy'" that preoccupied commentators on linguistic propriety such as Bache, due to their desire to re-establish distinctions based on socio-economic class (64). Indeed, many recent commentators have made precisely this point, arguing that changes in the English curriculum were driven by a deep cultural malaise brought on by rapid urbanization and the emergent dominance of monopolistic capitalism (Cmiel 124–125; Berlin 60). An insistence upon student proficiency in the grammatical and stylistic conventions of the upper middle-class was to serve as a bulwark against the encroachments of "vulgar[izers]" upon traditional class distinctions and provide a guarantee that the college-educated would be adequately trained in the "objectivity" and "correctness" valued by the managerial class (Berlin 75). Further, the push for "proper" grammar and word usage has been shown to coincide with a dramatic change in the demographics of the college population brought on by relatively more open admission policies in the years after the Civil War (Ohmann 234). No longer could the homogeneous student population of the pre-War years be assumed, as more and more young people from non-elite backgrounds came to fill the universities in search of access to the privileges of high socio-economic rank (Berlin 73; Rudolph 151).

Certainly, the strikingly congruent language employed by Strong and Bache in their attacks upon the "foreign" and "vulgar" is enough to suggest the essential validity of these efforts to conjoin the social and the pedagogical. But it is also important to realize that the virulent fervor with which our nineteenth-century authors condemn the deviant Other far transcends anything made necessary by changes in the economic sector. And even those critics like Connors, Cmiel, and Wallace Douglas who foreground issues of class anxiety in their discussion of the grammatical imperative in college composition tend to overlook the systematic manner in which such accusatory rhetoric is deployed in grammar texts and handbooks of the age. The mechanisms underlying the condemnations of "bad English" have to this point remained largely unexplored. Therefore, I would like to shift our attention from a consideration of mechanical correctness as a privileged pedagogical strategy promoting the linguistic marking of the "favored ones" to an investigation explicitly focused upon the dark side of this innovation; that is to say, to a reading of superficial correctness as a separating out of the linguistic Other into the category of a "bad English" that must be finally expelled, eliminated.

René Girard's Theory of Mimetic Desire

This interpretive move on my part owes much of its inspiration to the immensely exciting work of the cultural theorist René Girard and his development of a mimetic theory of human desire. Briefly, and with considerable oversimplification of a grand and intricate theory, Girard propounds a model of desire wherein the desiring subject is said to hold no original relation to the object of "choice" or desire, for he or she is incapable of spontaneously or autonomously desiring anything; rather, the subject is steered toward the object by a mediating Other who designates said object as desirable. Since the urge to possess an object already held or desired by the "model" (Girard's term for that mediating Other) leads inescapably to conflict as each seeks the object, Girard concludes that at the heart of all human relationships lies a proclivity for rivalry which must, at some point, "transform desire into violence" (*Violence* 169). To forestall the escalating—because mimetic—cycle of violence and revenge and establish instead an orderly, pacific site where some version of a sustainable cultural order might emerge; such is the fundamental task for the human organism that is so evidently predisposed to conflict and violent rivalry.

Girard therefore argues that all human institutions and cultural forms, from language and the sacred to the modern political state and judiciary system, owe their existence to the collective effort to deflect and defuse the ruinous impact of unchecked mimetic conflict. The educational system is by no means exempt from this agonistic orientation found within all institutions, and it is from just this Girardian insight that I seek to read the vogue of mechanical correctness sweeping the land during the latter stages of the nineteenth century. It is precisely through such key Girardian paradigms as the ritual accusation and the inevitable turn to the scapegoat mechanism to restore calm within the community that we can best grasp something of the cultural work undertaken by those seeking to eradicate "bad English."[5] Thus, when John Hart, in his *Manual of Composition and Rhetoric* (1870), blithely informs his readers that "purity" in diction is best attained through "habitual association with persons of education and refinement" (67–68), we see something akin to the sacrificial violence found by Girard to reside in all cultural institutions. Hart's bit of advice is intensely exclusionary because it serves to banish all those lacking "refinement," that is to say, all those with alternative political, cultural, and economic histories different from the one shaping the definition of linguistic "purity" proffered by the rhetorics and grammar handbooks of the era.

A Case in Point: William Mathews' *Words: Their Use and Abuse*

This is not the place to attempt a comprehensive survey of the widely diffused campaign for mechanical correctness which touched vast segments of the educational system and the culture-at-large.[6] Rather, I would like to focus on one exemplary text, William Mathews' *Words: Their Use and Abuse* (1876), as a means to suggest something of the sacrificial dimension so prominently residing in the movement to rid the culture of "bad English." *Words* works well in this regard because there is nothing subterranean about the text's accusatory rhetoric, and one can quite readily trace the accumulation of ritualized denunciations leading to the expulsion of the "alien" (327) Other. But the virulence of Mathews' language only serves to differentiate him in degree, and not in kind, from his fellow crusaders at all levels of the educational establishment. To cite only one example, consider A. S. Hill, the originator of Freshman Composition at Harvard and the author of the vastly influential textbook, *The Principles of Rhetoric*, who made as the first principle of his book the conviction that the "foundations of rhetoric rest upon grammar; for *grammatical purity* is a requisite of good writing" (1; emphasis added). I believe *Words* is representative of a generalized dependency in late nineteenth-century language pedagogy upon the mechanisms of sacrificial violence, mechanisms which reflected much more the perceived exigencies of the historical moment than the educational needs of novice writers.

Mathews composed his text while engaged as a regular literary critic for the *Chicago Tribune* during the early 1870s, and his commentary on language use first appeared in serialized form in the *Lakeside Monthly* (Cmiel 135, 137, 192).[7] Thus, as with Bache, we are again dealing with a text not specifically intended for classroom use. And although Mathews dedicates his book to the President of the University of Rochester, he is more properly associated with those "popular" verbal critics writing primarily for a non-academic audience, even if their linguistic agenda came to have a profound impact upon classroom practices throughout all levels of the educational system. By singling out a text such as *Words* that enjoyed considerable sales in the general marketplace, I seek to underscore the affinities between the vogue of mechanical correctness in writing pedagogy and a range of more broadly-based cultural phenomena. Indeed, as several scholars have recently suggested, composition as an academic subject was, in the late nineteenth century, intimately tied to popular energies and institutions. Susan Miller, for example, has argued that the establishment of composition as an academic subject on college campuses must be situated in relation to widespread cultural anxieties about populist discourse which date all the way back to the American Revolution (34). Similarly, Arthur Appleby reminds us that popular, non-academic texts like Noah Webster's *Grammatical Institute* (1783–5) and his *American Dictionary* (1828) played defining roles in the creation of the regularized grammatical forms of American English so favored by the textbook writers of the late nineteenth century (3). I would simply add to this the fact that A. S. Hill, of that august institution that was—and is—Harvard College, had his roots not in academia but in the popular press as a newspaper journalist, coming to Cambridge directly from his post with the New York *Tribune* (Kitzhaber 60).

One need not therefore feel particularly surprised to discover the same sort of siege mentality in *Words* as is so evident in Strong's best-selling *Our Country*. A sense of crisis, brought on by quite palpable fears of cultural disintegration, underlies much of Mathews' representation of good usage, and the text expends considerable energy warning its readers of the alien Other. Because "unity of speech is essential to the unity of a people" (46), Mathews judges the growing linguistic heterogeneity of the late nineteenth century (fostered in part by new patterns of immigration) to be "one of the greatest misfortunes" (47) facing the nation:

> The settlement of townships and counties in this country, by distinct bodies of foreigners is, therefore, a great evil, and a daily newspaper, with an Irish, German, or French prefix, or in a foreign language, is a perpetual breeder of national animosities, and an effectual bar to the Americanization of our foreign population. (47)

Echoing Josiah Strong, Mathews calls for active intervention "to check the deluge of barbarisms, solecisms, and improprieties, with which our language is threatened" (327). Non-sanctioned language practices (or, in the terms of the handbook, the "abuse" and abusers of words) are directly linked to the socially disruptive, though Mathews' wary eye is not focused exclusively on those newly arrived on North American shores. His battle is also fought along class lines, and a profound fear of popular, democratic movements activates much of his despair over the state of contemporary language practices. Mathews represents the perceived assault on the linguistic authority of the privileged classes as a manifest threat to their political power as well. He describes a kind of linguistic anarchy afoot in American culture, prompted by a "scorn of obedience, whether to political authority or philological," breeding "lawlessness," and demanding new "powerful securities against revolution" in a written language already too "hospitable to alien words" (327). As evidence of this threat, Mathews, like Bache, offers the case of the word "gentleman," that once venerable linguistic marker of class privilege:

> Perhaps no honorable term in the language has been more debased than 'gentleman' . . . Today the term has sunk so low that the acutest lexicographer would be puzzled to tell its meaning. Not only does every person of decent exterior and deportment assume to be a gentleman, but the term is applied to the vilest animals and the most contemptible miscreants, as well as the poorest and most illiterate persons in the community. (86–87)

Read out of context, Mathews' vitriol seems at times so excessive that it must surely be judged an aberration, even if *Words* did find a considerable readership. But as the examples of Strong and Bache would suggest, there is nothing particularly idiosyncratic about Mathews' fury against those perceived to threaten the social order; each of these authors instead reflects the generalized anxieties of a culture experiencing a profound sense of disequilibrium and social fragmentation. Girard's term for this conjunction of rapid change and the paranoia it tends to arouse among at least some segments of the populace is "sacrificial crisis," and its applicability to conditions in the late nineteenth-century United States surely merits consideration. By "sacrificial crisis," Girard means to describe that moment when long-standing cultural institutions[8] are no longer able to maintain an order based upon inviolable hierarchical classifications—be they social, religious, linguistic, etc.—and the community therefore falls into the maelstrom of unchecked mimetic antagonisms and the vertiginous confusion brought on by indifferentiation in the systems of representation (*Violence* 39–67). Mathews' display of fearful hostility toward those "miscreants" who mimic the airs of the truly noble through the indiscriminate use of "gentleman" suggests that the Girardian paradigm of a universal predisposition toward violence accompanying the loss of differentiation in sign systems and the attendant drift toward disorder which inevitably ensues has at least some relation to this period of American cultural life.

Indeed, the years between 1870 and 1915 were witness to considerable upheaval in the organization of social life, as rapid economic and demographic changes prompted the collapse of the localized, small rural community as the basic unit of the cultural order (Weibe xiv). The sovereignty of the local, clearly bounded community disappeared before the swift transformations in socio-economic life, setting off what the historian Robert Weibe has described as "a widespread loss of confidence" and a fearful preoccupation with "foreign" elements in the culture (44). Weibe entitled his classic study of the period *The Search For Order*, suggesting the pervasive sense of fragmentation in urban America and the restless quest to re-found the once-dominant structures of social stratification and distinction. Along with such powerful reformist political and social movements as the "Purity Crusade"[9] which promoted temperance and anti-prostitution legislation under the banner of repelling "threats to morality and social cohesion" (Pivar 160), the campaign against grammatical "improprieties" pursued a goal of cultural homogeneity in response to the disorientation of this late nineteenth-century sacrificial crisis.

Mathews' Drive to Expel the Linguistic Other

Mathews' affiliations with this cultural disposition are evident throughout *Words*, especially in those sections which describe the social implications of unauthorized linguistic behaviors. "[M]en are led into error," by "the fallacies in words" and usage, declares Mathews, because "in learning words we are learning to discriminate things" (247, 28). To manipulate words in a "master[ly]" (13) way is to reinforce the hierarchies of meaning and value which reside at the foundations of the cultural order. Therefore, much of the potential for social disruption which Mathews locates in deviations from the prescribed conventions originates in the capacity of "disordered" (56) language to deceive; such language is "hypocritical" (57) and aims to "mislead" (56). The "abuse" of words is a sign of the violator's predilection to subvert the truth, to abrogate by means of deception those recognized demarcations of the social order sustaining difference and thus ensuring cultural stability.

The improper use of words is thus seen to strike at the heart of those hierarchies of meaning and difference and to create conditions of profound linguistic—and epistemological—uncertainty; a confusion which must, in fact, give way to the search for a culprit. Fortunately, to Mathews' mind at least, the "confused" (57) and hypocritical abuse of language is a double-edged sword, and in its very "disorder" it betrays "the hollowness and unreality of the speaker's character" (57). This will invariably occur because, as Mathews assures his readers, "in every case, the beauty or ugliness of [a person's] moral countenance, the force and keenness or feebleness of his logic, will be imaged in his language" (192). Readers can therefore rest confident in Mathews' project to construct a linguistic Other equivalent to Strong's alien Other invading America; for the grammatical "improprieties" of that marginalized voice mark that individual in violation of the norm in both linguistic act and moral character and condemn the guilty party of the very crimes which the abuse of language would disseminate into the wider culture. This finally means, of course, that the catalogue of complaints about verbal and written behavior found in *Words* is no simple inventory, but it is rather a ritualized performance working to designate a surrogate victim that will be expelled for the presumed benefit of the cultural order.

In its representation of this linguistic scapegoat, Mathews' text resembles in a most striking manner the Girardian persecution text, that document characteristically produced by communities to "explain" acts of collective violence by assigning all responsibility for social unrest to an easily identifiable group or individual (*Scapegoat* 15). Such an association of mythological text[10] and nineteenth-century usage handbook is possible because *Words* reproduces, to a rather startling degree, the taxonomy of ritual accusations which Girard finds present in nearly all persecution texts. Typically, Girard reports, the scapegoat figure is charged with crimes which crystallize around the community's deepest anxieties concerning the stability of the social order (*Violence* 99). For Mathews, addressing an audience fearful of a loss in social prestige and power, the declaration that "as a garment may be honeycombed by moths, so the fine texture of a language may be gradually destroyed, and its strength impaired, by numerous and apparently insignificant solecisms and inaccuracies" (337), must have carried particular resonance. There is, in *Words*, that same preoccupation as we saw in Strong's best-selling text, that the walls have been breached, that the invasion has begun: "Even slang words, after long knocking, will often gain admission into a language, like pardoned outlaws received into the body of respectable citizens" (332). Mathews' criminalization of the linguistic Other recalls a frequent opening gesture in the sacrificial process because it serves to justify the policing of "common improprieties" (326) in order to protect society from their deleterious effects. Certainly, the author does not hesitate to make explicit his intention to apprehend and, presumably, incarcerate the linguistic offender; for he spends the entire text aligning himself with those "literary detectives who spend their time in hunting down and showing up the mistakes of others" (341).[11]

What is initially curious about this "criminal" investigation is that Mathews does not round up the expected group of suspects, especially if one is anticipating that the author's class prejudices will be routinely reflected in all his accusatory gestures. Such an expectation does not do justice to the complexity of Mathews' project, because instead of repeating his condemnations of "the vilest criminals and the most contemptible miscreants" (87), in this later investigation he takes up his pen against some quite respectable, and indeed thoroughly canonical, English writers. Addison, Swift, Hume, Gibbon, and Pope, to name only a few, are brought before the docket to be held accountable for their linguistic "sins" (341). These distinguished writers and, by inference, the elite class which most closely identifies with them, come under harsh criticism for their grammatical laxness. Their work is said to "swarm with errors of grammar and rhetoric" (342), and they display "numberless instances of slovenliness of style" (340); like the hordes of Strong and Bache, they seem to be carriers of "disorder" who must be ritually condemned and cast outside the orderly world of "our noble English tongue" (326). But Mathews' text does not finally work at cross-purposes to itself, and the attack on these criminally delinquent representatives of elite style and convention is not a retreat from, but an insistence upon, the primacy of class and tradition in the linguistic wars which *Words* enjoins.

To untangle the apparent paradox residing in Mathews' assault on Addison, et al., we must first of all remember mimetic desire, that most elemental of Girardian mechanisms, and the primary role of imitation in the inculcation of socially conservative behavior. Girard views human learning as geared toward the goals of cultural integration and cohesion, with imitation as the primary means by which individuals from infancy on learn appropriate patterns of behavior. As he points out, "there is nothing, or next to nothing, in human behavior that is not learned, and all learning is based on imitation. If human beings suddenly ceased imitating, all forms of culture would vanish" (*Things Hidden* 7). Near the conclusion of *Words*, Mathews propounds a similarly fundamental conjunction between culture and imitation when he turns to mimesis in the effort to relieve the anxieties of those seeking after "the niceties and delicacies of expression" (338–339). He advises his readers that:

> In language, as in the fine arts, there is but one way to attain to excellence, and that is by study of the most faultless models. As the air and manner of a gentleman can be acquired only by living constantly in good society, so grace and purity of expression must be attained by a familiar acquaintance with the standard authors. (338)

In other words, it is through imitation that one comes into possession of privileged verbal and written conventions and thus acquires, linguistically at least, "the airs and manner of a gentleman."

We are now at the heart of Mathews' apparently paradoxical attack on Addison, et al., for surely these writers must be classed among those "standard authors" which Mathews' readers are prompted to imitate. But Mathews desires only "the most faultless models," those writers whose work remains free of the "vulgar fineries of style . . . [which] barbarize our language" (108). Indeed, he is obsessed with constructing a "faultless model" of elite speech and written discourse because he fears that "our dear old English tongue" (108) has been invaded by a wave of vulgarisms that have left authoritative linguistic conventions corrupted and dangerously weakened. And the walls can only be rebuilt when those corruptions—and corruptors—are pushed away, beyond the margins of "good society," and models worthy of emulation again assume unchallenged ascendancy. Thus, Mathews' accusations that eminent writers of the past committed "impropriet[ies] of the grossest sort" (342)

are not so much attacks on individual authors as they are, much more fundamentally, complaints that popular conventions have invaded elite discourse;
indeed, his utilization of such class-specific adjectives as "common,"
"gross," and "vulgar" provides ample evidence of his fearful anti-
democratic sentiments.

His overriding preoccupation then is not really with a localized critique
but with a wholesale re-vitalization of that linguistic site where one might
"liv[e] constantly in good society," in order that imitative desire might
flourish and the mimetic mechanism work in support of socially conservative
ends. Addison and his linguistically careless associates must be "tried and
condemned" as "offenders" (342) of the English language because their
"common improprieties" are signs of an imminent peril threatening the
social order. To switch metaphors, they are injurious because their proclivity
for the "common" and slovenly interferes with the "proper" operation of
mimetic desire as a means of social control. As Mathews so frankly acknowledges, models can only be genuinely exemplary when the last vestiges of the
"vulgar" are driven from the lips and pens of the elite, and it is only at that
longed-for moment that one can entertain hope for the return "to grace and
purity of expression."[12]

Grammatical "Monstrosities" and Contagion

Such a reversal in prognosis requires drastic medicine, which for *Words*, as
with so many of Girard's persecution texts, consists precisely in the marking
of the sacrificial victim through a sustained association of the scapegoat figure with an array of criminal acts against the social order. As we have
already seen, Mathews does just that, and his accusatory rhetoric culminates
with the characterization of misused words or phrases as "monstrosities"
(334), a designation which both signals the fear of a radical destructuring of
the social order and conclusively identifies that dangerous Other who must
be expelled. Mathews condemns those "grammatical monstrosities" which
"correct taste will shun, . . . as it does physical deformities in the arts of
design" (334). The abnormalities of this grammar imply the moral monstrosity of the writer as well, since for Mathews the "abuse" of language constitutes "an expression corresponding to the irregularities within [an individual's mind]" (56). Defined by their subversive Otherness, Mathews'
"grammatical monstrosities" produce fear and hostility because they seem
to stand in direct violation of the most fundamental categories of proportion
and the natural order. They are grotesque, they "disfigure" (340), they challenge, by virtue of their very existence, every easy confidence in the invio-
lability of a traditional order.

Mathews herein employs a motif common to the rhetoric of ritual accusation, for the monstrous generally makes an appearance at the most intense
moments of cultural crisis. The arrival of the monster, who by its very

definition violates the essential categories of differentiation (think for a moment of Empedocles and his account of the birth of the monster: "We find creatures with revolving legs and countless hands. ... Others are born with two faces, two torsos; there are cows with human heads and men with the heads of cows" [quoted in Girard, *Violence* 163]), signals the effacement of all meaningful cultural differences and the reign of non-difference (Girard, *Violence* 64). Thus, when Mathews remarks that employing an inappropriate word is like "hanging a giant's robe on the limbs of a dwarf" (29), he describes a linguistic world dominated by the unnatural and freakish, where all categories of difference are dissolved in the "monstrosit[y]" that is the Other.

Mathews' accusatory rhetoric would thus represent the "abuse" of certain grammatical and stylistic conventions as an aberration meriting expulsion from the social field. When deviations from the prescribed linguistic norms are not described as "monstrous," they are often characterized as "contagion" capable of inflicting "an irreparable injury to our English tongue" (109, 108). *Words* constructs these "abuses" as constituting an invasive disease which imperils the good health (i.e., the social stability) of the culture's most fundamental institutions:

> It has been justly said that the corrupter of a language stabs straight at the heart of his country. He commits a crime against every individual of a nation, for he poisons a stream from which all must drink; and the poison is more subtle and more dangerous, because more likely to escape detection than the deadliest venom with which the destructive philosophy of our day is assailing the moral and religious interests of humanity. (91)

Like the medieval persecution texts which helped prepare the way for the pogroms by accusing Jews of poisoning the community's drinking water and thus causing the Black Death (Girard, *Scapegoat* 1), Mathews' handbook on grammar and style inscribes the linguistic Other within a space occupied only by those guilty of crimes striking at the heart of the cultural order. Grammatical "improprieties" are in this text infectious plagues, cancers which "disfigure" the language with "blemishes" (327) and threaten to "drag down [all] into the general gulf of feeble inanition" (109). They must be excised, "excommunicated" (357), from the field if the homogeneity of the inside is to be sustained.

Mathews' turn to the tropes of religion and the sacred (a realm Girard has shown to be structured by exclusionary violence) to represent the fate of his grammatical offenders is utterly consonant with the sacrificial dimension of his rhetoric which I have so far outlined. Near the conclusion of *Words* he will even combine the disciplinary power of the secular and the condemnatory force of the religious as he rails against "all inaccuracies of speech, whether offenses against etymology, lexicography, or syntax. To pillory such offenses, to point out the damage which they inflict upon our language, and to expose the moral obliquity which often lurks beneath them, is, we believe, the duty of every scholar who knows how closely purity of speech, like personal cleanliness, is allied to purity of thought and rectitude of action" (335). "Excommunicated," "moral obliquity," "personal cleanliness," are all powerful metaphors which reverberate with the aura of guilt and religious censure. They are also essential elements of the curative process Mathews' text works to enact; for the assignation of guilt is vital to the sacrificial mechanism because it fixes responsibility for the sinful world on a clearly defined agent (in this case, those who commit the "common errors of speech") and thereby frees the community-at-large of all accountability in the crisis-at-hand (Girard, *Violence* 76–78).

It is equally clear that the deployment of the trope of the "monstrous," in its rhetorical function as a sign of non-difference, cannot be permitted to stand, and the monster must finally become, in Girard's words, "the very exemplar of difference, a classic monstrosity" in the ritual economy (*Violence* 64). Therefore, Mathews directs his readers to see in the "monstrosities" of language "abuse" not the reflections of their own class fears and anxieties but rather the marks of a unique and dangerous alien presence whose deformity will serve as the foundation of a new hierarchical stratification organized around the collective decision to "shun" this linguistic Other. In other words, a ritualized expulsion must and will take place.

Girard has argued that the social value of ritual has always resided in its capacity to transfer generalized cultural anxieties onto a single figure(s) whose elimination brings forth a renewed sense of order and calm. So too in *Words*, for Mathews' project involves the expulsion of the linguistic Other as a means to recover that "delicacy of shades of meaning, and a power of awakening associations" (35) which derives from the renewed capacity to discriminate, to make confident distinctions based upon a secure hierarchy of difference. To conclusively mark the other as monster, to banish it from cultural field, makes possible that pre-lapsarian hope in a reconstituted homogenous linguistic collectivity built on the belief "that unity of speech is essential to the unity of a people" (46). It rejuvenates the exemplary "mastery" (16) of men like Milton, Webster and Lord Chatham, models of good usage who put "language completely under [their] control" (23) and "make language always the flexible and obedient instrument of thought; not, as in the productions of a lower order of mind, its rebellious and recalcitrant slave" (17). The kind of rhetorical attack performed by *Words* must then be finally judged as a ritualized cleansing of the linguistic field, with the usage handbook transformed into a quasi-liturgical manual, or at the very least, into a text written from the characteristic perspective of the persecutor in his struggle with the Other (Girard, *Scapegoat* 9).

While Mathews' vision of social renewal through linguistic prescription never materialized in the anxious reality of late nineteenth-century American culture, his text does provide considerable insight into the sacrificial impulse so manifestly at work in the broad movement to promote mechanical correctness and the avoidance of "grammatical improprieties." And the recovery of Mathews' rootedness in the mechanisms of ritual behavior also helps explain something of the rhetorical and institutional vigor with which the goal of superficial correctness was pursued, not just in *Words*, but throughout the nation during this period. If *Words* does indeed have paradigmatic value, it is in suggesting in a most powerful fashion the mechanisms underlying the construction of a deviant, transgressive category of language practices that was then driven to the outside in the attempt to restore social hierarchies and reinforce the cultural order. Of course, this conclusion necessarily raises the question of how much the composition textbooks and usage handbooks of today, which continue to devote a considerable number of their pages to admonitions against "unacceptable grammar" (Kroitor and Martin 280) and "street-English" (Howell and Memering 223), remain determined by the mechanisms of ritual sacrifice. Unfortunately, this is a question best left to another time and place. However, I am convinced that any consideration of the cultural work performed by composition and particularly by the teaching of mechanical correctness, either in the present or the not-so-distant past, must be informed by a recognition of the "dark" side of the discipline and what that silenced Other can tell us about our academic and pedagogical practices.

Notes

1. Jurgen Herbst estimates that as many as 175,000 copies of *Our Country* had been sold by 1915, and individual chapters of the book were widely reprinted in pamphlets, newspapers, and magazines. Contemporaries compared the impact of *Our Country* to that most influential of publications, Harriet Beecher Stowe's *Uncle Tom's Cabin* (ix).

2. Strong devotes a chapter of the book to each of these "perils" facing the nation.

3. Cmiel's phrasing here is derived from the title of a popular usage manual published by George Washington Moon in 1868.

4. During the period from 1880 to 1910, the typical writing course enrolled between one hundred forty and two hundred students, with paper loads for each instructor in the hundreds of student essays per week (Connors 66). Even at Harvard, where eleven instructors were responsible for six hundred thirty students during the 1899–1900 academic year, the load was staggering: each composition teacher read and responded to something in excess of 10,000 pages of student writing per year (Copeland 1). Little wonder that A. S. Hill, the head of English A at Harvard, characterized the teaching burden of composition instructors as "onerous and often thankless" (*Our English* 84).

5. An important caveat is therefore necessary. This essay means to be extremely limited in its claims; I have no interest in using this investigation of late

nineteenth-century grammar and usage handbooks to support the sweeping attempt of the Girardian hypothesis to explain so much of human behavior. Furthermore, this essay does not seek to argue that the sacrificial mechanism was deployed to a unique degree in these particular grammar texts. Clearly, the tropes of "purity," "vulgarisms," etc. were present in rhetorics and handbooks long before and long after the peculiar socio-historical circumstances of this era were manifest. My project is one of heuristic exploration rather than historical reconstruction aimed at narrating a unitary "story" of the rise of mechanical correctness as a pedagogical preoccupation. For while this essay is deeply historicist in orientation, it is more properly understood as an investigation of a particular—and limited—hypothesis concerning how the organization of grammar instruction and "advice" may have been shaped by such powerful mechanisms as mimetic desire and the scapegoating of the alien "Other."

6. My essay in *Rhetoric Review* does attempt to provide at least a cursory survey of this phenomenon.

7. In his very fine book, *Representative Words: Politics, Literature, and the American Language, 1776–1865,* Thomas Gustafson treats *Words* as an antebellum text, apparently assuming that the 1876 publication stands in very close relation to that late 1850s lecture given by Mathews under the title, "Words,—Their Significance, Use and Abuse" (151). However, it seems more appropriate to assign a primarily post-Civil War composition time to *Words,* if for no other reason than that Mathews himself describes the composing process as continuing "from time to time" over the twenty years following that initial lecture (7). Furthermore, the outside sources Mathews claims to have drawn upon for his book chiefly post-date his first public utterance on this subject. In the list of "Principal Books Consulted" provided by Mathews at the end of his text, twenty-nine of the thirty-five books or editions of books cited by the author and bearing copyright dates come from the years after 1859. And, as the 1884 revised edition of *Words* demonstrates, Mathews was not averse to re-writing substantially previously published material if the circumstances so dictated. Thus, it seem prudent to regard the 1876 edition of *Words* as a post-War document.

8. Girard primarily has in mind the collapse of ritual as a mechanism to check mimetic violence when he speaks of the sacrificial crisis. However, since all social institutions, according to his hypothesis, arise out of ritual, the collapse of any modern institution can be taken as a sign of an impending sacrificial crisis.

9. A term devised by the social historian David Pivar to designate this broad reform movement, though organizations with names such as the Maryland Purity Alliance did indeed exist.

10. For Girard, myths "are the retrospective transfiguration of sacrificial crises, the reinterpretation of these crises in the light of the cultural order that has arisen from them" (*Violence* 64). In essence, they are narratives designed to cover up real acts of persecution by assigning all responsibility for this violence to a surrogate victim.

11. In fact, in the passage just cited, Mathews is actually "hunting down" other "detectives" and charging them with "grievous . . . sins" against the "laws of grammar and rhetoric" (341-342).

12. Mathews' obsession with "purity," which he shared with so many other authors of rhetorics and handbooks, carried deep socio-political ramifications. As Susan Miller suggests, "the pedagogic obsession with mechanical correctness also

participated in a broadly-based nineteenth-century project of cleanliness'' which sought ''to convince the masses of their dirtiness while saving them from it'' (57). For example, the powerful social hygiene movement of this era (funded in part by John D. Rockefeller, Jr.) made personal cleanliness into an issue of one's relative conformity to hygienic laws, with obedience said to bring good health and disobedience represented as leading only to disease (Pivar 171,244).

5

The NCTE Commission on the English Curriculum and Teaching the Grammar/Writing Connection

Garry Ross

In 1945, the National Council of Teachers of English appointed a Commission on the English Curriculum. Its purpose was "to study the place of the language arts in life today, to examine the needs and methods of learning for children and youth, and to prepare a series of volumes on the English Curriculum based on sound democratic principles and the most adequate research concerning how powers in the language arts can best be developed" (I vii). The Commission began as a 177 member group who divided their work among five committees: "The Committee on Reading and Literature," "The Committee on Language and Writing," "The Committee On Speech," "The Committee on Listening," and the "Production Committee for the Elementary School." Three of the committees were further divided into subcommittees with responsibilities for primary grades, intermediate grades, junior high school, senior high school, first two years of college, and graduate school and senior college. "The Committee on Listening" and the "Production Committee for the Elementary School" were not divided into subcommittees. The first volume of the Commission on the English Curriculum, *The English Language Arts*, appeared in 1952 after seven years of work by its members. Their work coming shortly after the end of World War II, the members of the commission saw their efforts as closely bound to the maintenance and continued development of American democracy. They saw the purpose of teaching language arts in these terms: "The goals of teaching the

Language Arts are as old as the ideals of Western civilization. Yet each generation faces the task of interpreting these goals anew in the light of the conditions of its own age. To think clearly and honestly, to read thoughtfully, to communicate effectively, and to listen intelligently have always been basic to the perpetuation of democratic ways of living'' (3) and identified its mission as the need

> to discover ways in which the knowledge now available of the nature and
> uses of language and literature, of the way children grow, and of the problems of American and world society can be used in American education for
> the improvement of teaching the language arts, to the end that young people may be better prepared to deal effectively with the critical problems of
> life in the mid-twentieth century. (5)

The final volume of the Commission's work was published in 1965, twenty years after the appointment of the members of the original commission.

For the purpose of looking at how the Commission's five volumes—*The English Language Arts, Language Arts for Today's Children, The Language Arts in the Secondary School*, and *The Education of Teachers of English for American Schools and Colleges*—influenced the teaching of grammar and more particularly how they treated the interrelatedness of grammar instruction and composition instruction, it is important to note that the commission's work is roughly bounded by the heyday of structuralism (Fries' *Structure of American English* appeared in 1952) and the Chomskyan revolution (*Syntactic Structures* appeared in 1957 and *The Aspects Theory of Syntax* in 1965). The work of the commission began at a time when, at least in linguistic circles, descriptivism had pretty much fully discredited prescriptivism which had, from its beginnings, tried to force English grammar into Latin paradigms. Therefore, a reader of the commission volumes would hope to find sound advice about grammar teaching and its relationship to writing. Indeed, when this research was begun, it was hoped that a connection between the commission's work and the production of useful texts at all educational levels would be found. However, there is no useful advice for the teacher of writing present in these volumes. Even without reading the names of commission members, a reader of their volumes can readily tell that their production was dominated by scholars of *belle lettres*, not by serious scholars of language and how it functions. Quite simply there was nothing in the commission's curriculum series to build on as far as education in grammar and composition is concerned. Dominated by literature experts, the volumes outline ways of teaching literature quite successfully; but they offer little to teachers or students of writing. They are typical of the attitudes about writing instruction outlined in *Education for College* (1961) when the authors ask why so many English teachers are inadequately prepared to teach writing: ''The fault lies with college and university departments of English, which continue to assume that, if they prepare a student to teach literature, a kind of osmosis will endow him with the knowledge and ability to teach language and writing'' (91).

This chapter presents a discussion of each of the five volumes produced by the commission, paying particular attention to its discussion of grammar, and concludes with an estimate of the opportunity lost in the production of these volumes to develop a grammar of writing that would be helpful to students and teachers of writing.

The English Language Arts

In Volume I, *The English Language Arts*, the authors attempted to ''(1) give an overview of the curriculum in English Language Arts from the preschool through the graduate school, (2) to bring the best thinking in the field to bear upon major issues faced by curriculum committees throughout the country, and (3) to describe as illustrative for local committees a method of approach to curriculum-making found useful in this study'' (2). The book is divided into four parts: ''Making the Curriculum,'' ''Suggested Programs,'' ''Problems Faced by Curriculum Makers,'' and ''Evaluating the Outcomes of Instruction.'' Though the authors make occasional references to grammar throughout the text, only one chapter is dedicated to a discussion of grammar and its relationship to study in the English language arts. Chapter 12, ''The Modern View of Grammar and Linguistics'' is twenty-eight pages long. It begins with a discussion of what the authors label the five ''Basic Concepts Evolved by Linguistics'': Language changes constantly; change is normal; spoken language is the language; correctness rests upon usage; and all usage is relative. In the five and one half pages of discussion about the science of linguistics, two and one half deal with writing, but only in a cursory way. No suggestions are made about how a curriculum could be changed to incorporate any linguistic ideas into the teaching of writing. The basic argument of these pages is twofold: eighteenth-century authors relying on Latin and Greek models created rules that made correctness rest not upon usage, but upon prescription; and contemporary linguists do not recognize a distinction between good and bad English except in a relative sense. There are no absolutes, only appropriateness based on linguistic occasion.

The chapter's discussion of grammar is also inadequate. After pointing out ''that English grammar, as it is generally taught, is far from being a satisfactory explanation of English as it is actually used'' (280), the authors suggest that there are ''three major factors to be taken into account in planning a program in grammar: (1) individuals differ in the extent to which they can profit from instruction in grammar; (2) the desire to improve one's language is fundamental to success in doing so; and (3) knowledge about language is not the same thing as ability to use language effectively'' (288). The authors do not, however, offer any curriculum plan for integrating grammar instruction into English education. Indeed, in the chapter section headed ''A

Planned Program—Continuity without Grade Placement," the only advice given are platitudes such as "development of language power is a matter of individual guidance." "Growth in language power is slow." "Concepts develop over a long period of time." The chapter offers no practical advice about how to integrate grammar instruction into writing instruction or about how a student can use knowledge about grammar to become a better writer. Grammar, for the authors, is too much a part of the tradition of English instruction to be ignored or left out of the curriculum. Yet it is not important enough for them to give meaningful attention to it. The inclusion of only a twenty-two page treatment in a volume of 501 pages suggests the intent of the authors.

Language Arts for Today's Children

Volume II of the curriculum series appeared in 1954, nine years after the NCTE Commission had been formed. Divided into four sections, the book brings together four related parts: "the sources from which any effective program in the language arts stem"; "the four strands of the language arts program—listening, speaking, reading, and writing"; bringing "the four phases of language ... back into functional relationships among themselves"; and "basic considerations involved in setting up and appraising a sound language arts program" (v).

Controlling the relationship of the four elements of the language arts program to each other is the concept of the "Teachable Moment, the time when a child is ready for what he is to be taught." (23). The Teachable Moment includes physical, mental, social, and emotional readiness to be taught. However, that which is "as important as physical and mental maturity is the child's attitude toward what is being taught" (23). Without the proper attitude, the child will not make use of his or her intelligence. Thus the teacher not only must be aware of the students' physical and mental readiness to learn but also must be aware of students' attitudes toward what is being taught. Teaching, then, must take place when the attitude is right:

> Efforts to improve usage in a child's speech will bring little result until the child himself wants to improve and until his ear is tuned to the better forms so that they "sound right." The book material the child uses, on the other hand, may be predominantly better in usage than his speech. He becomes accustomed to patterns of usage in print which he does not carry over into his speech, at least beyond the teacher's presence. In writing, the child can become accustomed to higher standards and may learn to write better English than he speaks. Filling in blanks probably does not aid him much; improvement comes through many experiences in doing real writing that is important to him. (233)

The role of grammar, then, in the *Language Arts for Today's Children* is little more than emphasis upon usage problems—a common confusion even today. The authors write that "concerted attack on individual items of usage in the intermediate grades helps greatly in clearing the way for more mature elements of speech and writing in later years" (238). The crucial matter becomes "the *use* of language, not the classification of forms" (238). Instruction in proper use rather than proper classification "means that instruction will be focused on improvement in the pupil's own speech and writing" (238). The committee's emphasis on what is really a false division between classification and function does not support a language arts teacher's effort to develop a vocabulary and technique that can be used in teaching mature writing and speaking skills. The committee's assertion that "research indicates that run-on sentences, fragments, and garbled expression occur more frequently in [the intermediate grades] than at any other level of the school system" (240) becomes hollow because they offer no guidance in how to teach students to correct these problems. Their advice is to offer platitudes such as "clear thinking is the only adequate basis for clear sentences."

The committee's lack of concern for grammar instruction is reinforced by their acceptance of the linguistic truth that children learn language by hearing it and imitating what they hear. By accepting this truth, they adopt a cloak of linguistic respectability; but they fail to recognize that speaking and writing are different processes. It is true that children formulate rules to help them reproduce the language that they are exposed to; however, the committee ignores the differences between spoken and written language when they write that "Children can learn very early that conformity to accepted patterns of grammatical usage and spelling are as important as the use of commonly understood letter forms in writing " (348–349). Writing has to be taught and standard English is primarily a written dialect; whereas speaking is learned independent of explicit instruction. To argue that spoken forms are learned in the same way as the forms of business letters is to argue from a naive position. The authors do not recognize that spoken forms are modified by instruction in standard English and that as William Labov pointed out in *The Logic of Nonstandard English* (1969) instruction can make use of the grammar of both nonstandard and standard English to facilitate the learning of "accepted" forms.

Divorcing grammar instruction from an emphasis on how language is used in the real world makes such instruction the bore that it can become to students who are never given a clear reason why they are studying the parts and structure of sentences. However, grammar instruction that is used to teach a vocabulary and technique for the analysis of language both spoken or written can provide useful insights into components of writing as small as the relationship of phonology to style or as large as the role of discourse markers in developing coherent texts. The purpose of grammar instruction is to empower the language user to manipulate language so as to be able to master his or her work and play experiences rather than be mastered by them.

The English Language Arts in the Secondary School

Volume III of the NCTE Curriculum Series is *The English Language Arts in the Secondary School*. It was published in 1956, eleven years after the formation of the Commission on the English Language. All members of the committee which produced Volume III had been members of the production committee for Volume I. The authors see this continuity as a plus: "Volume III has had full benefit of those earlier years of co-operative planning and discussions of the language arts curriculum in the entire range from nursery school through graduate study" (vi). However, the continuity in membership meant a continuity in myopia as far as language study versus literary study is concerned, and the committee still does not formulate a meaningful curriculum that would help school teachers incorporate grammar instruction into the teaching of writing.

The volume is divided into two parts, "The Adolescent and the World Today" and "The Language Arts Program." One chapter of Part II deals with "the teaching of grammar, usage, and spelling" and attempts "to bring order out of the many viewpoints expressed in these fields today" so as "to give the teacher concrete help for classroom practice" (v). This chapter, "Chapter 10, Developing Competence in Grammar, Usage, and Spelling," is fifty pages long and is divided into two sections, "Grammar and Usage," and "Spelling." Section I makes up 30 pages of the chapter with section II being allotted 20 pages. Six pages of section I deal with usage, and twenty four deal with grammar. This same committee had given grammar only 26 pages in Volume I and had reached no clear-cut curriculum suggestions there. Here in Volume III, the committee offers a little more specificity under such headings as "Elements Requiring Instruction" and "Problems of Teaching Method," but their trying to be specific merely emphasizes their inadequacy for the task before them.

The introduction to Chapter 10 ends with the following paragraph:

> What is the relationship in the secondary schools between the teaching of English grammar and the development of the students' ability to use language well? The teaching of systematic English grammar to a student does not automatically result in his speaking and writing better. On the other hand, the teaching of grammar cannot be ignored, for through a functional knowledge of the basic structure of the English sentence and of the terms used in identifying language forms, an intelligent student can be assisted in the revision of his writing and in the self-analysis of recordings of his speech. (357)

These three observations are an accurate description of the importance of grammar instruction at the time the report was written. However, they do not offer the teacher suggestions about what to do nor do they answer the questions What should be taught? Why should it be taught? and When should it be taught? Subsequently, the authors make no suggestions about how to integrate grammar instruction and writing instruction. As applied linguists have shown, the place to teach grammar is at the point in writing where grammatical knowledge can be of use to the writer. But the committee does not recognize that the why and the when of grammar instruction are closely intertwined. Knowledge of grammar provides a vocabulary and a technique of analysis by which the writer can identify and remedy writing problems. The need to know how to revise then is the why. And during the revision process is the when. Grammar instruction in isolation from real language use—either that of the student or that of someone else—cannot be beneficial to a student. As the committee points out "a knowledge of grammar cannot be learned 'all at once' or 'once and for all.' Neither can it be effectively acquired apart from a situation in which the pupil is grappling with the specific improvement of his own writing" (365) or someone else's. Grammatical knowledge provides two types of knowledge for writers, one about how to revise and another about what to revise. These two types of knowledge though different are clearly connected. The teaching of English grammar, then, should be done when the students' "need for understanding and using [a] particular point [in grammar is] in connection with his own problems of writing" (367). Yet the committee suggests no instruction for prospective teachers about teaching strategies that take advantage of grammatical knowledge.

What is to be taught? Sentence structure, modification and subordination, agreement, nouns and pronouns, verbs, and adjectives and adverbs. For a committee whose guiding principle was the need to move away from traditional grammar, this list seems to be no move at all. And their discussion of these topics is as vague and unrewarding as the earlier discussions in volumes I and II. The following selections are illustrative of the generalizations offered: "As they grow, [students] need help in understanding the operation of an effective sentence. They need practice in writing and in appraising sentences which are complete, clear, and varied" (371). "Grammar becomes increasingly useful in helping the able students to understand the general ways in which words and phrases and clauses can modify each other and indicate directly or indirectly degrees of primary or subordinate importance" (371). The authors point out that English is no longer highly inflected, but that there are "still a number of words in English which require a change of form to indicate a change of relationship to another word" (372). *You sing* but *He sings* and *There is one* but *Here are two* are given as examples. Another example is the observation that there often is confusion in agreement when words intervene between two words which are supposed to agree

with each other. However, the committee supposes that instruction in agreement is not needed because "a student learns sentence patterns uncon-
sciously" (371). This unconscious learning will enable the student to
develop grammatical facts inductively which the student can apply "in handling the problems of agreement" (372). The authors fail to recognize that
in order for a student to be exposed to the entire domain of knowledge that
constitutes the basic rules of agreement would require a great amount of
reading. Whereas, the basic rules can be presented in a fairly brief passage
of a handbook. Why require the student to formulate rules inductively that
have already been clearly established and published? Wouldn't it make more
sense to ask the student to apply the rules deductively to what he or she has
written than to ask the student to read perhaps endlessly before finding any
clues to his or her immediate writing problem? Refusing to provide basic
principles because they are best learned inductively leaves room for large
gaps in knowledge and is extremely inefficient as a means of instruction.

The heading "Verbs" offers more generalizations: "The student needs
to use accurately not only one-word verbs, like *sing* but also verb phrases,
like *will have sung* or *was going to sing*" (374). "Often [the student] must
choose from among different verb forms the one which will agree with the
simple subject of his sentence" (374). "Both logic and teaching experience
indicate that direct practice of the correct pattern, with little if any regard to
grammatical framework, is usually successful in connection with teaching
the proper use of strong verbs" (374). "Having the student repeat many
times orally and in writing the same correct pattern establishes it" (375).

And under the heading "Adjectives and Adverbs," the authors offer the
following: "Many problems of choosing the right adjective or adverb are
good-usage problems, in which direct memorizing is worth while; but many
others are problems in which grammatical knowledge can be helpful. Perhaps most important about the latter is the use of adjectives and adverbs in
making comparisons" (375).

After establishing the elements requiring instruction, the authors turn to
methods of instruction. In this section of Chapter 10, they deal with "The
Need of Relating Instruction Directly to Speech and Writing," "The Value
of an Inductive Approach to Rules," "The Avoidance of Mere Definition
and Identification," "Provision for the Needs of Individuals," and "The
Measurement of Results." The section begins with the suggestion that teachers give grammatical instruction only in those "usages and principles [stu-
dents] have need of learning" and suggests that these principles should be
taught "by direct application to the effective and ineffective expression of
pupils themselves" (376). Whether the need to learn is established by testing
or solely by the teacher's analysis of student writing is never stated. It is not
made clear how the teacher will determine what part of the domain of standard English it is that students don't know.

The teacher is then encouraged to use the inductive method to teach grammar. By preparing a number of sentences for analysis the teacher allows the student to arrive at the proper principle through induction. This approach has some merit and certainly is preferable to a multiple-guess or fill-in-the-blank worksheet. The authors are correct to assert that "the important point here and elsewhere in the teaching of grammar is that the student shall not be tempted to memorize a statement instead of developing a clear concept. He must be helped to see that grammatical knowledge is a useful framework for analysis of the language he is using every day in speaking, listening, writing, and reading" (377). This grammatical knowledge can be used by students to revise their own writing and to develop a mature, readable style. According to the authors, "the real evidence of a students' grasp of grammatical concepts lies in his ability (1) to write good sentences, (2) to manipulate parts of sentences easily, and (3) to improve sentences which need improvement" (378). Grammatical knowledge provides a vocabulary and technique for analysis of and discussion about pieces of writing—analysis and discussion that should result in better writing.

The Education of Teachers of English for American Schools and Colleges

The fifth volume of the NCTE Curriculum Series, *The Education of Teachers of English for American Schools and Colleges*, appeared in 1963, two years before the fourth volume and 18 years after the formation of the 1945 commission. In many ways, it was the most difficult of the volumes to produce because it covered so much. The purpose of the volume was to recommend how best to train language arts teachers for all levels of education from the primary schools all the way through graduate school, areas that could have used a volume each. Therefore, the suggestions, based largely on programs already in use, were once again too general to be of much use to those institutions revising or setting up teacher training programs.

The committee which drafted Volume V divided it into four parts: "Educating Teachers of English for the Elementary School," "Educating Teachers of English for the Secondary School," "Providing for Continuing Education," and "Preparing Teachers of College English." Unlike earlier volumes which were written by the committee with the intention of presenting a unified voice, the twelve chapters of Volume III have been written by separate authors or separate groups of authors. The committee supports the overall need "to improve the preparation of teachers" (2), but leaves the analysis and suggestion up to the individual or group authors of the various chapters.

However, in this volume, there is still much confusion over what needs to be done and over how to implement effective programs. Typical of the dichotomy are the suggestions the various authors make about the teaching of composition in the elementary school. The purpose of the education program is "to help prospective teachers to understand the importance of teaching composition and of stimulating in children a desire to write and recognition of the value of writing" (36). However, the implementation of a scheme for the realization of these purposes revolves around the testing of prospective teachers:

> It seems particularly appropriate in institutions devoted to the education of teachers that a year before the candidate enters student teaching he should be required to take a standardized test in English usage, punctuation, and spelling on which he may be expected to reach a designated norm before he is permitted to stand before an elementary school class. If he fails to meet the standard set, he then has one year in which to do remedial work and an opportunity for a second testing before applying for admission to student teaching. (56–57)

There are no suggestions for a course of study that will lead to the prospective teacher's being able to achieve the purpose of teaching composition in elementary school. He or she is just simply not instructed in the teaching of composition or in the relationship between grammar instruction and writing instruction.

The program falls back upon the usual approach of the curriculum series, reliance on the vague generalization with no concrete suggestions for a course of study. The following are illustrative of this usual approach: "The prospective teacher should leave college recognizing that the problem of usage is not so much a question of right or wrong, of grammatical rule, or of scholarly edict as it is a matter of social convention in a wide variety of formal and informal situations" (59–60). The teacher "should know the basic patterns of the English sentence, why the grammar of Latin is inadequate for describing the locutions of his native tongue, and the relationship between grammatical structure and usage" (61). The elementary school teacher should know that "the composition should exhibit a feeling for style, displaying both precision and fluency, exhibiting mastery of the varieties of English sentence structure and the mechanics of writing" (65–66). The authors offer no clear-cut suggestions for a plan of study that will make these generalizations meaningful to the elementary teacher nor do they offer a plan for how these generalizations should be implemented. They assume that if an educator knows enough about language to recognize the importance of these generalizations, he or she is prepared to teach writing to elementary students.

Preparation of the teacher for the secondary level is primarily literature-based. The report suggests that "the mimimum major in English should include at least one course in composition beyond the freshman year, courses in the history of the language and in modern grammar and . . . a balanced program in literature'' (151). The authors later explain that "courses in the history of the language and in modern grammar" means a course in the history of the language and one in modern grammar, not multiple courses in each. "The balanced program in literature" means a program in which all upper-level English courses but three are literature courses. The required advanced composition course does not offer students any composition theory; it merely asks students to write longer papers, following various modes. The teaching of writing, then, is not addressed in any concrete way. And the connection between writing and grammar is ignored except for the ususal comments about usage. The "Standard of Preparation to Teach English" is given on page 181. The standards require the following in language:

1. A fundamental knowledge of the historical development and present character of the English language; phonology (phonetics and phonemics), morphology, syntax, vocabulary (etymology and semantics), the relations of language and society.

2. A specialized knowledge of the English language which is appropriate to the teacher's particular field of interest and responsibility.

3. An informed command of the arts of language—rhetoric and logic; ability to speak and write language which is not only unified, coherent, and correct but also responsible, appropriate to the situation, and stylistically effective.

It is unclear why the authors in part 3 should require a "command of the arts of language—rhetoric and logic" when they suggest that no university-level instruction in either be required for certification or graduation. And the main proposal of those high school English teachers surveyed by NCTE to find out their suggestions for ways to improve the education of English teachers was to require instruction in how to use a "teaching machine attack on grammar, mechanics, [and] spelling" (184), though they also suggested more emphasis on composition and the use of structural grammar to teach writing. The committee which prepared this volume of the curriculum series agreed with the NCTE Committee on the National Interest which had found that "in short, most of the English majors who were graduated in June, 1960, and are now teaching in high school are simply not equipped either to deal with problems of teaching the language and composition or to keep up with current developments in the application of linguistics to the teaching of English" (185). To remedy this problem, they offered the following recommendations for the preparation of teachers of English. In the English language, students who are going to be language arts teachers should take courses in the history and structure of the language, including attention to modern English grammars and to usage, lexicography, and related studies and in basic and advanced composition. These recommendations were just

more of the same for future teachers. No instruction in rhetorical or composition theory was recommended, and those courses recommended in English
grammar were divorced from writing instruction.

The most damning approach to writing instruction presented in Volume
IV is the introduction of programmed learning. Its benefits come from its
emphasis on individualized instruction; and had the approach not relied on
"automated teaching devices," it might have worked. However, all programmed learning did was to replace the mimeographed worksheet with a
teaching machine. It did not provide a mechanism whereby what was learned
at the machine was integrated into the student's future experiences with language. The approach had the same failing as the worksheet approach. It gave
students a lot of information which was never clearly integrated in their own
writing. Knowledge of grammar and mechanics was divorced from knowledge
of the writing process, and teachers were not trained in how to integrate the
two types of knowledge. The committee recognized that "for both teacher and
student the study of English usage was held to be identical with the study of
grammar" (250). The teaching machine provided quick and easy instruction
in usage. It could do little for grammar, particularly that knowledge of grammar that could be applied beneficially to the revision of student writing.

The lack of sound suggestions for improving the requirement for instruction in language is odd because the committee makes reference to the pitiful
amount of instruction that had been done before. The committee writes that
"ironically, one of the anomalies in the traditional preparation of teachers of
English is that they have been given virtually no instruction in the nature of
language" (246). But their recommendation to provide this instruction is a
requirement of only three courses: "a description of English grammar," "a
theoretical and more advanced course in language analysis," and "a historical course covering American as well as British English" (256). Any connection between these courses and writing instruction is ignored. Preparation
in writing consists merely of more writing. No instruction in the theory or
methodology of composition is suggested, and no discussion about the relationship between grammar instruction and writing instruction is given.
Unfortunately, this knowledge must be developed by the prospective teacher
through his or her own resources of generalization and analysis because no
instruction is proposed to be given to the prospective teacher in the connection between grammar and writing.

The National Interest and the Teaching of English (1961) had found that
the methods courses on the teaching of English devoted "more than twice as
much time to the teaching of literature as to the teaching of language and
composition combined" (340). If the time were divided equally between
language and composition, that means that time spent in methodology classes
would have worked out roughly two-thirds literature, one-sixth language,
one-sixth composition. However, having urged a better balance in light of
these findings, the only suggestion the committee came up with was for

methodology courses to require more "practice in writing exposition" and more review of "the essentials of English spelling, capitalization, and punctuation" (341).

The preparation of the college teacher of English was at the time the committee produced Volume IV equally biased in favor of literature even though the committee recognized that most candidates working on the doctoral degree would spend their career teaching first-year composition courses as a major part of their workload. The committee writes that

> the college teacher of English faces many of the same problems [as the secondary teacher]. He is very likely to be assigned the teaching of freshman English, which includes attention, formal or informal, to matters of language, of syntax, of usage. Yet conventional preparation gives him little, if any, instruction in the nature of the English language, even less in the nature of language itself. He is likely to have a course in the history of the English language and perhaps another in traditional grammar and conservative usage . . . [but] seldom does he have work in rhetoric and composition beyond freshman English. (527)

As the curriculum committee points out, the college English teacher is left up to his or her own intuitions about the nature of language—intuitions that are as apt to lead in the wrong direction as in the right.

However, to overcome this glaring deficiency in the preparation of college English instructors, the committee offers little. They would have required the Ph.D. candidate to take courses in the structure of modern English, the history of the English language, Old English, American English, and linguistic applications to the study of literature and composition. But the relation of these course requirements to writing instruction is never defined beyond the truism that "the future college teacher . . . ought to be a good writer and a good critic of writing" (554). The work in linguistic application to composition is to provide "a detailed knowledge of the structure of English sentences [and] encourage [the teacher] to develop a reasoned attitude toward matters of usage" (555). That there is or can be a connection between grammar instruction and writing instruction is ignored. And, of course, rhetoric and compositon theory make up no part of the committee's recommendations.

The College Teaching of English

The last volume of the Curriculum series to be published but the fourth in the list of the commission's work is *The College Teaching of English*, which appeared in 1965, twenty years after the commission had begun its work. The volume is edited by John C. Gerber, John H. Fisher, and Curt A. Zimansky; and it consists of thirteen chapters, beginning with a "Prospect" by John H. Fisher and ending with "The Department of English: Organization

and Administration'' by Robert W. Rogers. It appeared as a joint venture of
NCTE, the Modern Language Association, the American Studies Association, and the College English Association. Four of the thirteen chapters dealt
with composition–chapter 5, ''Freshman Composition,'' by Robert Gorrell;
chapter 6, ''Advanced Composition,'' by Richard Lloyd-Jones; chapter 7,
''Courses in Creative Writing,'' by Richard Scowcroft; and chapter 8,
''Courses in Language and Linguistics,'' by Albert H. Marckwardt. None of
these chapters offers any concrete suggests for teaching the writing and
grammar connection. They all tend to rely on the traditional dictum that if a
student reads a lot he or she will mature as a student and learn how to write.

Fisher's introductory chapter is a reaffirmation of the centrality of literary studies to English education. The teaching of English at the college level
is the teaching of literary interpretation. A reader of the introduction would
assume that neither writing nor grammar is taught in college English departments. This attitude dominates chapter 2, ''The Study and Teaching of
English'' by William C. De Vane, as well. De Vane praises the rise of literary studies or *belle lettres* over philology and admits that he is not competent to address the other, minor area of English, namely composition. He
suggests Strunk and White's *Elements of Style* as the best and perhaps only
book needed for first-year composition instruction.

Robert M. Gorrel in chapter 5, ''Freshman Composition,'' laments what
he sees as the fact that American high schools are not doing their jobs. The
best thing for first-year composition instruction is to abandon it and let each
department be responsible for teaching its own students to write. His argument is that students cannot write from a vacuum and need the subject matter knowledge that their majors give them in order to have something to write
about. Too many English departments are ''strongly wedded to prescriptive
grammar and to readings which have become familiar by appearance in collection after collection'' (96). They just simply do not provide students with
a body of knowledge about which first-year students can write. If the student
becomes ''comfortable in standard English, '' (98) the goals of the English
department have been reached.

Gorrel sees a shift in attitude toward English grammar and its role in the
first-year composition class:

> the most important change is a slow but persistent shift in the general atti-
> tude of teachers and directors of the course toward efforts to show students
> how language works rather than to tell them what not to do, toward the
> teaching of grammar based on the grammar of English rather than Latin,
> focusing on word order and sentence patterns more than on drill in the clas-
> sification of parts of speech or memorization of artificially contrived para-
> digms. (102)

He suggests that the new grammarians have provided insights about both oral
and written language that can be very helpful in the first-year course:

for purposes of teaching composition, we need more than a grammatical
description of patterns of subordination; we need to know the effects of the
patterns, the relationships the device reveals, the purposes for which the
device can be used by the writer. Or, as another illustration, we might consider the basic predication patterns of the sentence. The new grammars,
particularly generative grammar, have shown us a good deal about how
sentence patterns work. (113)

However, he does not give a clear or full description of how the newly discovered facts about language that linguists have found can be integrated into
writing instruction nor does he provide a methodology for teaching the
writing/grammar connection. This absence of concrete suggestion is particularly disappointing when Gorrell writes "we cannot conclude that the teaching of formal grammar is a waste of time or even that it should not be
included in the composition course" (106-107).

Chapter 6, "Advanced Composition" by Richard Lloyd-Jones, discusses
the traditional advanced composition course, business writing, and technical
writing. The only reference to grammar in the essay is to what Lloyd-Jones
sees as a need to remove "grammar" sections from technical writing books
so that the emphasis of the technical writing course will be "rational thought
and clear explanation." Those students who have not mastered the usage of
standard English are to be sent to remedial courses.

In chapter 7, "Courses in Creative Writing," Richard Scowcroft does
not mention grammar at all. He has written his essay to justify offering creative writing in universities. And after admitting that what the course does
for writers cannot be determined, he asserts that a creative writing course
does "something to help the student improve his writing." However, the
main benefit of a creative writing course is to "widen his capacities in reading, criticism, literary craft, and human awareness" (133). Scowcroft then
describes what is done in various classes at different institutions. In none of
them is the case made that a knowledge of how language works would be of
benefit to the beginning novelist or poet.

Albert Marckwardt begins chapter 8, "Courses in Linguistics," by making a distinction between philology and linguistics: linguistics is the scientific study of speech, and philology is the study of culture as revealed in language. He then argues for the inclusion of linguistics study in the
undergraduate program. He deplores the traditional grammarian's emphasis
on correctness and praises the structural grammarian's emphasis on how language works in different contexts. Prescriptivism is not as rewarding to students as descriptivism because prescriptivism sets up models of correctness
rather than describing what language really is and how it works. He admits
that his contemporaries in linguistics had done little work with the English
language beyond the level of the sentence, but suggests that the work Zellig
Harris was doing in discourse analysis was leading linguists into looking at

broader stretches of language. In discourse analysis, he believes, will rest the most help for teachers of writing.

The NCTE Commission, Literature, and Linguistics

Marckwardt's discussion of the differences between linguistics and philology reminds the reader of the split in English studies between philology and *belle lettres* which began late in the last century and reached completion in the 1930s and 1940s. The tensions between the advocates of these two approaches to learning, one German-based and the other British- and American-based, led to a division in the study of English that has not been healed. Linguists have been looked upon by their colleagues in literature as wanting to push English departments back into the rigorous scientific study that had been philology. And linguists have been looked upon by their literature colleagues as viewing literature as nothing more than grist for the mill of scientific language analysis. Since literature specialists have dominated most English departments for quite a long time, efforts by NCTE to establish what should be done in the teaching of English have been dominated by literature specialists. The five volumes produced by the 1945 commission clearly show that the commission's primary concern was to teach teachers how to teach literature. They paid a little attention to writing and grammar because writing and grammar had made up most of the teacher's work for so long. But after reading these volumes, we come away aware that the work of Bloomfield, Pike, Fries, Harris, and Chomsky has been ignored. And grammar studies could have been made more meaningful to the student and more useful to the writer if the panel had not been dominated by a group of scholars who were beyond doubt expert in their own areas but whose main belief about writing and writing instruction was that successful writing is the product of osmosis as the student reads great literature.

The work of the commission in developing the NCTE Curriculum Series took twenty years—years in which knowledge about grammar and writing grew in the field of linguistics. However, the commission did not take advantage of the increase in knowledge and, while developing a strong curriculum for the teaching of literature, did little, if anything, for the teaching of writing. The final volume of the series to appear shows that the commission had not progressed beyond "the Woolley or Scott and Denney handbook approach" (158) to writing instruction. And the valuable insights linguists were making into the grammar/writing connection played no part in developing a curriculum for writing instruction.

II

Present Concerns About Grammar and Writing

Opening this section with the linguist's point of view that Garry Ross found missing from the NCTE Commission's reports, John Edlund borrows Bakhtin's metaphor in "The Rainbow and the Stream: Grammar as System Versus Language in Use" and uses the familiar *langue/parole* distinction to investigate a number of contemporary linguistic contexts where the concepts of grammar and literacy must interact. He focuses on the particular case of ESL writers to urge college writing teachers to find ways to negotiate a compromise between grammar as an abstract system and language in individual use. Moving from Edlund's theoretical perspective to practical questions about grammar and writing, in "The Use of Grammar Texts: A Call for Pedagogical Inquiry," Joan Mullin uses survey research to prove that when we relegate grammar to handbooks, we cause our students to misperceive its relative importance for writers. R. Baird Shuman uses his experiences in writing classrooms to support the view that for practical and social purposes students should master Standard Edited English. In "Grammar for Writers: How Much is Enough?" Shuman provides a pragmatic answer to this question by identifying the grammatical information most useful to students and teachers of writing.

The next four essays in this section explore contemporary sites where we see grammar and writing conjoined. We need to read these situated discussions in terms of the theoretical and practical concerns that Edlund, Mullin, and Shuman have put forth: the tension between grammar as a fixed system and a fluid response to time and place that Edlund describes, and Mullin's and Shuman's admission that grammatical knowledge ensures social acceptance. In "Grammar in the Writing Center: Opportunities for Discovery and Change," Carl W. Glover and Byron L. Stay posit their writing center as a context where grammar instruction and writing necessarily happen at the same time. Glover and Stay show that the nature of the writing center tutorial is such that when a peer tutor interacts with a particular writer about a specific paper, together they seize the moment when grammar and writing can intersect. Donald Bushman and Elizabeth Ervin shift our attention to the all–too–familiar dominance grammar as a fixed set of rules holds among teachers of writing across the curriculum. In "Rhetorical Contexts of Grammar: Some Views from Writing-Emphasis Course Instructors," Bushman and Ervin use their experiences in WAC workshops and survey data that they collected at the University of Arizona to establish the rhetorical importance of grammar.

Finally, in our search for contemporary connections between grammar and writing, Stuart C. Brown, Robert Boswell, and Kevin McIlvoy and Wendy Bishop take us into writing classrooms where concerns with grammar, rhetoric, and the composing process coalesce. In "Grammar and Voice in the Teaching of Creative Writing: A Conversation," Brown, Boswell, and McIlvoy base their reflections on years of writing and teaching experience, claiming that grammatical understanding is central to creative expression. In "Teaching Grammar for Writers in a Process Workshop Classroom," as Bishop examines what it means to teach in a process theory writing classroom, she too argues that grammar for writers is essential. But, drawing on the work of Winston Weathers, she would have us add to the dominant grammar of Standard Edited English a diversity of grammars or stylistic alternatives in our process workshop classrooms. Bishop concludes her chapter and this section on present concerns about grammar and writing with journal entries written in Weathers' Grammar B to invite writing teachers to see teaching writing as teaching grammar.

6

The Rainbow and the Stream: Grammar as System Versus Language in Use

John R. Edlund

The question of whether or not to teach grammar appears on the surface to be a simple one. If a writer produces a paper which contains numerous grammatical errors, and if these errors appear to be one of the main difficulties for a reader in reading and understanding the paper, the logical course of action would seem to be to address these problems by teaching grammar. This is the view of most faculty in disciplines other than composition, of most university administrators, of most students, and of most parents. For people in all walks of life this is common sense. If you are a writing center director, as I am, you could make a long and happy career out of providing clear, well-organized, coherent grammatical instruction, with little fear of criticism from your clientele, colleagues, or supervisors.

In reality, however, the question is not simple at all. Common sense can be wrong, even dangerous. A substantial body of empirical research has accumulated that shows that teaching grammar does not improve writing, and *no* studies exist which show that teaching grammar *does* improve writing. George Hillocks Jr., in his book-length survey of recent empirical studies in composition, concludes:

> The study of traditional school grammar (i.e., the definition of parts of speech, the parsing of sentences, etc.) has no effect on raising the quality of student writing. Every other focus of instruction examined in this review is stronger. Taught in certain ways, grammar and mechanics instruction has a deleterious effect on student writing. In some studies a heavy emphasis on mechanics and usage (e.g., marking every error) resulted in significant losses in overall quality. (248)

Rei Noguchi, in his recent book *Grammar and the Teaching of Writing: Limits and Possibilities*, responds to the above passage by asking, "Assuming that such studies are valid and reliable, *why* does formal instruction in grammar fail to produce any significant improvement in writing quality?" And he asserts, "Just because formal instruction in grammar proves generally unproductive in improving writing does not necessarily mean that we should discard all aspects of grammar instruction" (3). In other words, what aspects of grammar instruction, if any, should we keep?

Noguchi's questions are important and must be answered clearly and definitively if composition, as a discipline, is ever to escape from the trap of being at odds with both colleagues and students concerning teaching practices and theories. Empirical studies have shown that grammar instruction does not correlate with writing improvement. We must know why, and we must know what we should be doing instead.

However, the core of the problems which are called grammatical is at the intersection of a number of different theoretical perspectives, and although each perspective reveals different problems and implies different solutions, they also overlap and confuse one another. Our attempt to answer Noguchi's questions will unavoidably raise even more fundamental linguistic and philosophical questions, such as What is language?, Where and how does it exist?, and How do we acquire it?

The study of language involves an inherent and as yet unresolvable contradiction that is perhaps analogous to the Heisenberg uncertainty principle in physics, which states that the position and velocity of a subatomic particle cannot be measured at the same time. In linguistics the opposition is between language as abstract system and language in individual use. Thus the Belgian linguist Fernand de Saussure divided the study of language into *langue*, the system and relationships of the language considered in a timeless moment, and *parole*, the realm of individual utterances. Noam Chomsky made a similar distinction between "competence" and "performance," and M. A. K. Halliday means much the same thing when he talks of "intra-organism" versus "inter-organism" linguistics (*Language as a Social Semiotic* 57). Saussure argued that *langue* was the proper object of study for a science of linguistics, because utterances were too various, unpredictable, and changeable.

Bakhtin, recognizing this split, divides linguists into two camps: "individualistic subjectivists," best represented for him by Vossler, and "abstract objectivists," represented primarily by Saussure. He represents the relationship between these two views with an image: "If, for the first trend, language is an ever-flowing stream of speech acts in which nothing remains fixed and identical to itself, then, for the second trend, language is the stationary rainbow arched over that stream" (*Marxism* 52). This image is especially apt if we imagine the stream of language to contain not only currents and eddies of ongoing linguistic change, but also mud and wreckage, unseen obstacles, and the other debris of life. The rainbow, on the other hand, is ideal, pure, logical, and timeless. The co-existence without connection expressed in this image is at the heart of our grammarian/anti-grammarian debate. In theory, system and use can be, perhaps must be, divided. In practice, language is a complex interaction of system, intention, history, and context.

In this chapter, I will apply this split perspective to a number of different linguistic contexts in which the contradiction of language as system and language in use play out: the descriptivist/prescriptivist debate, historical linguistics and the problem of ongoing linguistic change, Stephen Krashen's language acquisition theory, M. A. K. Halliday's vision of a grammar-constructed reality, and finally, the writing teacher's perspective.

The Descriptivist/Prescriptivist Debate

The common sense view is that knowing grammar will enable you to speak "correctly." The prescriptive type of grammar found in standard college handbooks, commonly called a "school" grammar, is designed to define the standard of what is "correct" and what is not, and to teach those principles. Edward Finegan, in his useful and interesting book, *Attitudes Toward English Usage: The History of a War of Words*, notes that in the view of many linguists this school grammar "has given the impression that nonstandard *spoken* varieties of English (and sometimes merely informal standard ones) are 'bad' or 'ungrammatical' English," and has provided "too-narrow and too-rigid definitions of 'standard English' itself, definitions that reject the usages of many educated and cultured speakers and writers" (9).

In fact, Finegan observes, many Americans consider bad grammar to be a crime or a sin against the national language, and evidence of questionable moral character. It is no surprise then that self-appointed "language guardians" emerge in every generation. When, for example, a cigarette company began using the slogan "Winston tastes good, like a cigarette should," *New York Times* writer John Kieran responded "Such things . . . persuade me that the death penalty should be retained." And poet John Ciardi confessed that he'd rather hear his first grade son swearing "*As*, damn it!" than using *like* as a conjunction. (6). It would seem that making a grammatical mistake is considerably worse than swearing and just about equivalent to first degree murder.

The core of Finegan's book is a chronicle of the battle, in 1962, between the linguists and the language guardians over *Webster's Third New International Dictionary*, the first dictionary created according to the principles of descriptive linguistics. The editors of the dictionary were accused of basing their definitions "simply on current usage" and of "refusing to distinguish good from bad," assertions which were, of course, quite true by design (122). Most commentators believed certain words, meanings, and usages to be right and others wrong, and they wanted the "wrong" ones eliminated or

clearly marked. The controversy was so heated that the American Heritage
Publishing Company attempted to buy out G. & C. Merriam, intending to
suppress the dictionary. That being unsuccessful, they published their own
dictionary, including "extensive notes on how to use the language" (136).

We might ask, what does it matter if *like* becomes a conjunction? What
can possibly be at stake? There are many contradictions here. On the one
hand, there is the idea of progress. If the linguists simply describe the status
quo, without judgment, how can we improve our language and our society?
On the other is the conservative fear that a valuable legacy of the past is
being corrupted or debased through careless, inattentive use. Sheridan Baker,
in the guardian camp, finds a political motivation and puts the conflict in
terms of class struggle:

> Good English has to do with the upper classes—and there's the rub—with
> the cultural and intellectual leaders, with the life of the mind in its struggle
> to express itself at its intellectual best. Linguistic relativism has a fervently
> democratic base. 'Science' is only an antiseptic label for a deep social belief
> that we ought not to have classes at all, even among our words. (quoted in
> Finegan 124)

It is as if the structure of society is threatened by linguistic variation. And,
indeed, perhaps it is.

Ivan Illich and Barry Sanders, in their strange book *ABC: The Alphabet-
ization of the Popular Mind*, point out that the first grammar of any modern
European language, the *Gramatica Castellana*, was published by a Spaniard
named Elio Antonio de Nebrija on August 18, 1492, just fifteen days after
Columbus had set sail on what he thought was a new route to India (65).
Nebrija argued to Queen Isabella that "the unbound and ungoverned speech
in which people actually live and manage their lives has become a challenge
to the Crown," (66–7) and that a standardized Spanish grammar would
increase the power and reach of the throne, because it would allow con-
quered barbarians to learn Spanish and make them easier to govern.

But Nebrija had another reason for replacing the people's vernacular
with the grammarian's language. He says:

> Your majesty, it has been my constant desire to see our nation become
> great, and to provide men of my tongue with books worthy of their leisure.
> Presently, they waste their time on novels and fancy stories full of lies. (67)

On the surface, Nebrija's reasoning seems incomprehensible. How
would a standardized language improve taste in reading material? However,
Nebrija was born thirteen years before the first moveable type was put into
use. When he published his Spanish grammar, he was 35 and Europe was
awash in books. Illich and Sanders observe:

> An argument for standardized language is also made today, but the end is
> now different. Our contemporaries believe that standardized language is a

> necessary condition to teach people to read... Nebrija argues just the
> opposite: He was upset because people who spoke in dozens of distinct
> vernacular tongues in 1492 had become victims of a reading epidemic.
> They wasted their leisure on books that circulated outside of any possible
> bureaucratic control. (67)

Nebrija saw the standard language as a way to exert governmental control over publication and reading. Before the printing press, books were expensive and readers few. Most important documents were in Latin, a language which required years of study to master. Reading belonged to the elite. Nebrija wanted to put this genie back into its bottle.

By and large, Nebrija's vision has come to pass. Is it not true that in our own age those who speak and write only so-called "non-standard" dialects are shut out from publication and reading, as Nebrija desired, even in the midst of a surge in interest in ethnic literature? Enforcing a standard language has the effect of ensuring that only those who were born to a particular experience and world view, or who have worked hard to assimilate that world view, have a public voice. On the other hand, while a prescriptive grammar can be used to intimidate and shut out, we cannot ignore the fact that it might also be seen as a tool of social mobility, a way to transcend the social class into which one was born. Speakers of non-standard dialects often welcome prescriptivist approaches, just as they are baffled by attempts to validate or valorize their own dialects. Linguistic forms have social meaning and social consequences, and whether your language is good enough depends on who you want to talk to and what you want to do.

Nebrija was a man ahead of his times. He was fully aware of the fact that his grammar was an *artificio*, an abstract construct, a linguistic system. Illich and Sanders argue that Isabella initially rejected his project for this very reason, because she thought such a book could only be useful to a teacher, and she believed that the vernacular was something that could not be taught but could only be acquired naturally. Today, for the language guardians, and for nearly everyone else in our society, there is a unitary ideal national language, and usage is either correct or incorrect. However, we should keep in mind that this idea, as ubiquitous and powerful as it has become, is relatively new. It may turn out that Queen Isabella of Spain was correct in her linguistic views, in 1492.

The Historical Perspective

As noted above, another source of the vehemence demonstrated by language guardians is the fear that the language is decaying or deteriorating through the influence of unsophisticated users. Prescriptive school grammars are conservative, oriented toward preserving past usages and staving off new ones. However, ongoing linguistic change is an essential feature of any natural language. As Bakhtin says, language is not like a ball tossed from generation to generation, but "endures as a continuous process of becoming" (*Marxism* 81).

Like Bakhtin, American linguist Edward Sapir saw language as a river flowing through time, with a current of its own making, a "drift." Sapir argues that "If there were no breaking up of a language into dialects, if each language continued as a firm, self-contained unity, it would still be constantly moving away from any assignable norm, developing new features unceasingly and gradually transforming itself into a language so different from its starting point as to be in effect a new language." (Sapir, *Language* 150) This process of change has continued in spite of printing, standardized spelling, grammar books, and language guardians.

While most individual variations die out without a trace, others are cumulative in some special direction. Sapir argues that this direction may be inferred from the past history of the language, but it is by no means easy to predict the future state of the language from the present, because the forces that direct this change are so complex and manifold.

> In the long run any new feature of the drift becomes part and parcel of the common, accepted speech, but for a long time it may exist as a mere tendency in the speech of a few, perhaps a despised few. As we look about us and observe current usage, it is not likely to occur to us that our language has a "slope," that the changes of the next few centuries are in a sense prefigured in certain obscure tendencies of the present and that these changes, when consummated, will be seen to be but continuations of changes that have been already effected. We feel rather that our language is practically a fixed system and that what slight changes are destined to take place in it are as likely to move in one direction as another. The feeling is fallacious. (Sapir, *Language* 155)

Sapir argues that it is "the uncontrolled speech of the folk to which we must look for advance information as to the general linguistic movement." And he prophesies (in 1921) that within a couple of hundred years "not even the most learned jurist will be saying 'Whom did you see?' By that time the 'whom' will be as delightfully archaic as the Elizabethan 'his' for 'its'" (156). From our perspective more than seventy years later it appears to be safe to cut about one hundred years off of Sapir's prophecy.

As writing teachers, we are in an excellent position to chart the general direction of certain elements of the drift. These are the very features of student writing that we mark over and over again, things like *alot* for *a lot*,[1] or *their* used with a singular subject. When students write "Every student should bring their book," and get a red mark for it, they are being squeezed between massive linguistic change and the conservative resistance.

The resisters are afraid that the language is losing its ability to make subtle distinctions, and, of course, it is. The language guardians lament loudly every time someone confuses *compose* with *comprise*, or *lie* with *lay*, or forgets to use the subjunctive. However, those resources that are lost or diminished are reinvented and renewed elsewhere. In a lecture about *Attitudes Toward English Usage*, Finegan argued that any existing language is constantly being pulled toward two contradictory extremes of ideal language, a desire for the complexity that would offer a unique expression for every single nuance of thought, and a competing desire for simplicity and economy—a single expression for every (all) thought. On the one hand, we have a poet attempting to express the ineffable; on the other, we have a group of teenagers who know each other and their own world so well that they can communicate using a single expression over and over again.

From the historical perspective a grammatical error might be an anachronism, evidence of the advance of the drift, or a minor eddy in the current, soon to be canceled out. It is harmless variation, a part of the vast process of linguistic change. For this reason it is clear that we should not waste massive amounts of ink and class time fighting against the drift, which is like taking up arms against the sea. If our purpose in teaching grammar is to halt linguistic change, we have chosen an impossible and useless task, and should not teach it. To return to Bakhtin's image, it is to impose the view of the rainbow on the view of the historical stream.

Language Acquisition Theory

Many composition teachers who have rejected grammar teaching as a method for improving writing ability still believe that grammar is a necessary part of the curriculum for foreign students who are learning English as a Second Language (ESL). However, grammar teaching is almost as controversial in the ESL community as it is in composition.

I began my teaching career as a writing teacher in an intensive English as a Second Language program. Grammar was taught, but in a different room, by a different teacher, in a different part of the day. On occasion, students would ask grammatical questions in my class, but by and large our issues were not grammatical, although, of course, their papers were filled with grammatical errors. One of the questions they asked was why is it that you can say:

> He likes looking at paintings.
> > and
> He likes to look at paintings.
> > and
> He enjoys looking at paintings.
> > but not
> *He enjoys to look at paintings.

This is a very common type of problem in ESL writing, but one rarely encountered in the writing of native speakers. According to *The Grammar*

Book: An ESL/EFL Teacher's Course by Celce-Murcia and Larsen-Freeman, the usual way of addressing this particular problem is to have students memorize lists of verbs that take infinitives, verbs that take gerunds, and verbs that take both. These are long lists, as you might imagine. Another approach is to teach "the Bolinger Principle," which states that there is an underlying semantic principle governing the choice: the infinitive very often expresses something "hypothetical, future, unfulfilled," whereas the gerund typically expresses something "real, vivid, fulfilled" (434). But the Bolinger principle doesn't seem to apply to the situation above, and there are, of course, other exceptions.

As an ESL composition teacher I often encountered situations like this one. Grammatical explanations were either too specific to cover the case at hand, or too vague or complex to be useful. It was this situation that made Stephen Krashen's language acquisition theory attractive to me, and it became the basis of my own teaching for many years.

Krashen distinguishes between conscious learning, such as memorizing the list of verbs that take the infinitive, and language acquisition, an innate human ability that takes place at an unconscious level. He also argues that second language acquisition is very similar to first language acquisition (*Principles* 10–11). Babies, after all, do not study grammars and dictionaries, but acquire language naturally from their linguistic environment. Acquisition is a very powerful process, both in children and adults. On the other hand, conscious learning has a very weak influence on language use.

The core idea of the theory is what he calls the "input hypothesis." This states that language acquisition takes place when "comprehensible" input is available. Krashen argues that we acquire language when we are exposed to input that contains structures and vocabulary a bit beyond our current level of competence (i+1). Context or extra-linguistic information can help make input comprehensible. When communication is successful, when the input is understood and there is enough of it, (i+1) will be provided automatically. We acquire by "going for meaning" first, and as a result, we acquire structure. Simple codes—caretaker speech, foreigner talk, teacher talk—facilitate acquisition by making input more comprehensible (*Principles* 20–23).

For example, on one occasion teachers from the ESL program took all of the students to see a baseball game. On the bus a conversation was going on across from me in Spanish. I could not understand everything the students were saying, but I had some Spanish, and I knew that they were talking about Mexican popular music, specifically songs about drinking. That conversation provided a degree of comprehensible input for me, and I could acquire further ability from listening to it. On the other hand, in back of me a conversation was going on in Indonesian. I have no Indonesian, and the context provided no clue as to what they were talking about. No acquisition is possible under these circumstances. However, if I had lunch with the Indonesians, and it was clear that we were communicating about the food, the utensils, and things in the immediate environment, acquisition could begin. Context can make input comprehensible.

Krashen argues that conscious learning does not affect acquisition in any way and can only be used to "monitor" output to a small degree. This position, which Rod Ellis calls the "non-interface" position, holds that conscious and unconscious knowledge are entirely separate and unrelated (229–230). If we imagine a continuum of language teaching methods that has at one pole the direct teaching of grammar rules, vocabulary and syntax, Krashen's model, which relies on pure acquisition untainted by conscious learning or teaching would occupy the other extreme.

William E. Rutherford stakes out a position he calls "Consciousnes-Raising" (C-R) that is solidly in the middle of these two extremes. Rutherford argues that language learners build, test, and discard hypotheses about how the target language functions, based on linguistic universals, the grammar of the first language, and input. Furthermore, grammar teaching, in his view, can aid in the formation of such hypotheses by increasing awareness of certain linguistic features. For Rutherford, target-language grammar enters the learner's experience not as a body of knowledge to be mastered or as an obstacle to be overcome but "rather as a network of systems in which the learner is already enmeshed, the full grammatical implications of which he alone has to work out on the basis of what he comes in contact with in interaction with what he himself contributes as an already accomplished language acquirer." In this sense grammar is not "in command of learning," but "in the service of learning" (153).

The nature of the "interface" between learning and acquisition is crucial to the question of whether grammar should be taught. In Rutherford's model, unconscious acquisition is the primary factor, though learning can provide a context or a framework that focuses attention and facilitates acquisition. Today's grammar defenders tend to take a similar "interface" position, albeit reluctantly. Noguchi notes that

> Startling as it may sound at first, all students who have acquired English as a native language (as well as many who have acquired it non-natively) already possess an immense knowledge of the operations (i.e., the descriptive rules) of English, including its syntax. . . . This knowledge, however, is largely unconscious. (43)

Noguchi recommends teaching grammar in a manner that takes advantage of the student's naturally acquired knowledge of the grammatical structures of the language through a procedure that emphasizes the sentence and its major components—subject, verb and modifier. Although Noguchi does not refer to Krashen's language acquisition theory, he argues that we should use naturally acquired knowledge as a foundation for *teaching* a grammatical system.

Martha Kolln makes a similar argument in the preface to the third edition of her book, *Understanding English Grammar*. She says that the book is designed "to help students understand the system of rules underlying the grammar of English, to help them understand in a conscious way the system they already know subconsciously.... The more that speakers and writers and readers know consciously about their language, the more power they have over it and the better they can make it serve their needs" (v–vii). Noguchi and Kolln are moving in the opposite direction from Rutherford, in that for them it is acquisition that makes the learning of grammatical concepts possible, rather than grammar facilitating acquisition.

The conscious/unconscious or interface/non-interface opposition is, in fact, the most problematic aspect of language acquisition theory. Behind the controversy is another version of the *langue/parole* distinction, language as system versus language in use. Krashen's theory is a theory of *parole*. The argument that Noguchi and Kolln have with Krashen is a version of the argument Nebrija had with Isabella.

A Grammar Constructed Reality

M. A. K. Halliday's concept of grammar is quite different from traditional views, and perhaps more than any other linguist he is able to avoid splitting *langue* and *parole*. The price for this is considerable obscurity, as we will see. Halliday argues that while it is possible to separate lexicon and grammar for certain purposes, it is better to think in terms of a "lexicogrammatical" system. He says "The lexical system is not something that is fitted in afterwards to a set of slots defined by the grammar," but is "simply the most delicate grammar" (*Language as a Social Semiotic* 43). There is one grammatical system, and lexical choices are the most specific level of realization.

For example, in the discussion above of *look* and *enjoy*, we found that certain verbs "take" the infinitive, and others the gerund. Some verbs "take" certain prepositions, and not others. Clearly part of the grammatical system is built into the lexical choices.

In "Language and the Order of Nature," a later article, Halliday characterizes the grammatical system as constructing both our social and natural realities. In other words, grammar does far more than structure our language—it creates our world. For Halliday natural language is a "dynamic open system" which is "metastable, multi-level ('metaredundant')" and "metafunctional" in that "it is committed to meaning more than one thing at once, so that every instance is at once both a reflection and action—both interpreting the world and also changing it" (145). This complexity is part of the reason grammatical rules are insufficient to the task of teaching language. The problems of ESL writers are both symptom and confirmation of this complexity, in that redundant systems are often in conflict, such as when the lexical choices indicate that the action is in the past, but the tense system indicates it is in the present.

Halliday notes that it is impossible to recover a fixed and stable meaning from discourse, but that one *can* recover a meaning that is complex and indeterminate. It is hard to make this meaning-making process explicit because

> We can do so only by talking about grammar; and to do this we have to construct a theory of grammar: a 'grammatics', let us call it. But this 'grammatics' is itself a designed system, another scientific metalanguage, with terms like 'subject' and 'agent' and 'conditional'— terms which become reified in their turn, so that we then come to think of the grammar itself (the real grammar) as feeble and crude because it doesn't match up to the categories we've invented for describing it. But of course it's the grammatics— the metalanguage—that is feeble and crude, not the grammar. (145)

Halliday borrows the term "cryptogrammar" from Benjamin Whorf to describe grammatical features of a language that function below the usual level of consciousness, features "which create their own order of reality independently of whatever it is they may be used to describe" (142). One feature of the cryptogrammar described by Halliday is patterns of transivity. For example, a recent memo I saw argued that one of the duties of a new committee should be to "cohere" various writing programs. *Cohere* is normally described as an intransitive verb, and we could argue that it is ungrammatical to say that one should "cohere" something. However, for a moment, imagine what *cohere* would mean as a transitive verb, what it would mean to be able, as an action, to *cohere* something. To me it implies a magical power of the *fiat lux* variety, a radical restructuring of human powers. This is not to say that we cannot translate this error into something that fits our world view better like *coordinate* or *supervise*, but it is enough to see that normally unconscious grammatical processes do structure our sense of what is possible and potential, what is connected and what is not.

Halliday argues that when we begin to reflect on the processes of the cryptogrammar, bringing them to conscious attention, we destroy them.

> The act of reflecting on language transforms it into something alien, something different from itself—something determinate and closed. There are uses for closed, determinate metalanguages, but they can represent only one point of view about a system. ... I don't mean that it is impossible to *understand* the cryptogrammar of a natural language, but that its reality-generating power may be incompatible with explicit logical reasoning. (1987 143)

Halliday is arguing that in a sense it is impossible to write a complete grammar of a natural language, not because the language is constantly changing, not because there are too many different varieties, but because a determinate representation of the grammatical system can never function as a real grammar.

Halliday's terms for the difference in function between grammar as determinate meta- language and the cryptogrammar are "automatised" and "de-automatised." I do not find these terms particularly helpful, but he explains that in semiotic terms, in the "automatised" function, the signified constructs the signifier—reality is described by the sign system. This is the common- sense view of how language works, that we choose our words and sentences to describe what we see. In the "de-automatised" function, the reverse is true, the signifier constructs the signified—the sign system constructs reality. In this mode, which Halliday argues is the normal mode of language use, our words and sentences structure what we see. In other words, "turning the cryptogrammar of a natural language into a metalanguage for reasoning" doesn't work because "it has to become automatised—that is, the grammar has to be made to describe, instead of constructing reality by not describing, which is what it does best" (144).

Halliday argues that as the structure of society changes, people want to change the grammar. For example, the fact that English does not have a gender neutral third person singular pronoun was not a problem before feminism. We are uncomfortable with locutions like "Every student should bring his book" for reasons which have nothing to do with grammar, but which exist in our social consciousness. The plural form, *their*, is clearly being pressed into service, and will eventually be acknowledged as grammatical. An analogous situation occurred in the late seventeenth century when the second person singular pronoun, *thou*, dropped out of English because it was too often used to imply contempt or superiority, and the plural form *you* was used in its place. (Burnley, *History of the English Language* 200). Halliday argues

> When people want to change the conditions of the dialogue, and the structures it is setting up, they do so by changing the grammar—thus illustrating how well the grammar is doing its job. The complaint is not that the language is not functioning properly, but that it is functioning all too well—it is the social order construed by it that is being objected to. But mostly the design for change is drawn up only at the surface of the language, rather that at the much less accessible, cryptotypic level of patterning by which the structures are really installed. (137)

Halliday's viewpoint reintegrates elements of language and discourse others have divided, including, to an extent, *langue* and *parole*. Lexicon, syntax, grammatical structures, social structures, and our view of the natural world are all integrated in one dynamic open system. When we write a grammatical metalanguage, it is but a two-dimensional sketch of a small corner of a three dimensional universe.

In the light of these difficulties, can a case be made for teaching such a metalanguage? Even Halliday admits that "there are uses for such a closed, determinate metalanguage," and we can assume that one of the uses he has in mind is pedagogical. And Bakhtin characterizes such a metalanguage as

> Language as a ready-made product, as a stable system (lexicon, grammar, phonetics), is, so to speak, the inert crust, the hardened lava of language creativity, of which linguistics makes an abstract construct in the interests of the practical teaching of language as a ready-made instrument. (*Marxism* 48)

Should we teach grammar because these linguists believe that teaching is one of the only uses for such a construct? It seems to me the answer depends on whether there are alternatives to teaching this "inert crust."

In my view, Krashen's language acquisition theory provides just such an alternative, just as Halliday's perspective provides insight into why the theory works and why direct teaching of a grammatical metalanguage is not sufficient for language improvement. Concepts like the "Bolinger Principle," mentioned above, represent attempts to describe the complex patterns of the cryptogrammar and thus fill in the inadequacies of the structural description, but such attempts are by their nature incomplete and insufficient. Without real linguistic input, without a language acquisition base, any grammar is but a pale shadow of the real language.

Halliday's analysis also addresses why some people see grammatical error as a crime or sin. From Halliday's viewpoint, a grammatical error is a new or different way of structuring or seeing the world.

The Writing Teacher's Perspective

It is not my intention to argue that the perspective of *parole* is superior or more valid than the perspective of *langue*. The difficulty of language as an object of study has made this division of perspective necessary for most investigative purposes. However, each view is inadequate without the other. Any representation of the system of language is necessarily deficient for the reasons I have described. It is a description of a frozen moment in the life of a language in constant flux, as Sapir makes clear. It is a decontextualized analysis, and Halliday, and others, have shown that the disassembled parts don't add up to a language. Noguchi's question was "why does formal instruction in grammar fail to produce any significant improvement in writing quality?" I think this is the answer. Any attempt to use formal grammar as a way to get back to first principles and build the language up again step by step is misguided.

However, Noguchi also asks if we should discard all aspects of grammar instruction. I think we can now resituate that question in terms of *langue* and *parole*. The split between *langue* and *parole* that exists in linguistic theory is paralleled in popular linguistic thinking as a split between *grammar* and *"the way I talk,"* or *correct speech* and *ordinary speech*. Dictionaries and grammar books function as a physical representation of *langue*, and as a potential link between the rainbow and the stream. Unlike linguists, writers and writing teachers cannot remain comfortable keeping these two perspectives divided. We must negotiate a connection.

Thus, we cannot ignore usage. To deny that the linguistic precepts of the school grammar have social effects is indeed dangerous nonsense, whatever the logic, scientific validity, or intent of those precepts. Handbooks and dictionaries are useful, because they represent authority, define the unity, and take a position. A student can define herself and her language in relation to that unity; she does not have to let it define her. And each handbook is simply an opinion, a view of the linguistic unity. When handbooks contradict one another, as is often the case, they open up space for questions, redefinition, and a new unity.

One of the most unusual handbooks on our shelf is Douglas Cazort's amusing book, *Under the Grammar Hammer: The 25 Most Important Grammar Mistakes and How to Avoid Them*. Like Noguchi, Cazort has paid close attention to the Connors-Lunsford study of error frequency and the Hairston study of attitudes toward particular error (see Noguchi 19–31 for a summary). Both writers attempt to maximize the return on the effort spent contemplating grammatical problems. Cazort's small book, however, is the only grammar book I have ever perused which *reduced* grammar anxiety rather than increased it, and it makes no attempt to create a sense of monolithic authority. Cazort says:

> I hope to free you from the idea that the English language is the sole property of English teachers and other authorities on correct usage. It belongs to all of us who use it, and part of my purpose in writing this book is to help you feel more secure in your ownership, even in the presence of English teachers. (4)

Rather than simply representing the idealized rainbow of *langue*, Cazort negotiates a compromise for those who exist in the multi-variant currents and eddies of the linguistic stream. We cannot deny *langue*; neither can we simply follow our own linguistic current. As practitioners, not theorists, this compromise is the best we can do.

Notes

1. I gave up on marking "alot" when I discovered that about 50% of the writing tutors I hired, many of whom were English majors and quite literate, spelled it that way.

7

The Use of Grammar Texts:
A Call For Pedagogical Inquiry

Joan Mullin

The questions that built this chapter emerged from twelve years of writing center tutoring. While this tutoring included developmental and international students, mostly the writers have been "average," honors, and graduate students, as well as faculty. Yet, no matter the level of the writers with whom I worked, despite the use of a range of metaphors or strategies during tutorials, I found it difficult to undermine students' tendencies to equate good papers with good grammar. My question is and has been, why? I want to explore this question further, eliminate what may seem some obvious reasons, and suggest further areas for personal and public inquiry.

Students still come into the writing center with the expectation that if their grammar can be "fixed," their paper will receive approval. Not only do those students who come to writing centers believe this, but grammar proves one of the main concerns of students in classes across the curriculum. Writing center presentations in composition classes and in those of other disciplines inevitably lead to student questions about help with "grammar." At the University of Toledo we first assumed that students were lumping "grammar" into a category of "writing;" we have found instead that students really do want to know "how to make my verbs agree."

While I would not deny that, presently, verb agreement is important, students' questions during tutorials made me wonder how grammar contributes or detracts from their ability to complete a writing task. For these students and this exploration, "grammar" refers to what may be called traditional grammar—those categories of language associated with workbooks, multiple choice exams, and faded "grammar" school dittoes. The legacy of these materials seems to dominate students' writing anxieties and writing abilities.

Tales from Elementary School

Since students do not come to us as blank slates, it could be concluded that prior education primed them for the assumption that good grammar equals good papers. A look at language arts curricula in five city and suburban elementary school systems shows that very different philosophies guide students' attitudes towards writing. The writing programs in and around Toledo, a metropolitan area of 450,000, forty miles south of Detroit, incorporate a wide variety of philosophy and pedagogy which range from writing across the curriculum to assigning the writing of one hundred sentences to students who misbehave. However, because of current assessment practices and proficiency tests, all instructors find themselves teaching traditional grammar alongside holistic approaches. Grammar is "testable;" questions can be graded and results easily calculated by the same machine.

One of the early elementary school teachers described herself as having "lived through" several writing workshops: writing to learn, collaborative writing, holistic scoring. She enjoyed the lively environment that the seminars helped her provide for her students, but she also found "that one of the bottom lines is grammar recognition. Students can be creative all they want, but if they can't pass the proficiency tests, all the creativity in the world won't get them a good grade." At another workshop, this time for a regional elementary-junior high English program, a passionate discussion about grammar was silenced by the declaration that all of us should

> Get real. For all the process, let-'em-write-what-they-want wonderful stuff I do, the reality is that I use and have my students use a grammar book and workbook. And, you know what? They use a book written by one of the theorists who promotes dumping emphasis on grammar in favor of composing! Who's kidding who?

My original intent for this chapter was to survey those writers of grammar books and respond to this last statement. But initial responses by a few authors proved clear and concise: the books are needed as reference tools. One author noted for a multi-disciplinary perspective in writing said that the grammar section was purposely placed in the back of the book—where reference sections should be. Another author noted for her cutting-edge views of collaboration and process pointed out that she had refused to write a grammar handbook, but she got tired of watching students try to use them: she decided to try to make one that was user-friendly. Publishers claim that teachers want grammar handbooks, and a recent survey conducted by the industry found grammar handbooks to be the most sought after books by teachers.

Tales from High School

While elementary teachers may integrate various writing pedagogies and philosophies, many of the high schools in the same districts now take primarily a content/process approach. Several standard public school curricula are guided by holistic approaches to language. In the Toledo Public School system, grammar may not be used as a unit; grammar must instead be integrated as individualized instruction related to content.

Though one of our National Writing Project veterans recently confessed, "I don't care what they tell me I can't do; I teach them grammar, and then they can write a decent paper," this does not *emerge* as the general sentiment. However, every district has basic or remedial workshops or tutorials which emphasize grammar either implicitly (through assessment responses) or explicitly.

High school teachers with whom I have contact have responded to papers as readers for their students. Their reports at workshops point to ways in which they let students know that grammar is a part of communication, not communication itself. In a recent workshop, teachers were asked to evaluate a particularly explosive essay in which the student argued that Hester Prynne deserves all the punishment she gets because "if a woman gets pregnant it's her fault." The paper itself contained organizational problems and identifiable dialect interference (verb endings, tense shifts, incorrect infinitive forms). Generally, teachers *in this workshop* steered clear of grammatical comments. One teacher listed nine comments in what appeared to be no hierarchical order. None addressed grammar or syntax specifically. Another instructor had four suggestions: three addressed organization and evidence, the fourth recommended the writer "Remember to stick with the same tense and point of view." The following comments gained loud approval by all:

> You have a well-organized paper; I can identify a beginning, middle and end. I particularly like the way you summarize your argument at the start of the last paragraph. Something else I like about your writing is your variety of sentence beginnings: "For Hester to commit . . . is wrong."
>
> A drawback of your paper is your tendency to over-generalize: "It is common to see . . ." in paragraph 2 is an example. You will find this a problem if you continue to write politically unpopular papers like this one. Those who evaluate your writing won't let you get away with it.

Teachers agreed that their students need to be encouraged to write.

University Tales

If readers agree with recent theories about the place of grammar in the classroom, then they will pleased to know that so do many university colleagues. Though some may complain that colleagues in universities still focus on grammar, a recent self-report of 156 composition instructors from thirteen institutions found general agreement that grammar "is a distraction from the teaching of writing." Most compositionists who participated in the survey approached "all grammatical problems from the perspective of the reader.

Such errors normally interfere with the easy comprehension of the text or they negatively affect those of the writer (or both!).''

The thirteen institutions surveyed responded to an inquiry sent out on WCenter, an electronic bulletin board for the writing center community (see Appendix I). Eight institutions reported student populations of 10–20,000; three institutions had 5–10,000 students, and the remaining two reported student populations of 20–30,000. Both composition and ''basic'' writing instructors were surveyed; responses from both groups reflected current language philosophies, but emphasis on grammar differed.

Basic writing instructors report being encouraged to use or ''cover different and sundry chapters in the [required] handbook.'' Most also agree that concerns about grammar ''should be employed after the first graded major assignment'' or approached ''from the perspective of the reader.'' Comments regarding evaluation emphasize taking up ''grammar concerns as they arise on student papers,'' and one group of instructors report using a rubric sheet which ''directs students to specific sections in the handbook for assistance.''

First-year composition instructors were not required, generally, to use a handbook, though many of their readers included sections on style and grammar. Instructors reported that they recommended their students ''read it [the section on grammar] quickly'' or ''develop the responsibility for correcting errors themselves.'' These composition instructors agree that they ''don't think we can afford to use much classroom time for teaching grammar. We have to assume that students have learned the basics before coming to college.''

To those in whole language education, ''basics'' refers to those elements of grammar and syntax that need to be addressed holistically, within the texts students write in elementary school. But two respondents offered the information that their institutions have a ''really basic'' writing course that emphasizes only grammar and syntax; this is not an uncommon college practice. Such classes usually require decontextualized grammar instruction, and the vocabulary of other writing instructors indicates that a basic writer needs more grammar: faculty request their students be given ''lots of grammar exercises'' in the writing center; they ask center staff to recommend computerized sentence practice exercises; they wonder out loud how a ''student whose verbs don't agree could have graduated from high school.''

Despite this underlying attitude, respondents from basic writing classes and about half those from the first-year composition classes reported that whenever there are ''common errors'' they ''cite and briefly discuss'' the corresponding rules or chapters in handbooks. Instructors generally believe that

> the handbook should be used as a reference guide . . . They [students] should develop the responsibility to refer to the handbook when they have a question about style or usage. If a student displays a large amount of

grammatical errors, the handbook can be utilized in a personal conference as a tool to help both the student and the instructor determine why some mistakes are being made and how they can be rectified.

The expectation, therefore, of many of the respondents to the survey is that "by the time students reach Composition I, they should be prepared for intellectual and personal writerly growth—grammar is only a MINOR component if at all a component." Composition faculty report turning to process writing and those studies which grew from Mina Shaughnessey's work when they discuss grammar. They report using sentences from students' texts to direct attention to usage, they devise plans for putting grammar into a "proofing" or last step category. For some, this means sending students to the nearest writing center—assuming (wrong as that may be) that these places are for "cleaning-up" grammar and "proofing."

These repeated responses support research which verifies that learning formal grammar does not guarantee that one will know how to write. Yet, as a history teacher recently recounted, a student will still come "to me with a paper loaded with comments about logic and organization and expect a better grade because she has no comma splices." One survey respondent explained at length that "students I've had ASK for grammar practice, and that motivated me to switch to a grammar-intensive text." Others reported similar incidents of students *wanting* grammar instruction; certainly the evidence at writing centers bears this out: students often come in and ask a tutor to "please, just check my grammar." A recent on-campus inquiry of honors students demonstrated that many do not use the writing center because "My writing has always been good; I don't have any problem with grammar."

Tales From Outside Educational Institutions

There is no question that grammar is important in American culture. Maxine Hairston's 1981 study of professionals surveyed their attitudes towards particular types of composition errors. Briefly, those surveyed showed a variety of tolerances towards certain stylistic features; they registered the most tolerance concerning punctuation (commas, semi-colons) and semantic differences (*among* and *between*, *that* and *which*), and the least tolerance towards syntactic errors (e.g., *He got*). Likewise, Connors and Lunsford's informative 1988 study describes not only what kinds of errors students make, but also points to the fact that not all teachers marked every error. Whether a lack of marking errors was due to grading "exhaustion" or to tolerance would demand further study, but there is every indication that teachers also have varying degrees of tolerance for stylistic error (see also Noguchi's discussion of grammar surveys 17–33). A look at teacher corrected elementary workbooks, interviews with teachers, as well as Connors and Lunsford's 1988 study demonstrates this lack of consistency in marking surface, grammatical errors. If we consider the time and importance given grammar in school, it is no wonder students are confused when various teachers place varying degrees of importance on different grammatical features.

What also proves significant for us here is the progression by which children may learn about formal grammar and academic writing: first and foremost, children are introduced to the concept of grammar after they have negotiated a level of oral proficiency. Different from language already spoken in their daily life, school writing and communicating appears to demand artificial sets of rules with *apparently* little reference to children's experiences.

Furthermore, students in elementary schools that have already incorporated process and collaborative models into reading and writing classrooms soon find out that assessments do not adequately measure what they have been doing. Later, in high school, students may find two grades on their papers: one for grammar and one for content. Teachers stress that students must concentrate on ideas, separate from grammar, and save their scrutiny of surface features for the last stages of revision. However, in order to graduate, students must pass proficiency tests which do not coincide with these assessment practices.

In their comparison of classroom practices and reading/writing assessment, Tierney, Carter and Desai uncover the source of many low scores on proficiency tests (29). In the same way, I am proposing that we question whether students' interpretations of our assessments parallel our objectives. As indicated in the Tierney, Carter, Desai portfolio study, the gap that exists between messages we send students through our classroom practices and those we send through our assessments may contribute to students' misunderstandings about the relationship between grammar and writing.

Nonetheless, students enter college and are told that they should know grammar by now. They are encouraged to freewrite, collaborate, and design personal narratives. Comments on their papers address issues of argument, warrants, claims—the grammar errors are circled or marked without explanation, though a comment in the final epistolary may include a "you have problems with verb tenses also." Despite what most of us would consider encouraging, non-directive comments on papers, students from all levels in the academy often sit down in the writing center and claim, "I just never get my tenses right," or, "It's those fragments; I always have trouble with fragments." One student whose teacher had exhaustively tried to explain the need for focus and direction in the paper continued to examine her commas, exclaiming, "You'd think by now I could avoid comma splices!"

Sixty-nine percent of the instructors responding to the sixth question on the survey (see Appendix 1) indicated that only ten to twenty percent of their evaluative comments addressed grammar issues. About fifteen percent of the respondents reported that twenty to thirty percent of their evaluative comments were grammar-related. Less than one percent of the respondents reported that fifty percent or more comments related to grammar. These last two groups of respondents, and many from the group reporting twenty to thirty percent grammar-related comments, taught basic composition.

Like most first-year composition respondents, seven years ago I would have reported that ten percent or less of my comments were grammar-related. However, I changed my assessment practices and now read my students' papers into a tape recorder, recording what I think while I read. During this assessment protocol, I try to turn my mind inside out, reading the student's text exactly as my mind hears it and reporting the impact the words have as I read. I never considered myself anything but a process/content/whole language person, yet the first time I recorded my responses, I was horrified at the emphasis I inadvertently placed on correct grammatical items. While some of my comments were about content, my reading picked up every error, and several comments registered disdain or surprise at "errors" in the paper.

This emphasis was so prevalent that I re-recorded the papers, and continued monitoring my own comments and examining the roots of my responses. I believe I finally reached a comfortable—and automatic—tone and repertoire of commentary that says: "I have a difficult time reading some of this because your codes are giving me mixed (or mixed-up) messages." Students react positively to this method of response: "I liked hearing how I misuse commas. I never understood what they were for until I heard the paper—and heard you misunderstand what I was trying to say, not because I had the wrong words down, but because I made you pause at the wrong place!" Or, "I never understood what teachers meant by *frag* on my paper. They would write "frag" and then say I had good ideas and give me a C–! When I heard you stop where I put periods I first replayed the tape because I thought it had skipped! . . . Nope, there it was . . . a "frag" but this time I could HEAR what it meant."

Whether instructors unknowingly focus on grammar during class time or within their evaluations, or whether students focus on grammar errors because of prior experiences, our instruction fails to change many students' perceptions about the use of grammar. Our profession, our research, our dissemination of research through journals and conferences, and our handbooks do not go far enough towards changing our students' or instructors' assumptions about the use of grammar either. By downplaying in language arts, English, or composition classes the importance of grammar, or by relegating grammar to handbooks, as is current practice, we may be avoiding a professional self-examination that is long overdue.

The Connection: Academic/Social Contexts of Grammar

Perhaps students and teachers look to grammar because it's the easiest thing to fix—there *are* rules for it. Speakers at the first CCCC illuminate what still may be the problem: "'there is a big difference between filling in blanks in a workbook and forging out of one's own chaotic thought a coherent piece of discourse[;] it is easier to teach the limited skill than the larger art of composition'" (Bartholomae 43). Thus, within the history of our own discipline, one can see the play between "Language as an abstraction, language as practice; an idealized English, a common English" (Bartholomae 44). But what is common English?

In the same article, Bartholomae traces the early foundations of CCCC to this very question. An idealized English communicates to an audience because of supposed agreements; in the United States these have for us long resided in grammar. Instructors teach these agreements, often without questioning or without allowing questions, about how or why these agreements were reached. Yet we know that "grammars" are both created and learned within environments. We further know that different groups create different dialectic forms of grammar, (not deep structure but the evident surface marks that determine success or failure in English classes). As the current controversy surrounding Richard Rodriguez attests (Spellmeyer chapter one; Mills 20), we must engage ourselves and our students in discussion about whose English—whose grammar—we are promoting.

Those involved in the black dialect controversy already have asked why they have to learn Standard English. In the recent *New York Times* article headed "Grappling With How to Teach Young Speakers of Black Dialect," a student pointed out that "'English is not our language. . . .Our language has more rhythmic tones'" (A8). Agreeing with the students, Geneva Smitherman, a linguist and English professor specializing in black vernacular, claims that "we are at the point where we need a multilingual policy that means that everybody would learn one other language or one other dialect" (Lee A8). This coincides with a "growing resistance of some black young people to assimilate their efforts to use language as a part of a value system that prizes cultural distinction" (A8).

While this controversy is not new, it serves as an example of the kind of cultural splits existing between those outside and inside the academy. Students theorizing cultural differences find positions from which they can choose to use or reject a convention. For Black, Hispanic, or regional writers that may mean breaking standard grammatical conventions; for all students it may also mean translating media conventions to academic texts. However, for those unaware of the gap between their language use and the criteria guiding instructors' responses to their texts, academic conventions seem unnecessarily artificial.

In *Voices of the Self*, Keith Gilyard examines the conflicts over dialect usage. He concludes that

> Social relations are a far more vital factor for Black students in school than
> differences of language variety. Black children, like all people, make
> decisions based on vested interests. If they were to perceive that the social

dialectic were in their favor, learning another dialect could not be a major problem. In fact it would be extremely difficult to *prevent* them from learning Standard English. For most Blacks in school such perception can form only within a setting in which teachers genuinely accept them as they come and respect them enough not to sell them myths of simple assimilation. (74)

The idea that "teachers genuinely accept them as they come and respect them enough not to sell them myths of simple assimilation" seems applicable in all school environments that teach Standard English through grammar. For students, evidence abounds in their mediaized worlds that the population does not write (advertisements, newspapers, magazines, fiction) in Standard English. They learn from books, or through comments on the personal narratives they are encouraged to write, that grammar is a necessary school constraint; they memorize it and study it, but they don't understand it. Our present teaching methods—and perhaps our present ideologies—have yet to convince them of grammar's necessity beyond the classroom.

Many teachers, influenced by these very same thoughts, report they have had to convince themselves of the justification of teaching grammar. Perhaps what we have is a lack of understanding on both sides of the desk. I think grammar texts and our present use of them lead to at least this one question: what is the purpose of our current grammar rules? If we can answer that question, we can begin to place grammar into the context of writing.

If we continue to assume that there is one correct way to think, and therefore one correct way to express that thinking, then grammar will continue to be taught as a series of external rules that ignore the already present set of oral customs internalized by students before entering any educational institution. Such patterns of speech, insofar as they may reflect patterns of thinking, need to be placed in play with other conventions of culture that equally reflect ways of expressing particular kinds of thoughts to selected audiences. Until our teaching reflects this philosophy, students will persist in misusing, not using, or not knowing how to use grammar handbooks as reference tools.

Questions for Further Inquiry

Several questions relating to present uses of grammar and classroom practices demand further inquiry *among teachers*, not just theorists:

- Has anyone taught students how to use a handbook or why they should use it? (Current practices resemble the directive that students should look up words they can't spell.)

- Are we up-front with students about grammar instruction and its place in writing?

- How closely do our assessment practices measure our classroom objectives—implied or stated?

- How can we measure the gap between what students think they hear about writing and grammar and what is being said?
- How do our concepts of and practices concerning the "basics" correspond to what students need to know?
- Finally, how closely aligned are our writing and grammar philosophies?

Until we ask these and other questions suggested by more intense data gathering and reflectivity, student perceptions about grammar will continue to undermine our classroom practices.

Appendix 1

Questionnaire

1. Does your English department or composition program require students to buy a grammar handbook? Yes _____ No _____
   1a. If yes, how is the text chosen?

2. Does your department choose a reader/rhetoric that has a section on grammar in it? Yes _____ No _____
   If you answered yes to 1 or 2 above, what text has the department recommended?

3. Does your department disseminate required or model syllabi for composition courses? Yes _____ No_____

4. Does the department syllabi incorporate use of the grammar text as part of the course of study? Yes _____ No_____
   4a. If yes, please briefly describe how the department suggests grammar be used in the classroom. (You may choose to send the syllabus or course description.)

5. If your department does not recommend a grammar handbook, do you require students to purchase a grammar handbook for your class? Yes _____ No _____
   5a. If yes, how do you choose the text?
   5b. Which text do you now use?
   5c. Please describe how you use the handbook in classroom or evaluative situations. You may choose to enclose syllabi or course descriptions.)

6. As best you can, please estimate how many of your comments or marks on student essays pertain to issues considered primarily grammatical.
   Less than 10% _____ 10–20% _____ 20–30%_____
   30–40% _____ 40–50% _____ over 50% _____

7. Freewrite: At the college and university level, please describe how concepts of grammar and grammar texts should be used in composition classes and in the evaluation of texts (Do not complete if you already answered this in #5a.)

8. Institutional demographics: State _____ Private _____
   Two year _____ Four Year _____ Four + Graduate _____
   Under 5,000 students _____ 5,000–10,000 students _____
   10,000–20,000 students _____ 20,000–30,000 _____
   More than 30,000 students _____

9. If you have any other comments on the use of grammar in the composition classroom, please use this space:

8

Grammar for Writers: How Much Is Enough?

R. Baird Shuman

Although people knowledgeable in recent rhetorical theory know that writing is a process, the public at large still views school writing—especially the writing students do in English classes—as a product which, after its errors are enumerated, receives a grade. It is not unusual for parents, politicians, and principals to assess English teachers' effectiveness on the basis of how scrupulous they are in ferreting out every infelicity students commit in their writing and downgrading them accordingly. Such tactics are generally applauded because they suggest to the public that teachers are maintaining high academic standards.

A half century of research has demonstrated that writing passes through many stages before it emerges as a finished product—if, indeed, a piece of writing can ever be called "finished." Most published authors of note eventually "surrender" their manuscripts for publication rather than "finish" them. Among the stages they pass through as they work on a piece of writing are invention, percolation, prewriting, organizing, drafting (often several times), and revising, revising, revising until the piece comes close to saying what the writer wants it to say.

At that point, proofreading, sometimes called editing, becomes important. In the editing stage, writers (and later their editors) catch surface problems whose elimination will result in a polished ("finished") piece of writing. The stages through which writers pass do not necessarily occur in the exact order given above. Before a piece of writing reaches what might be considered its final stage, however, it goes through each of these stages in one way or another.

Prewriting, intimately connected with invention, can consist of all sorts of activities—meditating, brainstorming, conversing, daydreaming and nightdreaming—that involve no actual writing as well as some activities—outlining, brainstorming on paper, freewriting—that do. "Percolation" is the term John Mayher and his coauthors use to identify "everything that happens to the writer apart from the actual setting of marks on paper" (Mayher, Lester, and Pradl 5). They differentiate percolation from prewriting because they consider it less linear than prewriting.

As schools have moved toward the whole language approach to teaching English and other subjects (for a discussion of the whole language approach, see Newman; Goodman; Goodman, Smith, Meredith, and Goodman), teachers have begun to understand that students will produce a great deal of writing that should not be graded, although it is productive for writers to discuss what they are writing with others—teachers, classmates (possibly in peer groups), siblings, and parents. Early talk and drafting represent steps in a process that eventuates in students' writing papers that communicate effectively in standard English.

What Is Grammatical Correctness?

People who talk about grammatical errors usually mean errors in spelling, punctuation, or usage, none of which relate directly to grammar in a sophisticated sense. Writing is grammatically deficient if it contains sentences like, "He to the market yesterday down the street went."

No native speaker of English—no speaker, indeed, who has internalized the rudiments of English grammar—would ever use the sentence above to convey the information contained in a more standard form of the same sentence: "Yesterday he went to the market down the street" (for a detailed discussion of how people internalize grammar, see Pinker). On the other hand, if someone says or writes, "Yestaday he goed to de mahket don de strcct," one can assume that the writer understands the structure of English (can put sentences together meaningfully) but has problems with spelling and with an irregular (strong) verb form. Certainly these problems cannot be ignored: teachers can, however, deal with them directly and, in many cases, quite easily.

One can assume that the writer cited above understands how to put verbs in the past tense, even though the rule for doing so does not work with the verb *to go* or with slightly more than a hundred other verbs in English that are irregular. One can also detect some dialect interference in the sentence above. A longer sample of this writer's writing might reveal problems in punctuation, in subject/verb agreement, in pronoun reference, or in a number of other areas that linguists generally lump together as problems that are only peripherally grammatical.

The public at large would, most likely, consider a piece that contains such problems or a piece that is badly misspelled to be ungrammatical even if one of these usage problems or frequent nonstandard spelling were its only problem. This same public might also reach conclusions about the intelligence of people who write this way even though little direct relationship has been shown to exist between people's intellect and their ability to spell, punctuate, make their verbs agree with their nouns, and make pronouns agree with their antecedents (Glowka and Lance).

Nevertheless, because the public is a harsh judge of surface errors in writing, teachers and school administrators would be remiss if they did not encourage students to write in ways that help them to avoid the displeasure and reproach of those whose judgments about such matters lead them to reach erroneous conclusions about people based upon such judgments. In short, for purely practical purposes, it is desirable for students to master Standard English.

Dangling participles are essentially grammatical errors because they defy logic, as in the sentence, "Driving her Chevrolet down the street, an eagle fell from the sky and hit it." Clearly, the eagle was not driving, although the sentence as written suggests that it was. Run-on sentences, comma splices, and unjustifiable sentence fragments also reflect inherent grammatical problems. Students who cannot write legitimate sentences have a grammatical deficiency.

Does a Knowledge of Grammar Help People Write Well?

Substantial numbers of researchers suggest that people can write well with little formal knowledge of grammar. (Hoyt; DeBoer; Meckel; Sutton; Hartwell; Sanborn). On the other hand, other researchers—fewer in number—have sought to demonstrate that a knowledge of grammar based on formal study contributes to good writing. (Neulieb; Kolln 1981; 1985; Neulieb and Brosnahan). Regardless of the camp to which one subscribes, most people who have thought the matter through acknowledge that people's backgrounds have more to do with the way they speak and write than does the study of formal grammar. People brought up hearing Standard English usually speak and write something that resembles Standard English. People who do not have such childhood exposure often do not speak and write Standard English.

Children who are read to early in life, children who are later encouraged to read independently and to discuss books, predictably grow up preferring to read and to discuss books than children brought up in bookless environments. Children who are encouraged to write are likely to develop better writing skills than those who, as children, are seldom expected or encouraged to write. These early relationships, although they do not apply to every student, are valid for large numbers of students at all educational levels in contemporary schools. One must remember that the communicative skills are intricately and intimately interrelated. The decoding skills—listening and reading—and the encoding skills—speaking and writing—all contribute to each other. Early exposure to rich communicative environments gives some young people a definite advantage over others who come from different backgrounds; this advantage often follows them into adult life. These earliest language experiences have nothing to do with a formal study of grammar, although it is in their earliest years that people internalize the grammar of their language, be it a standard or a nonstandard grammar (Pinker).

An awareness of how language operates helps students to write effectively, but this awareness comes from many sources, among the least of which seems to be the systematic study of formal, school grammar. Having said this, I must acknowledge that grammatical knowledge of various sorts can help students to become effective, linguistically-aware writers. In the following sections, I will attempt to identify the grammatical information that students and teachers in writing contexts should find most useful. Individual teachers will wish to modify my suggestions to accommodate their immediate teaching situations.

Learning Basic Grammatical Terminology

Teachers and students cannot discuss writing effectively or efficiently unless they share a common vocabulary that relates to language. Being able to use this specialized vocabulary affords valuable shortcuts for people who need to discuss a piece of writing analytically. Minimally, students should, by the time they enter sixth grade, know the most commonly used parts of speech by both name and function.

Although I am not sure that students need to know what interjections are, I think that students must have a working knowledge of nouns, verbs, adjectives, and adverbs, which grammarians call "form words." They should also know what kinds of pronouns exist and how they are used. They need to know such structure words as determiners, conjunctions, prepositions, auxiliaries, and qualifiers in their various forms and functions.

Teachers who work with student writing at the sentence level need assurance that their students know the difference between active and passive voice and that they know what is meant by such terms as subject, predicate, direct object, and indirect object. Students should, by the sixth or seventh grade, have a working knowledge of simple, compound, complex, and compound-complex sentences, which also implies that they know something about subordination and coordination.

Students need to know what dependent and independent clauses are; to do this, they also have to be able to differentiate clauses from phrases. It will help them to know the difference between a comma splice, a run-on sentence, and a sentence fragment.

Where Do Most Student Errors in Writing Occur?

Robert Connors and Andrea Lunsford analyzed the kinds of errors they found in some three thousand essays written by college students across the United States. Their study showed that the largest number of errors fell into three areas: punctuation, particularly the use of commas and apostrophes; irregular verbs; the use and reference of pronouns. Although the writers in this study were of college age, a similar survey of student writing at the elementary and secondary levels would be likely to show similar results. Maxine Hairston, who has also surveyed considerable quantities of student writing, has devised a hierarchy of errors that she designates by such labels as errors that are "minor or unimportant," errors that are "status markers," and errors that are "very serious." Her designations are derived from information that professional colleagues in fields other than English supplied about their reactions to types of student error in written work.

Working from the base provided by these two studies, Rei R. Noguchi has offered valuable suggestions about how much grammar to teach and what elements of grammar to include in instruction if the ultimate aim is to produce competent writers. Noguchi points out that teaching grammar involves many pitfalls, such as overcoming many of one's own pre- and misconceptions about language. He urges teachers to help students develop operational defini tions of grammatical terms because such definitions force students to define terms in ways that they understand rather than to learn age-worn definitions by rote. He also urges teachers to keep in mind that all language is systematic and functions according to rules, although the language conventions that apply to various dialects of English at some major junctures diffe r substantially from those by which Standard English operates (Noguchi 38–63).

Clarifying Punctuation

Punctuation is no problem for speakers of English or of any other language. Voice inflections and pauses indicate where one syntactic structure ends and another begins. Marks of punctuation serve functions similar to those that road signs serve along the highway. They call attention visually to things like termination, series, omission, insertion, mood, and direct address, all of which are handled in oral English simply by pauses or by the rise and fall of one's voice.

The apostrophe in possessives is not heard; context (possessives are usually determiners followed by nominals) reveals possession. In speaking, it is strictly context that differentiates *its* from *it's* or *there* from *their* and *they're*. When we say *isn't* or *don't*, the apostrophe is not heard, although the contraction that requires it is clearly understood.

Because commas and apostrophes are generally thought to give students the most trouble in their writing, it is sensible for teachers of writing either to teach the rudiments of their use from materials they prepare themselves or from a direct, simple, and accurate textbook. An excellent, rudimentary book that I have used for this purpose is Blanche Ellsworth's and Jack Higgins' *English Simplified*, any of whose six editions provides useful and dependable presentations of punctuation and of the me chanics of expression.

Teachers should diagnose student problems with commas and apostrophes from the student writing they read, and they must use judgment in determining what is worth teaching and what need not be taught immediately. It is of little consequence whether students place commas before the *and* in the next to last element of a series. Of much more consequence is students' regularly putting unnecessary commas between the subjects and verbs of their clauses. It is equally consequen tial to work with students who omit commas required to prevent misreadings.

Apostrophes have confounded generations of writers. Most students know that apostrophes are used to indicate possession or to indicate omissions. Not all students know where to put an apostrophe that indicates the latter. Therefore, teachers often receive writing in which students write *do'nt* or *is'nt* rather than *don't* or *isn't*.

Possessive plurals are particularly confusing for students, as are the possessives of words ending with *-s*. A few simple rules apply. It is not always easy to get students to apply these rules even when they know them. Peer editing should catch some of the problems and should also provide a basis for classroom discussion of the apostrophe. Teachers should be sure that students know when to use an apostrophe to prevent a misreading, as in the following sentence: "There are two i's in *idiom*." This maverick use of the apostrophe prevents the sentence from reading, "There are two is in *idiom*," which would not be immediatcly comprehensible to readers.

Up to a point, students can tell where some punctuation marks go by reading aloud what they have written. When they pause briefly, probably a comma is appropriate. A long pause requires a period or a semicolon. A rise in the voice at the end of a sentence usually calls for a question mark. The oral test, however, docs not work in all cases.

A good rule of thumb is to teach the most obvious things about punctuation rather than the arcane uses writers seldom have occasion to use. For example, it is probably helpful for writers to know that in ninety-seven percent of all cases, a semicolon has an independent clause before it and after it. It is useful for writers to know that a colon is not an appropriate mark of punctuation unless it has an independent clause before it; it is often followed by a list or an enumeration. Such generalized rules serve writers well. It does not take long to teach them. Students, however, tend to forget the conventions of punctuation, so they need to be retaught occasionally.

Teaching Pronouns

Pronouns come in many varieties: personal, possessive, demonstrative, intensive, reciprocal, relative, interrogative, and indefinite. Students have little difficulty using most of them, so teachers need to do little to teach about them if the purpose of their teaching is to give students information that they can transfer to their actual speaking and writing.

If students have pronoun problems, they usually occur in their use of personal, possessive, and relative pronouns. Problems occur with personal pronouns when the reference is unclear, as in the following sentence: "Jim and Martin played soccer together and then showered in his dormitory." Obviously, the reader cannot tell whose dormitory the sentence refers to. A personal, possessive pronoun is inappropriate here; for the sake of clarity, *his* needs to be replaced by *Jim's* or *Martin's*. It is also helpful for writers to know that the noun a pronoun refers to should not occur so far from the pronoun as to cause confusion.

Another problem surfaces when two pronouns follow a preposition, as in, "The coach shouted at him and me." Many students would use *I* rather than *me*; if, however, they read the sentence omitting the words *him and*, it will be clear to them instantly that the objective case of the personal pronoun is required. It is not really necessary in a situation like this one to discuss the objective case with students. They are most likely to transfer the information to their writing if they are given this simple test to apply. The same test applies with an objective pronoun without a preposition, as in "The principal recommended him and me for scholarships."

An increased sensitivity to sexist language has brought about a change in thinking about some of the conventions that have traditionally been applied to agreement. Currently, it is more politically acceptable to say "Everyone cast *their* vote for the underdog" than "Everyone cast *his* vote for the underdog." This shift indicates how arbitrary English usage sometimes is as language adjusts to meet social constraints.

Possessive pronouns cause confusion because many of them—*its, hers, yours, ours, theirs*—do not use the apostrophe that people generally associate with possessives. Once they learn the possessive pronouns on this list, writers should be able to avoid this looming pitfall.

Few accomplished writers pay much conscious attention to whether their relative clauses are restrictive or nonrestrictive. In fact, the distinction between the two is less and less frequently reflected in the choice of *that* or *which* as the relative pronoun. It helps to know that in formal English, the relative pronoun *that* is always restrictive, meaning that it does not have a comma before it; *which* is sometimes used in restrictive clauses, although it is preferable to use *that* in- stead.

Writers who understand that *which* clauses usually provide parenthetical information rather than information essential to the meaning of the clause will understand the logic of putting commas around them. Perhaps it is best to suggest that student writers test their *that/which* clauses in the following way: In a which-clause, can *which* be replaced by *that* without distorting the meaning? If it can, then replace *which* with *that*. Then ask whether *that* is essential to the meaning. If it is not, drop it. The following three sentences illustrate this technique:

1. The car which I wanted to show you is not here.

2. The car that I wanted to show you is not here.

3. The car I wanted to show you is not here.

Learning About Verbs

Students need to be aware of the verb tenses in English. It may help to introduce them—probably by eighth or ninth grade—to the verb expansion formula that makes possible all the tenses of the verbs in active, declarative sentences. This formula, which is without exception, states that all verb phrases have at the very least two elements, tense (T) and a main verb (MV); *paint* (present tense plus MV) and *painted* (past tense plus MV) are examples of the simplest of verb phrases. Each word has a form of the main verb plus tense. The past tense has the characteristic *-ed* marker that regular (weak) verbs use to indicate past time.

All of the other elements in the verb expansion formula are optional (as indicated by parentheses in the formula below). When they are used, however, they are, without exception, used in the order given:

T + (Modal) + (have + *-en*) + (be + *-ing*) + MV

From this powerful rule are generated all of the verb structures used in active, declarative (indicative) sentences in the English language. Using the main verb *paint*, the full formula would result in a verb phrase like "may have been painting." Dropping one optional element, would yield something like *could be painting, will have painted,* or *had been painting.* Using just one op tional element, the result would be something like *can paint, have/ has/had painted,* or *is/are/am/was/were painting.*

Although the percentage of irregular (strong) verbs among all the verbs in English is small, some of the most commonly used verbs in English are irregular, including *to be, to go, to eat, to drink, to sing, to run,* and *to drive.* It is not unusual for people to say or to write, "They have went" or "She has swam" or "I have drank." Such locutions quite frequently weaken people's writing as well as their speaking. Young writers seem particularly resistant to such verb phrases as *have swum* or *has drunk,* neither of which, one must admit, is notable for its euphony.

Most writers who experience problems with irregular verbs have diffi-culty with the past perfect tense, although a few have trouble with the sim-ple past tense of some verbs as well, being unsure whether to say "I drank (or drunk) a gallon of water yesterday" or "She sang (or sung) two songs at the rally." The irregularity in irregular verbs occurs—with the exception of *to be*—exclusively in the past and past perfect tenses. Strong verbs are like weak verbs in their base forms, present tenses, and present participles.

The Importance of Rhetorical Grammar

Papers without problems in spelling, in punctuation, in the reference and agreement of pronouns, and in verb tense may still be problem papers. Indeed, in grading them, teachers might mark no surface errors but might be keenly aware of other inadequacies that make the paper weaker than some papers that have flagrant errors in the mechanics of expression, spelling, and usage. Such papers usually suffer from rhetorical deficiencies ranging from problems with style and rhythm to immature or ineffective expression of ideas.

Martha Kolln deals effectively with these sorts of problems both in chapter 14 of the third edition of *Understanding English Grammar* and in *Rhetorical Grammar: Grammatical Choices, Rhetorical Effects*. Her com-ments on rhetorical grammar give substantial attention to the rhythm of lan-guage, a point that is worthwhile for writers to consider seriously. Many people who speak effectively forget that when words are represented by symbols on a page rather than by sounds, the words still have sound.

A class session can profitably be devoted to looking at a selection of sentences from various sources. I use samples of a sentence or two each from the King James Bible, a current news magazine, the L. L. Bean catalogue, *The New York Times*, the local newspaper, and works by Charles Dickens, Henry James, Lewis Thomas, Barry Lopez, Richard Powers, Harold Brod-key, and Loren Eisley—enough to fill about a page and a half of paper, sin-gle spaced.

When I use this activity, I have students work in groups to discuss the sounds of the sentences I have chosen, asking them to mark the major emphases in each one. I make sure to include some sentences that do not have appealing rhythms and some that are hypermetric, making them hard to understand. Many students have told me that this activity made them realize for the first time the importance of reading aloud any important piece of writing before they submit it to someone.

Interrupting the Rhythm of a Sentence

Kolln offers valuable information about how writers can control the rhythm of sentences by interrupting their rhythm, thereby shifting the emphasis. The pairs of sentences below, for example, provide essentially the same information, but they have vastly different rhythms, therefore vastly different impacts upon readers:

A. The typhoon had subsided by midnight. However, the old man was too fearful to leave his home before noon the next day.

B. The typhoon had subsided by midnight. The old man, however, was too fearful to leave . . .

C. The typhoon had subsided by midnight. The old man was too fearful, however, to leave . . .

D. The typhoon had subsided by midnight. The old man was too fearful to leave his home before noon the next day, however.

Each of these sentences affects readers differently. The first uses *However* essentially as the conjunctive adverb it is, employing it largely to provide transition between the two sentences. In this version, the words *fearful, home, noon,* and *day* each receive almost equivalent emphasis, thus robbing the writer of the opportunity to control the impact of the sentence as fully as he or she might. The sentence, in other words, has too many points of emphasis. In the B version, *man* and *fearful,* because of the interrupted rhythm, receive greater stress than they do in the A version. In the C version, *fearful,* for the same reason, receives greater stress than in any of the other versions. The D version (which is the least effective of the four) essentially puts its major stress on *day,* hardly the word that warrants major stress in this sentence.

Moving Adverbials Around

The major characteristic of adverbials is their moveability. Writers who consciously use their adverbials to full advantage usually gain increased control over their writing. Note the impact each of the following sentences makes:

A. The specifications in the work order are not clear about the kinds of quality control the buyer will demand.

B. In the work order, the specifications are not clear about the kinds of quality control the buyer will demand.

C. The specifications are not clear in the work order about the kinds of quality control the buyer will demand.

D. The specifications are not clear about the kinds of quality control the buyer will demand in the work order.

Note the difference in meaning that occurs in the D version. The B and C versions have essentially the same meaning as A, although each achieves a slightly different emphasis.

People who begin to experiment with moving words around within sentences to vary impact should also be encouraged to move sentences within paragraphs and paragraphs within longer pieces of writing. Word processors give writers more freedom to experiment than they had in the pre-computer era. People who wish to improve their writing may be pleasantly surprised when they begin to tinker with the fundamental components of their writing—words, phrases, clauses, sentences, paragraphs.

Using Parallelism, Absolutes, and Cleft Constructions

Orators have long recognized the effectiveness of parallel structure. Successful writers also capitalize on this rhetorical device. Charles Dickens used it effectively in *A Tale of Two Cities*, which opens with the nicely balanced sentence, "It was the best of times; it was the worst of times," a classic example of the effective use of parallel structure.

Coordinating conjunctions usually demand parallel structures because they join grammatically equal elements. The semicolon is another device that invites parallel structuring, which also occurs in series and is often established through the repetition of key words, such as those that are repeated in the Dickens example above.

Writers often achieve immediacy by turning relative clauses into absolute constructions. Note the heightened impact of the B version of the sentence below, which is achieved by using an absolute construction:

A. The fleeing girl, who was exhausted from running and was half dead from hunger, collapsed on the bishop's doorstep.

B. The fleeing girl, exhausted from running, half dead from hunger, collapsed on the bishop's doorstep.

The B version of this sentence, by omitting the subject and verb from the relative clause (thereby turning it into an absolute) and by omitting the coordinating conjunction *and*, both alters the rhy thm of the original sentence and adds to its impact and immediacy.

The cleft construction also permits writers to control the emphasis in their sentences, although—as is the case with any rhetorical device—experienced writers use the cleft construction in moderation only to achieve specific, well-defined stylistic ends. A cleft construc tion permits writers to achieve an emphasis that speakers often can achieve simply by intonation. Note how this construction allows a writer to direct attention to various ideas within the sentence: "Tennessee Williams wrote *The Glass Menagerie* in 1944." The versions below emphasize the element suggested following each version.

A. It was Tennessee Williams who wrote *The Glass Menagerie* in 1944. (Emphasis is on who wrote the play)

B. It was *The Glass Menagerie* that Tennessee Williams wrote in 1944. (Emphasis is on which play Williams wrote in a given year)

C. It was in 1944 that Tennessee Williams wrote *The Glass Menagerie*. (Emphasis is on the date of authorship)

The cleft construction achieves its end by using a dummy subject (*it*), which permits it to delay the real subject until later in the sentence where it will receive increased emphasis.

Gaining Experience in Sentence Making

People working individually or in groups can gain valuable experience in composition by working with sets of individual facts that they are asked to combine into a single sentence without distorting any of the information provided. Teachers and members of peer groups can generate such exercises quite easily. The following simple sentences are all to be combined into a single, more mature sentence:

1. Jane and John have a dog.

2. Their dog is named Friskie.

3. Their dog wandered away one day.

4. Their friend, Michael, found Friskie.

5. Michael took Friskie home.

6. Soon Michael called Jane and John.

7. Michael told Jane and John that he would return Friskie.

The combined version:

> Jane and John's dog, Friskie, wandered away one day, but soon their friend Michael called to tell them that on finding Friskie, he had taken him home and would return him to them.

This is a very simple set of ideas that can easily be incorporated into a single sentence. A more complex set would require a restating of relationships within the combined sentence:

1. Frieda is my doctor.

2. Frieda's husband, Frank, is an architect.

3. Frank designed a house for Frieda's father.

4. The house was built in Toledo.

5. The house was built on a lot owned by Frieda's sister's son.

The combined version:

Frank, an architect who is married to my doctor, Frieda, designed a house that was built in Toledo for his father-in-law on a lot owned by Frieda's nephew.

The most challenging set of facts I give to students in this activity are drawn from a sentence in an essay I wrote about the rotary (Wankel) engine and published in a reference work. The following set of facts emerged as I labored to unravel (deconstruct) my unwieldy sentence that initially did not communicate clearly. Once I enumerated the facts I wanted to include in my sentence, I arrived at the solution given following these individual facts:

1. The Wankel engine offers motorists many appealing possibilities;
2. At present, the engine lacks popular acceptance;
3. The engine can propel automobiles smoothly;
4. The engine can run on 75–80 octane fuel;
5. The engine is quiet at high speeds;
6. The engine produces less air pollution than conventional engines do;
7. The engine consumes little fuel;
8. The engine operates on fuel that is not highly refined;
9. The engine can produce significant power.

A possible solution:

Despite its present lack of popular acceptance, the Wankel engine offers motorists many appealing possibilities, particularly in its ability to produce enough power to propel automobiles smoothly and quietly at high speeds with much less air pollution than conventional engines create and with relatively little consumption of fuel that, at 75–80 octane, need not be highly refined.

It is important to emphasize to people who work on such sentence combining activities that these exercises will help them achieve flexibility in their own writing. It would be unfortunate to leave anyone with the impression that long sentences are, *per se*, better than short sentences. The message writers should take away from this exercise is that in writing, variety is better than sameness.

Editing and Deconstruction

People who write can learn a great deal from reading and commenting on each others' writing. Incredible amounts of grammatical knowledge reside in any group of four or five writers. Sharing this knowledge through discussion and editing, challenging this knowledge through healthy debate in peer editing groups, will result in some sophisticated learning experiences for those involved.

It is valuable in class to expose people to some of the practical writing tasks that we all face as professionals. For example, ask students to read an article and then write a fifty-word abstract of it or give them a 450-word book review and ask them to reduce it to three hundred words. Such tasks confront writers regularly and force them to make rhetorical decisions. Performing these sometimes onerous tasks sharpens their writing skills.

Finally, it serves writers well to be able to take relatively complicated sentences (at least four or five printed lines) and study how they are put together and what their discrete elements are. The first task in such an exercise is to put brackets around every clause in the sentence. In many cases, this will result in putting brackets within brackets, because many clauses have other clauses imbedded within them.

Next, those doing the exercise should identify the main clause, indicating its subject, predicate, and, if it has them, direct and indirect objects. The next task is to identify every other clause by type (subordinate clause, relative clause, etc.). After that, absolutes and appositives should be noted. The rhythm of the sentence should be discussed: long sentences are often rhythmic disasters.

Once writers start to take sentences apart, they begin to understand more accurately the dynamics of sentence structure. If they are ever to write well, they will have to internalize these dynamics so that they can apply them as automatically as possible to their own writing.

A Word in Closing

Good writing is hard work. A great deal of outstanding writing results from unique talent, but even those with such talent need to work hard to develop it. The best—probably the only—way to learn how to write is to write. If writing is not a daily activity for those who are working to develop their skills, the results will probably disappoint.

A comprehensive knowledge of grammar will not assure one's ability to write. Grammarians, after all, are not among the world's most alluring writers. Grammar, however, and rhetorical grammar in particular, can offer a great deal to those who are learning to write. Fundamentally, writing, while it is developing, needs to be discussed from a technical standpoint; it is most efficiently discussed by people who can use a grammatical vocabulary.

Writers at all levels need to know as well what options in writing are available to them. It is useful for them to know that replacing a relative clause with an absolute can tighten up a sentence or that using parallel structure can create an environment in which ideas are presented effectively.

It helps writers to know how sentences are made, and they can learn this through some of the exercises on grammatical structure suggested in this essay. Everyone who teaches writing must determine what individual writers need. It is necessary in evaluating student writing to assess areas of weakness, but it is more important to find in it the rhetorical assets on which fledgling writers can build and to communicate with students about their strengths as well as about their weaknesses.

Once people come to realize that effective writing gives writers control over their language and permits them to communicate their ideas convincingly with force and vigor, they begin to develop an enthusiasm for writing that most of us have to work hard to develop. Writing is, after all, a most unnatural act. Good writing instruction strives essentially to make it seem a little more natural to those whose instincts tell them to shy away from it.

9

Grammar in the Writing Center: Opportunities for Discovery and Change

Carl W. Glover and Byron L. Stay

Did you know that the correct way to pronounce the name of the town we live in is "F-ederick," or that the railroaders in the western part of our county live in Bruns-ick? That to exclaim displeasure with the appearance of your car is to say "This car needs cleaned?" Parents say to their children "Let it on the table" or "Leave go of that." Where do these terms come from?

[Young people] now say: "We seen 'em jes' las' night when we was at the mall." Or, "That don't matter none."

It does matter. Limited English skills limit opportunity.

Good grammar and diction, correct usage and pronunciation help our graduates achieve success in college courses, in job interviews, and in business and social situations.

The teaching of formal grammar has negligible or, because it usually displaces some instruction and practice in composition, even a harmful effect on improvement in writing.

These three passages—the first two from letters to the Frederick (MD) *News Post*, the third from Richard Braddock, Richard Lloyd-Jones, and Lowell Schoer's *Research in Written Composition*—illustrate a serious dilemma for teachers of writing. On the one hand, they face pressure from a skeptical public and vocal conservatives who decry what they perceive as a decline of literacy. On the other hand, many compositionists, like Braddock, Lloyd-Jones, and Schoer, have reservations concerning the influence of grammar on writing instruction. Other compositionists have begun to look for ways to teach grammar within the spirit of the process approach. In this chapter we will argue that the writing center, not the writing classroom, is the context where grammar instruction and writing instruction meld together.

Compositionists typically identify three distinct kinds of grammar:

grammar 1. The formal, internal patterns of language.

grammar 2. The linguistic science concerned with description

grammar 3. Linguistic etiquette or "school grammar."

Those supporting instruction in grammars 2 and 3 often argue that it improves writing by making the student aware of grammatical resources and by providing students and teachers with a common vocabulary for analysis (Kolln; Williams). Of course, this justification begs the question of whether grammar instruction makes better writers or thinkers. In fact, the justification that instruction in grammars 2 and 3 improves student writing remains unsubstantiated, and, as Patrick Hartwell suggests, "it may well be that the grammar question is not open to resolution by experimental research" (1985, 107). The justification for teaching school grammar, the kind of grammar this article will address, is that it makes students "appear" educated (Tubbs; Tabbert). As the second letter writer put it at the beginning of this article, good grammar helps "achieve success in college courses, in job interviews, and in business and social situations."

It's hardly surprising that this pragmatic argument has not washed well with modern compositionists who advocate a process approach to composition. Grammatical correctness has taken a back seat to the "making of meaning" for practitioners who emphasize invention, revision, audience, occasion, and collaboration. While composition process theorists are correct in assuming that no link exists between traditional grammar instruction and learning to write well, they ignore a more fundamental issue: the link between *understanding* grammar and writing proficiency. Learning to write well through a better understanding of grammar means addressing the growth and development of the whole person, since writing is a way of coming to know—the self, others, and the world. Through an understanding of grammar, as opposed to rote memorization of forms, students can begin to see the connections between grammatical choice and audience, and, more important, they can begin to understand what these choices say about themselves as writers and as human beings.

Mina Shaughnessy recognized this difference between grammatical understanding and grammatical correctness. The goal of teaching grammar, she argued, ought to be a "shift in perception which is ultimately more important than the mastery of any individual rule of grammar" (129). For Shaughnessy, having the right answers is less important than having grammatical reasons for what a writer does, because "grammar is more a way of thinking, a style of inquiry, than a way of being right" (129). In other words, the development of grammatical understanding enables a student to build a paradigm through which to view the world and act in it through language, a paradigm that a student can apply in a variety of contexts. By extension, approaching grammar as a way of thinking, as a style of inquiry, and as a way of seeing the world, means approaching grammatical questions within the larger context of audience and purpose.

A number of studies over the past decade have argued for such contextuality. Eleanor Kutz has advocated classrooms "that encourage risk-taking [and] reward experimentation with new forms versus the production of error-free papers" (390). Robert de Beaugrande has called for a "learners' grammar" rather than a "teachers' grammar." "The further grammar is removed from natural communication," he writes, "the more likely average people are to lose control of it" (67). If grammar is taught as a dualistic exercise in finding correct forms, students will likely see it as something that has little or no relevance to their lives. If, on the other hand, grammar is taught within the context of its personal, moral, and political implications, then it's an opportunity for discovery, growth, and even liberation.

Unfortunately, there are significant pragmatic obstacles to the classroom teaching of grammar as a way of thinking. It's very difficult to imagine teaching contextually to classes of twenty or more students. There are simply not enough hours in the day to explore the grammatical implications and possibilities in a traditional classroom setting. If grammar 3 instruction becomes a required component of courses, as it often is, it will likely be relegated to workbooks and, perhaps, computer-assisted instruction. While the practical problems are daunting enough, they are subsumed by the larger political obstacles as instructors weave their way through the competing demands of students, the profession, and the public.

Grammar 3 instruction is more than anything a question of power. It suggests a classroom where the teacher actively hands out grammatical truth to the passive students; it suggests a classroom where instructors must choose between teaching grammar and using the process approach; and it suggests an academy forced to choose between pedagogical effectiveness and a public demand to return to the "basics."

First, grammar 3 instruction, at least the way it is normally employed, threatens to undermine process writing by allowing power to remain in the hands of the instructor. Hartwell, referring to the work of Janet Emig and others, writes that "the thrust of current research and theory is to take power from the teacher and to give that power to the learner. At no point in the English curriculum is the question of power more blatantly posed than in the issue of formal grammar instruction" (1985, 127). Instead of transferring power from the teacher to the student, grammar instruction often does the opposite.

Second, grammar 3 instruction is hampered by a power struggle within the discipline of composition studies. As Hartwell argues, those who dismiss grammar "have a model of composition instruction that makes the grammar issue 'uninteresting' in a scientific sense." Those who defend the teaching of grammar often "tend to have a model of composition instruction that is rigidly skills-centered and rigidly sequential" (1985, 108). Few who embrace the process approach to composition want to be associated with those who teach "skills."

Third, grammar 3 instruction reveals the power struggle between a public demanding "back-to-the-basics" instruction and a resisting educational establishment. In each of these three power struggles the student loses. In the first case the student is treated like a vessel into which teachers pour acontextual grammatical rules. In the second case the student becomes lost in the struggle between competing pedagogies. In the third case the student becomes a pawn in the struggle between correctness and personal and intellectual growth. Despite these obstacles, we wish to suggest that grammar can be taught effectively as long as such instruction is seen as a tool for empowerment and not as merely a rite of passage to the world of the educated and that such instruction must occur within full view of the power implications described above. We call this a "grammar of discovery."

Writing centers offer the best place to teach such a grammar of discovery because they allow learning to occur contextually within a framework of personal, moral, and political growth and because one-on-one instruction can mitigate the political obstacles of the classroom. Writing center instruction ought to address the issues of power clearly and honestly. Writing center tutors have an obligation to make students aware of the implications of the grammatical choices they make, whether pronoun or verb choice, active or passive constructions, or agreement. In a one- on-one tutorial a peer tutor can say, "I understand what you mean here, but your readers may make some assumptions about you and about your subject that you don't want them to make." Thus, the focus of the tutorial can shift from "correctness" to "implication." It's not unusual for writing center tutorials to close with open-ended discussions of politics, power, and the correct use of the semicolon.

Opening up the study of grammar, a one-on-one tutorial not only circumvents political obstacles, it can even become politically liberating. While the back-to-basics movement is usually identified with public pressure from outside the profession and conservative traditionalism inside it, a renewed emphasis on basic grammatical skills need not be allied with any competing political agenda. As Donald Lazere has pointed out, this back-to-basics movement might be a "force for liberation—not oppression—if administered with common sense, openness to cultural pluralism, and an application of basics toward critical thinking, particularly about sociopolitical issues, rather than rote memorizing" (9). The resistance of the educational establishment, particularly those on the political left, to the renewed emphasis on standard English, according to Lazere, diminishes an opportunity for liberatory education. Learning to take a measure of control of academic language could be a tool of liberation:

Teachers may unavoidably have to "coerce" students and "lay on" academic culture and standard English in the cause of showing that they contain the potential to be a force for *either* conformity or nonconformity. For teachers to use this opportunity to empower students ultimately to decide for themselves which ends they should use their education for would seem to be a pedagogical endeavor that is legitimate from any political viewpoint. (20)

If, as Lazere argues, there are sound social and political reasons for grammar 3 instruction, we still need to find effective ways to teach it. The writing center is not only effective in teaching traditional grammar 3 concepts in non-traditional, personal ways, but it also allows the instructor to consider the larger personal and political implications of grammar. As Christina Murphy observes, writing centers have the capacity to operate as a bridge between competing educational philosophies and political ideologies on campus. According to Murphy, this intermingling of rhetorical communities gives writing centers the potential to become "agencies for change" within the academic world "by extending and redefining the dialogue on literacy education" (284). Grammar instruction, redefined and recontextualized in the writing center, can bring this same transforming power to the relationship between student and tutor.

Writing center peer tutors can facilitate empowerment and self-actualization in a number of ways. Consider, for example, the use of verb choice as an occasion for both grammatical and personal understanding. In a recent study, psychologists William McGuire and Claire McGuire point out that individuals tend to use verbs of action to describe in concrete terms what they do but use static verbs (verbs of state) to describe in "abstract dispositional terms" what others do. Individuals generally think of themselves as "dynamically changing" and think of others as more static. Thus, they use becoming verbs to describe themselves and being verbs to describe others. McGuire and McGuire further observe that our propensity to see ourselves as more introspective than others hampers interpersonal communications: "These failures to appreciate that others have as rich an interior life as oneself, and particularly that their interior life is as full of likes and dislikes as one's own, may account for some of the insensitivity and inconsiderateness in interpersonal relations" (1142). The research of McGuire and McGuire, although it addresses spoken rather than written language, is important to writing instruction because of its potential to re-direct grammar studies away from a justification of social mobility toward a justification of interpersonal responsibility. Our use of grammar indicates more than our social/political station in life; it indicates how we see ourselves and others.

Not unlike verbs, pronouns also can promote discovery and change in both grammatical and personal ways. Repeated uses of "he" as a referent to both male and female subjects constitutes a lack of rhetorical sensitivity, if not an error in the modern grammatical use of the pronoun. This lack of grammatical sensitivity creates the occasion for student and tutor to explore together not only a more inclusive use of pronouns, but also to examine ways in which language both mirrors and shapes the forces of alienation in our society (Scholes 768–769).

A writing center tutorial enables the tutor to carry the grammar of the pronoun one step further. Following the work of Martin Buber, it can be argued that every use of the pronoun "I" implies one of two possibilities: "I-Thou," or "I-It." I-Thou is grounded in relationship, dialogue, and mutual respect; I-It suggests de-personalization and alienation.

Understanding I-thou relationships is important for grammar instruction not only because of its usefulness in revealing student-audience relationships but also because it informs student- teacher relationships. Just as students can be victimized when they become vessels for grammar instruction, they can also be victimized when they fail to be seen as partners in the learning process. In *Pedagogy of the Oppressed* Paulo Freire recasts the issues in terms of "banking" and "problem-posing" education. In the banking model, like the "I-it" relationship, the teacher pours knowledge into the "it"—the patient, passive, receiving students (57). One might call this the "grammar of oppression." By contrast, in problem-posing education, like the "I-thou" relationship, the subject-object dichotomy is broken apart—"the teacher-student and the students- teachers reflect simultaneously on themselves and the world" (71). In seeing the world in a process of transformation and in becoming a part of that transformation themselves, students and teachers "develop their power to perceive critically *the way they exist* in the world *with which* and *in which* they find themselves" (70–71). In this case the transformation from "I-it" to "I-thou" might be termed a "grammar of liberation."

The relationship of teacher and student in the teaching of grammar raises a number of ethical and philosophical questions, one of the most serious of which is the instruction of basic writers. Not only are these writers far more likely to have fallen victim to well-meant but stultifying grammar instruction, but they are also likely to embrace a more rigid stance toward grammar instruction (Hartwell, 1984, 58). Basic writers have traditionally seen themselves in I-It relationships to grammar and to the world. These students, who most need to learn and experiment and take chances in the writing process, are the ones most likely to be assaulted by the rigidity of grammar instruction. They feel de-personalized, alienated, and victimized, not only by grammar but also by the larger political structures of the university and of society in general. In other words, weaker writers relate to language and the world as the "it" of the "I-it" dichotomy. If we work with these students in traditional error-based instruction, we run the risks of counter-productivity identified by Braddock. But if we teach such students grammar within the context of self and other, we open up new possibilities for instruction. Rather than teach students that commas never function as sentence boundary markers, we might teach them that punctuation is a dynamic, negotiated signal between writer and reader that establishes expectations that are either followed through or thwarted. The peer tutor and student thus become partners in looking at the audience, a partnership that is itself a dynamic negotiation, helping students gain a position of control over their language and their world.

Writing centers can help to alleviate the problem of rigidity and depersonalization by teaching grammar in the context of students' own papers. Muriel Harris has written extensively about the potential of writing center grammar tutorials. "The conference setting is particularly appropriate for working on grammar as an editing skill," she writes, "because specific errors evident on the page make up the agenda for discussion" (120). Her strategies for teaching grammar are particularly helpful since she avoids much of the traditional rule-based language in favor of more immediate and focused responses. Since writing centers focus attention on individuals as well as on texts, they occasion discussions of meaning in full view of author, audience, and purpose. The question of grammatical structure in a one-on-one tutoring session is completely different from workbook grammar. The writing center session, since it is already highly interactive, allows student and tutor to focus on the intersection of grammar and meaning.

Teaching the grammar of discovery is no easy task, inside or outside of the writing center. Even in the collaborative, process-oriented, student-centered classroom, it is difficult for teachers to sacrifice the classroom agenda for the grammatical needs of each individual student. On the other hand, the situational nature of grammatical error makes the writing center better suited for the teaching of grammar. Since grammar instruction is most effective within the context of the moment, the writing center provides the situation for tutors to respond to the specific needs of each individual student according to the demands of each paper. But the teaching of grammar ought to be more than merely teaching about words. It is about empowering students. It is about helping students come to know themselves, others, and the world around them. It is about teaching students the possibilities and responsibilities of transforming themselves and the world through language.

10

Rhetorical Contexts of Grammar: Some Views from Writing-Emphasis Course Instructors

Donald Bushman and Elizabeth Ervin

All is not well in the city of Tucson—at least not where college writers are concerned. Recent headlines in three newspapers, the local *Arizona Daily Star* and *Tucson Citizen*, and the University of Arizona's *Arizona Daily Wildcat*, resounded the bad news: "Writing skills weak at UA, exam reveals," "UA looking for ways to improve writing," "More students failing on writing assessment." The outcries were part of the fallout of a report released by the University's Intercollegiate Writing Committee (IWC), a faculty group assembled to monitor the University's ongoing commitment to undergraduate writing instruction. In part, the IWC's report questioned the effectiveness of the Upper-Division Writing-Proficiency Exam (UDWPE), a two-hour timed writing test currently used to screen students before they enter writing-emphasis courses in their major. According to the report, twenty-five percent of the students who took the UDWPE over the course of the last academic year were judged by faculty to be unsatisfactory, and an additional forty-one percent were found to be only minimally satisfactory.

Although the statistics themselves are in line with those from previous years, what's different is that members of the campus and local communities have shown any interest in them. This newfound interest appears to stem from one of the boldest claims in the IWC report— namely, that current efforts to assess student writing at the mid-career level are not working, and that the University needs to rethink these efforts, particularly the UDWPE. The report warns that the University may need to reaffirm its commitment to writing instruction altogether. One faculty response to these figures was voiced by math professor Donald Myers, who "questioned the consistency of campus departments in dealing with their own writing-emphasis courses" (Wabnik 2B). "I don't think the faculty is sufficiently organized on the question of what [is] expected in the way of writing proficiency," Myers was quoted as saying. He added: "It's not just an English department problem. It's a campus problem" (quoted in Wabnik 2B).

Thus, while the University's assessment "crisis" is somewhat misleading, it has jolted many faculty across campus out of their indifference to writing instruction. At an UDWPE holistic scoring session in December 1993, the first after the IWC report was made public, a number of faculty who were participating for the first time praised the usefulness of the scoring sessions as a forum for exchanging views about the state of student writing; many showed tremendous insight into the "logic" of ineffective writing. But through their well–intentioned comments, two faculty members exemplified the difficulties surrounding WAC efforts in general. The first came during the "norming" process, which Don explained was a necessary step in holistic scoring— required, in part, to expose differing ideas about what constitutes effective writing among the different academic disciplines represented by the scorers. A psychology professor objected to this assumption, saying, "I think we all would agree on the qualities of good writing: logical structure, clear purpose, sound mechanical skills." The second comment came at the end of the scoring session, when a University administrator exclaimed confidently that "With this many committed individuals [there were about sixty faculty members in six scoring sessions for the December UDWPE], we ought to be able to fix this problem we've read so much about lately."

These remarks illustrate some entrenched attitudes about writing which dovetail neatly with the IWC report, and which suggest that while English composition teachers may understand concepts such as grammar in complex terms, writing teachers in the disciplines may see it as a simple, straightforward skill. This leads us to ask: are we speaking the same language when we talk about writing with colleagues across campus?

Many of our colleagues across campus are interested in issues concerning writing—indeed, in some cases passionate about such issues. However, they may never have carefully thought through their convictions about what makes writing "good," and they may not have the critical vocabulary that allows them to discuss their ideas productively with other writing teachers. Writing-emphasis faculty, in particular, have valuable ideas about writing instruction, but they may consider themselves "non-experts" and thus doubt the validity of their contributions. The psychology professor, for example, had only to be asked to consider the possibility that a colleague in, say civil engineering, might have very different ideas than she about what was logical or clear or sound. As for the University administrator, her enthusiasm inspires hope that faculty and administration will make writing instruction a higher institutional priority, and that faculty collaboration can bring this change about. But at the same time, her belief that poor writing is a "problem" that can be "fixed" with a little concerted effort simply echoes her colleague's idea that good writing is a uniform thing, uncomplicated by such factors as race, social class, and disciplinary conventions. This belief indicates that the university community in general lacks an understanding of how writing is taught and theorized in English and other disciplines. While, as composition teachers, we value the teaching of writing-as-content-area, we don't necessarily think that writing-emphasis instructors simply need more "specialist" knowledge about writing—and, besides, many of them don't want it. Instead, we advocate a greater awareness of *specific* rhetorical contexts—and the *variety* of rhetorical contexts—in which writing occurs. Awareness alone doesn't improve student writing, of course, but, like "norming" in holistic scoring, it prepares us to define more specifically our issues and to explore them from a shared perspective.

This series of events provides the context for our study. As writing teachers committed to writing across the curriculum, we are interested in soliciting the expertise of writing teachers in the disciplines. Our purpose is not simply to "indoctrinate" these teachers with the expertise of writing teachers in the English department; rather, we hope to understand more fully the variety of rhetorical contexts that writing-emphasis courses represent so that we may more effectively incorporate these contexts into the curricula of our own classes.

Are students getting consistent writing instruction in their first-year composition courses and in the upper-division courses they must take in other disciplines? If not, what sort of writing instruction is appropriate in "content" courses? What is the most judicious manner of our providing support to teachers and students in writing-emphasis courses? How do writing-emphasis teachers provide guidance for students preparing to revise? What is the place of grammar in this guidance? Our preliminary goals were to bring together, compare, and synthesize faculty members' attitudes about grammar and their strategies for helping students to improve this element of their writing. After speaking with writing–emphasis instructors and examining our data, however, we have become convinced of the need to discuss grammar not simply as an isolated aspect of the writing product, but as part of the shifting rhetorical contexts of college writing. Thus our revised goals for this project include the following: encouraging writing- emphasis instructors to develop a greater self-consciousness about how important grammar is in relation to other writing concerns; sharing pedagogical approaches to responding to student writing in a way that responds to the specific rhetorical contexts of their classes; and promoting greater continuity in university-wide writing instruction.

Our study included twelve instructors from across campus, all of whom teach required writing-emphasis courses within the disciplines, and it took place in three parts. First, we distributed three sample student essays written to fulfill the UDWPE requirement, asking participants to "make written comments on these essays in a way that is faithful to the manner in which you comment on drafts written by undergraduates in your department." Several days later, we brought the participants together for a focused discussion, using the student essays as a springboard for understanding what they considered to be "grammatical problems" in student writing, how they dealt with such problems, and how serious those problems were within the rhetorical contexts of their classrooms. This discussion was audio- and videotaped, and later transcribed. Finally, we distributed an attitudinal survey to participants, which solicited general views about the relative importance of grammar within the writing process, and suggestions for effective writing support for writing-emphasis faculty and students. Our results are primarily descriptive, although we draw some tentative conclusions and offer limited suggestions about how greater continuity in university-wide writing instruction might be achieved.

The qualitative part of our study provides the bulk of our evidence, and will be described later in this essay. First, however, we would like to define some terms and survey some of the territory already covered by others interested in grammar, specifically as it applies to writing in the disciplines.

Rhetorical Contexts of Grammar: An Extended Definition

The renewed debate about how to teach grammar was recently addressed in an open letter published in the NCTE *Council Chronicle*. Martha Kolln, President of the Assembly for the Teaching of English Grammar, acknowledges that the very word *grammar* "conjure[s] up visions of do's and don'ts and fill-in-the-blank exercises on purple ditto pages" (14). But she is also concerned that the conflation of traditional or "school" grammar with *all* grammar has effectively eliminated discussions of grammar from the agenda of the National Council of Teachers of English. According to Kolln, "The only question ever asked [in studies of grammar] is whether or not we should teach 'formal grammar'—that isolated class, usually in junior high, based on traditional 'school grammar.' . . . But the next logical question has not been asked: If formal grammar doesn't work, what does? What other method should we try?" (14–15).

In fact, though, many studies have asked this question, and most have concluded not only that an emphasis upon grammar instruction does not translate into improved writing skills, but that it may also result in a decreased level of interest in writing among students. One solution to this dilemma is to conceive of grammar in a rhetorical rather than merely "formal" context. David Bartholomae justifies such a stance in "The Study of Error," in which he defines *errors* not as what the student failed to do, but "as evidence of intention"—the writer's idiosyncratic way of negotiating individual style of expression with "the language of the tribe." He continues:

> A writer's activity is linguistic and rhetorical activity; it can be different but never random. The task for both teacher and researcher, then, is to discover the grammar of *that* coherence, of the "idiosyncratic dialect" that belongs to a particular writer at a particular moment in the history of his attempts to imagine and reproduce the standard idiom of academic discourse. ... [W]e cannot identify errors without identifying them in context, and the context is not the text, but the activity of composing that presented the erroneous form as a possible solution to the problem of making a meaningful statement. (305–307)

According to Bartholomae, the presence of errors in student texts foists upon teachers two responsibilities they may not want to accept: the first is to read for rhetorical intent as well as for content; the second is to be more self-conscious about their expectations within the rhetorical context of composing for a specific assignment, course, or discipline. As Robert J. Connors suggests in "Mechanical Correctness as a Focus in Composition Instruction," these responsibilities—in particular, finding an appropriate balance between formal and rhetorical considerations—may be the most central, difficult, and ongoing professional task writing teachers face: "We cannot escape the fact that in a written text any question of mechanics is also a rhetorical question, and as a discipline we are still trying to understand the meaning of that conjunction" (71).

But what exactly does it mean to "rhetoricize" grammar? Part of the answer may lie in the disassociation of grammar—including the responsibility of defining and "enforcing" grammar—from English departments. Elaine P. Maimon explains in "Knowledge, Acknowledgment, and Writing across the Curriculum: Toward an Educated Community" that "Instructors create writing communities by teaching students that those who write determine what becomes characteristic within a discipline and that writing is essential to the ongoing formulation of what constitutes a field of study" (90). In other words, although it is clear that scholars in all disciplines depend on writing as a way of defining themselves professionally, it is not so clear what writing means in those various disciplines—mainly because it doesn't receive the same self-conscious attention that it does among English teachers, especially composition specialists.

Problems occur both when people outside of English neglect to define the conventions of writing in their own discipline or profession, as well as when English teachers fail to relinquish their traditional authority where grammar is concerned. Joseph Williams illustrates this problem in "The Phenomenology of Error," in which he describes an incident that occurred when he "was consulting with a government agency that had been using

English teachers to edit reports, but was not sure they were getting their money's worth'':

> When I asked to see some samples of editing by their consultants, I found that one very common notation was "faulty parallelism" at spots that only by the most conservative interpretation could be judged faulty. I asked the person who had hired me whether the faulty parallelism was a problem in his staff's ability to write clearly enough to be understood quickly, but with enough authority to be taken seriously, [sic] He replied, ":If the teacher says so." (154–155)

Rather than working within the rhetorical context of the government agency ("write clearly enough to be understood quickly but with enough authority to be taken seriously"), the English teachers were working within their own rhetorical context. More specifically, they were looking for errors—in this case, errors that were irrelevant, or at least relatively unproblematic, within the rhetorical context of writing government reports. In short, the English teachers—presumably "experts" on writing and editing—showed themselves to be unaccustomed to writing and editing conventions outside their own field, and therefore, as the agency suspected, not particularly useful.

If indeed writing conventions are socially constructed, then, Williams argues, errors of grammar and usage may be viewed as forms of "social errors," much like the inappropriate obscenity or racist joke, or mentioning our painful hemorrhoids in the presence of strangers. "[O]riginating in ignorance or incompetence or accident," these "flawed verbal transactions" typically evoke a judgment from the audience that requires a response from the offending party (153). If we view errors in written usage in the same way that we view social *faux pas*, "it is also necessary," Williams advises, "to shift our attention from error treated strictly as an isolated item on a page, to error perceived as a flawed verbal transaction between a writer and a reader. When we do this, the matter of error turns less on a handbook definition than on the reader's response . . ." (153). This comparison introduces Williams's main proposition in "The Phenomenology of Error"—namely, that we can discuss error "at the level of consciousness that places all error at the very center of our consciousness. Or we can talk about how we experience (or not) what we popularly call errors of usage as they occur in the ordinary course of our reading a text" (159).

Like Williams, Patrick Hartwell believes that grammar can be defined broadly and from multiple perspectives. In "Grammar, Grammars, and the Teaching of Grammar," Hartwell attempts to make sense of the deluge of composition studies that explore the usefulness of grammar instruction to the teaching of writing. If the argument is ever to advance beyond the experimental research stage (of which Hartwell is highly critical), he proposes that one question we must ask is: "What definitions of the word *grammar* are needed to articulate the grammar issue intelligently?" (108). He surveys five possibilities: the set of formal patterns according to which language is arranged for the purposes of communication, or "the grammar in our heads"; transformational grammar, the linguistic science that concerns itself with the formulization of language patterns; "linguistic etiquette," or usage; "school grammar," often based on unwieldy rules of logic or adapted from Latin; and "stylistic grammar" which employs grammatical terms in the interest of teaching prose style. The last of these, stylistic grammar, offers the most productive definition for our purposes. As an illustration of how this grammar has been conceived, Hartwell points to Kolln's defense of sentence combining exercises as a form of grammar instruction (see 1981, 149). Such exercises stress how an understanding of the rules of grammar can be used to create discourse appropriate to specific rhetorical purposes and audiences.

But the question of what is appropriate in the context of any given writing task is open to discussion. Recall the views of the psychology professor at the UDWPE scoring session; clearly, faculty are not always conscious of the ways that different rhetorical contexts require different discourse styles. Mimi Schwartz addresses this phenomenon in a fascinating study in which she polled twenty-two faculty and 105 students from across her campus about their writing preferences. She developed a handout with three pairs of passages, each of which discussed the same general idea in two different discourse styles; or as Schwartz puts it, "Each set of passages has a different rhetorical conflict" (56).[1] Her survey results tell us "both what twenty-two faculty thought [about the passages] and what 105 students *thought* faculty thought" (56). While the reactions of the students are enlightening—they typically preferred the more straightforward passage of the pairs and wrongly predicted that the faculty would prefer those that were jargon- filled and complex—it is the responses of the faculty and Schwartz's analysis that concerns us here.

Faculty responses were far from uniform. In at least one instance, different passages evoked nearly identical responses. As Schwartz tells us,

> The business professor likes [passage] A because "It's clearer, more descriptive, better organized." But a writing professor likes [passage] B for the same apparent reason: "It's tight, clear, unlike the first which, though descriptive, rambles." Same text, same vocabulary, opposite meanings. No wonder students are not sure of what we mean when they see "Be more clear!" in the margins of their papers. (57)

Schwartz adds that we (and our students) mistakenly assume that terms such as "clear" and "wordy" have some sort of universal meaning, and that rules such as "Never use I" are accepted by faculty in every department. Therefore, students writing in a variety of classes are forced to "rely upon a generalized rhetoric, independent of context" (61), and this rhetoric often manifests itself in jargon-laden, convoluted prose that students utilize to sound authoritative. As our psychology professor revealed, faculty, too, are often confined by the notion of a generalized rhetoric. Because faculty may not "articulate their rhetorical values" to their students, these values go unnoticed *by both students and faculty*; but they are nonetheless "at work, shaping our responses as readers" (61). The sorts of comments that our students will be able to make the best use of, Schwartz says, are those that "tell the writer what an individual reader needs to know about a particular text. We must play more the role of reader than of judge . . ." (61).

Those of us who have interacted with faculty across campus know that while many of them are intuitively very sharp with respect to writing, many have never been asked to articulate clearly their "rhetorical values." That's one reason why writing–across–the–curriculum efforts are so important— both to the successful teacher-student dynamic, and to the ongoing dialogue among faculty in all disciplines. And it's also why we need to ask larger questions about grammar and grammar instruction, like what role it plays in specific rhetorical contexts. Because other scholars have already demonstrated (at least to our satisfaction) that such contexts exist in great variety, this issue will not be the focus of our study. Instead, we offer a qualitative analysis, relying on conversations with writing-emphasis faculty and their comments on student essays; its immediate area of application, therefore, is writing instruction outside of English departments.[2] As will become evident below, this study illustrates the profound frustrations about writing instruction experienced by many writing-emphasis instructors, and their strategies— sometimes effective, sometimes not—of dealing with those frustrations.

How Writing-Emphasis Faculty Respond to Grammar: Five Profiles

The teachers we spoke with represented a variety of disciplines across campus: Architecture, Art, East Asian Studies, English, Math, Nursing, and Pharmacology and Toxicology; one participant was an independent writing and communications consultant.[3] As either members of the University's Intercollegiate Writing Committee, frequent UDWPE scorers, and/or writing-emphasis course instructors, all had demonstrated a commitment to undergraduate writing instruction at the University of Arizona, and all had strong opinions about student writing. Many of them echoed Mina P. Shaughnessy's characterization of the writer's relationship with his or her audience as part of the "economics of energy": "Although speakers and listeners, writers and readers, are in one sense engaged in a cooperative effort to understand one another, they are also in conflict over the amount of effort each will expend on the other" (11). And as far as grammar is concerned, the participants in our study agreed with Shaughnessy's notion that mechanical errors are in general "unprofitable intrusions upon the consciousness of the reader":

> They demand energy without giving any return in meaning; they shift the
> reader's attention from where he is going (meaning) to how he is getting
> there (code). In a better world, it is true, readers might be more generous

with their energies, pausing to divine the meaning of a writer or mentally to edit the errors out of his text without expecting to be rewarded for their efforts, but it would be foolhardy to bank on that kind of persistence except perhaps in English teachers or good friends. (12)

Writing-emphasis course instructors seldom fall into either of these categories—English teachers or good friends. Still, in spite of their frustrations over having to deal with grammar, and their doubts about their *ability* to deal effectively with grammar problems (which we will discuss later), the teachers we spoke with were not unusually conservative in their attitudes toward grammar problems. For example, one professor said, "If you teach grammar you're in trouble—because it's not the grammar that's important, it's what you do with it." Another said, "I think of [grammar] as a step in the learning process." Several maintained that if a paper was "well-written with mistakes," then they would not lower a student's grade because of grammar problems. Many of these professors, at least, are less concerned about the intrusion of grammatical problems in the meaning-making process than we (and Shaughnessy) would have guessed.

Results from a 1992 survey of writing-emphasis faculty at the University of Arizona are illuminating here. Only seven percent of the respondents felt that poor spelling and punctuation are the most serious writing problems among college students; thirty-four percent believed that teachers who want to improve student writing will point out all errors on each paper they read; only thirty percent thought that spelling and grammar instruction in writing-emphasis classes will solve most student writing problems; and forty-one percent thought that there are fixed rules which govern all good writing. The faculty representatives in our micro-study were even more liberal in their attitudes toward grammar. In a similar survey, no respondents felt that poor spelling and punctuation are the most serious writing problems of college students; none believed that teachers who want to improve student writing will point out all errors on each paper they read; and none thought that spelling and grammar instruction in writing-emphasis classes will solve most student writing problems. Additionally, only forty-three percent of the respondents felt qualified to respond to the sorts of grammar problems they saw in their students' writing, whereas seventy–one percent agreed that providing evaluative and summative comments on student essays is more important than marking grammatical errors, and the same amount expressed interest in learning to respond more effectively to such problems. Despite this interest, though, forty percent considered grammar instruction the responsibility of the English department. Seventy-one percent of respondents claimed that they would react differently to student writing if grammatical problems were not so distracting, but only twenty-nine percent said that they would consider assigning more writing in their classes.

But surveys and statistics can only approximate teachers' attitudes about writing. The issues becomes more complex when we allow participants of a study—especially those speaking from perspectives outside of English or composition—to talk openly and to set the agenda for discussion. From our discussions with this group, we attribute the attitudinal discrepancies illustrated by the survey to two factors. First is a conviction that grammar problems *will matter eventually* (e.g., in a professional context), even if they don't matter much to that particular teacher. As one participant wrote, "We cannot simply leave [the responsibility for writing instruction] to someone else; if we do, students come to think the only time they have to pay attention to their writing is in English classes. Fostering that attitude is a disservice to the students. We should teach them instead that how they write is important *whenever* they write." The second factor is the belief that being a good writer doesn't necessarily qualify a person to teach writing, and vice versa. Indeed, as one respondent put it, "I am quite uncomfortable with the idea that the teaching of writing can be delegated to other professionals, who may very well be experts in their own fields, but who can only work part-time as teachers of writing and cannot possibly be familiar with current writing theory and practice." Another teacher agreed that writing is important throughout the college curriculum, but thought that outside of English courses, the goal of general writing competence should be considered secondary to content-area competence. He wrote, "But also I feel that one of the most important perceptions for a student to develop (except if s/he is becoming a novelist or a poet) is that writing is a *tool* to be used in pursuing some other goal associated with the course, work, career, foreign policy. . . ."

As mentioned earlier, we began our study by distributing to participating faculty copies of three essays written during a recent Upper-Division Writing-Proficiency Exam. The exam was based on Wendell Berry's essay "In Defense of Literacy"; thus not only were the student essays *about* issues of grammar and literacy, but they also embodied such literacy issues as grammar skills. Participants brought their copies of the essays with them to a discussion, complete with written comments, and we began from there. Feelings of nervousness and insecurity set the initial tone of our session. "I'm not really sure why I was asked to be here—unless I'm being recruited to grade those [UDWPE] exams again," one professor confessed as we went around the room making introductions. Everyone laughed; many seemed equally bewildered as to why *they* were being consulted about grammar. One professor said, "I don't teach any writing classes; I'm actually a little afraid of writing. . . . But I actually think that I'm a writer sometimes." More laughter. Another added: "I feel a little bit like you. I'm in defiance of writing. Glad to know we're not alone!" "Misery loves company."

It was immediately clear to us that although the faculty who participated in this study were successful writers and/or writing teachers in their disciplines, few of them were outwardly confident about their abilities to talk about writing. As our discussion progressed, however, it also became apparent that each of them practiced specific strategies—some more effective than others—to address what they perceived as grammar problems in students' writing.

What follows are five composite sketches of these strategies. Each profile is based on the comments and written responses of one or two faculty members, with comments and examples from other participants added as they seem relevant to that profile. All pronouns used in the profiles are arbitrary.

The Advocate

Most of our faculty participants agreed on the importance of encouraging students to develop their writing skills—even when the texts they produced had many problems. One professor in particular put this conviction to frequent use in her comments. On one essay, her end comments read, in full:

> I think you are beginning to understand the joy of *becoming* literate. Discovering the literature of your heritage has reinforced the value of recording ideas and feelings, and made you a part of your culture in new and exciting ways. I hope you continue to develop *your* communication skills so that someday you can make *your* contribution to the body of Hispanic knowledge—and that your own literacy continues to grow and enrich your life.

The end comments were signed with the professor's first name, adding a personal and collegial touch to her comments. The tone, furthermore, is enthusiastic and encouraging, with only an indirect assessment of the quality of writing in the essay: "I hope you continue to develop you communication skills ... and that your own literacy continues to grow and enrich your life." Within the text, however, the professor made several changes in the student's writing, ranging from word choice to spelling to sentence structure. She also posed questions or urged the writer toward revision—typically, improved clarity and development through specific examples—as when she says, "I'm not sure what you mean," and "like what?"

Looking at her marginal and end comments in isolation, it might appear that the Advocate is applying an uncritical pedagogy: ending on such a positive note when, as her comments throughout the text suggest, the essay has many problems. However, as the professor explained in our group discussion, "We all need to be responsible [for helping our students to improve their writing], but not everybody can teach writing." Instead, she sees her role as encouraging students to work on their writing; she devotes significant energies toward directing them to programs or services on campus where they can receive help, and informing them about what opportunities will be open to them professionally if they *do* improve their writing skills. Rather than try to "tutor" her students, or simply tell them to "Go to the Writing Center," she invites them in her end comments to come see her. For example, at the end of another essay she writes, "You obviously understand the importance of communication skills, but your poor grammar & spelling make your ideas less powerful. Please come see me. I would like to discuss with you how we might improve your writing—I think it could help you in all your classes." Thus the Advocate still takes responsibility for helping her students to improve their writing, but this responsibility manifests itself in resource sharing rather than in actual writing instruction.

The Confirmed Non–Experts

Two frustrated attitudes are represented by this term: helplessness ("I don't know *how* to deal with these problems") and indignation ("I shouldn't *have* to deal with these problems") in the face of students' grammar problems. While several of the participating teachers believed that grammar problems override an essay's strengths (or other weaknesses), one professor claimed that he felt ill-equipped even to write comments on the sample student essays. "I couldn't talk about these," he said. "I never see papers this bad. I was turned off by these because I think that the level of help these people need is so early, rather than high or low, that somebody should be able to sit down with them and explain what needs to be done." This Confirmed Non-Expert, though, *doesn't have to* deal with serious grammar problems in his classes: his department provides an English department instructor to work with his students on their papers before he ever sees them. And, as he explained on our survey, "I never mark on the finished work. . . . To do so seems rude and unproductive." In our discussion, he justifies his "hands-off" stance by drawing an analogy between developing literacy and going to the doctor: "I don't medicate myself. And if I have a paper like this, I'm not qualified to help this person. That's why I didn't write on [the sample essays]. I'm just flat not qualified."

Another Confirmed Non-Expert revealed a somewhat different perspective. Although she felt qualified to address her students' grammar problems (in fact, she told us that she used to teach composition), this professor felt that many of the problems were so severe that they would take too much time to address: "There's no easy way, no logical way to do it simply in a reasonable amount of time, and then give [comments] back to them and have them correct their papers." Part of the problem for this Confirmed Non-Expert was class size: she teaches a large general education course with an enrollment that regularly surpasses 100 students. Thus even with two teaching assistants, she can't spend the time commenting on drafts and final essays, even though she knows her students would benefit from it. Of course, part of her resistance stems from an impatience with the pervasiveness of grammar problems, including spelling and wordiness. "I tell them, 'I'm going to pretend I didn't see [those errors]. Do not ever turn in [an essay] that looks like this again.' And by the Lord Harry things are better the next time around." Later she expresses a concern that hers is a *general* education course, not what she regards as a forum for learning any kind of specialized language use: "This is supposed to be a part of being 'literate.' . . . [Grammar] is only a fairly small part in the whole course, but it is a mark of being *il*literate if you can't say what you have to say, and say it in a way that people can understand.''

Like all of the faculty in our discussion, the Confirmed Non-Experts expressed a clear understanding of the importance of grammar in the writing their students do. Both wanted to foster a challenging and "productive" environment, and both, in their own ways, took some form of responsibility to help their students—one by supplementing his own instruction with that of an English department instructor, the other by consistently sending her students to the University Writing Center. The first Confirmed Non-Expert proudly reminded us that his was "one of the first writing-emphasis courses on campus"; and although the atmosphere of his class sends the clear message that writing is important, he is not embarrassed to say that a certain level of grammar problems are beyond his area of expertise. Considering the size of the classes both Confirmed Non-Experts teach, they are to be commended for assigning as much writing as they do.

The Editor

One faculty member earned this tag for his practice of rewriting passages of students' essays to model clearer-sounding prose, a strategy he learned in graduate school. After his own professors had reworded parts of his essays a few times, he said, "it didn't take long for me to learn to do it myself." This teacher was quick to point out that he found some interesting ideas in the passages he rewrote in the sample student essays, noting that on a first reading of student papers he tends to ignore grammatical problems in order to concentrate exclusively on ideas. In a tentative effort to explain the rationale for his pedagogy, the Editor suggested that there must be some value in "maybe taking their ideas and just putting them in a different form—not the 'right' one because there is no 'right' one, necessarily—just so they can see them expressed differently." He knows he is at least providing some form of assistance to these writers, even if that assistance is problematic.

What was so striking about the Editor was that when he communicated with us, he seemed keenly aware of rhetorical considerations in his own writing and that of his students. For example, he works closely with graduate students in his department who are submitting their work to peer-reviewed journals. "Your fate is in this sentence you just wrote," he tells them, cautioning them against such assumptions as "my reader already knows all this," and directing them toward what he calls "reader-directed writing": "The more you can do to make it easier for the reader to just *read* [what you've written], the better off you are." In spite of this broad understanding of complex rhetorical situations, his comments on student essays consisted almost solely of rewritten passages. Consider the following sentences from a sample student essay:

> Another, would be to tell the community about a crise of a conflict that is
> occuring or has already occured in the business you work. A person that has
> poor communication skills would probably hinder the business for becom-
> ing really famous.

The Editor revises the passage to read like this:

> Another example would be to inform the community about a crisis at work
> that might affect their health or safety. Poor communication in a crisis could
> seriously damage a company's reputation and prevent them from being
> successful.

He even offers an alternative version of the second sentence:

> Effective communication could save lives and improve a company's public
> relations.

Although most would agree that his suggestions did in fact improve the clarity of this student's writing, we believe that other methods of responding
would produce more long-lasting effects for the student and ultimately save
time for the professor, as well. The clarity and coherence of the Editor's
rewritten passage is the result of an obvious tacit understanding of the elements of effective discourse. For instance, his repetition of the word "crisis"
in both sentences of the rewritten passage indicates his awareness of the need
to link consecutive sentences with overlapping information—à la Halliday
and Hassan's "given-new" contract. Other rewritten passages reflect revision strategies that further demonstrate his grasp of semantic theories for
creating clarity and cohesion on the sentence level and beyond.

Certainly, a writing-emphasis teacher need not be familiar with semantic theory in order to help his students write better. In this case, the Editor
might begin by explaining to students what he has done to improve their
prose when he rewrites, and to discuss with them how *they* might rewrite
their sentences to achieve the same sort of clarity. Although this strategy
would require an expanded critical vocabulary, it would still allow him, in
Schwartz's words, to respond to student writing more as a reader than as a
judge. Dale Holloway agrees: "If we can talk about subjects, verbs, and
objects (or other completers) as 'agents,' 'actions,' and 'goals,'" she says,
"we have a valuable terminology by which to link the grammar of our sentences with the actual (or 'real-world') actions they describe" (206). As we
mentioned earlier, the Editor insists that students' ideas are the most important part of any piece of writing—even those that might be dismissed by
some readers as substandard. On our follow-up survey, he also expresses a
willingness to attend a workshop designed to help him to respond more
effectively to grammar problems in student writing. He underscores his commitment to improved student writing with the idea that neither he, nor his
department, nor any single campus unit can assume all credit or blame for

the state of student writing: "[Responsibility for writing] has to be shared—only when students get a consistent message is it working."

The General Rhetorician

Our term for this profile alludes to the mindset that Schwartz uncovered in her study—one that assumes that universal standards of "good writing" and useful comments transcend disciplinary boundaries. The psychology professor in the UDWPE scoring session also would fit into this category. The General Rhetorician, while showing no less concern for student writing than anyone else, expressed frustration over students' reactions to her written comments. "Whatever you write [on students' essays] is worthless because they don't understand your criticism," she said in our discussion. The reason for this misunderstanding may lie with the comments themselves, which for this professor consisted mostly of general remarks, both positive and negative, in the form of a list at the end of the essay. For example:

1. Organization is clear and logical,
2. Seems to be discussing communication skills rather than literacy,
3. Not convincing,
4. Many spelling and some grammatical errors,
5. Does not answer the question.

Occasionally, this professor made specific marginal comments (e.g., "good point," "not clear what this means?") on the sample essays, but her end comments reiterate the problem Schwartz saw in her faculty sample—namely, that they don't "tell a writer what an individual reader needs to know about a particular text" (61). The General Rhetorician's students may not understand her written comments because it isn't always evident what they refer to. For instance, what about the essay's argument is "not convincing"? What could the writer have done to more effectively "answer the question"? Even when supplemented by the marginal comments, the general end comments don't answer these questions; neither do they tell a student what the instructor was thinking about, or how she was affected by the text, as she was reading it.

Of course, some teachers' comments were general and, in our opinion, quite effective. For example, one professor writes "be consistent" in a passage that shifts from singular to plural subject; she adds, "Before you write think about whether you want to talk about an individual or a group." Although her suggestion could be applied in virtually any writing task, it didn't appear in a vacuum as a generalized rule; instead, it responded to a specific problem in a specific sentence.

So the issue isn't simply whether or not general comments are effective. In fact, one teacher seemed to speak for the entire group when she said, "The example people get in the world is not good writing. It's pretty mediocre writing, really . . . and if you're trying to intuit what good writing is from the newspapers, advertisements . . . you're going to come to some wrong generalizations." Her remarks initiated a lengthy discussion about the difficulty many students have even *recognizing* good writing. As another teacher put it, "Some students have never had the experience of really understanding something. . . . Grammar is about clear and precise expression, and if they've never understood what the difference is, [then they won't understand] why it means nothing to have verb and subject disagreement, and why all of a sudden it clicks when you've got agreement."

For this reason, the General Rhetorician advocates providing models of effective papers for her students, something she frequently does in her own classes. As she explains, "If there's an essay exam or a paper due, I select one or two papers I think are well-done and suggest [that students] read them, because I can't go through [everyone's essay] line by line." The purpose of these papers is to show students what competent responses to an assignment look like. But the General Rhetorician explained in our discussion that she simply tells her students to "Read *this* paper in contrast [to yours] and do these things [that the paper does well]." That is, she provides no explanation of *what makes that model good*. Without that commentary, students may not infer the same "rhetorical values" that the teacher has.

The Contextual Rhetorician

All of our participants demonstrated a sensitivity to rhetorical contexts in at least some of their comments. In a survey response, for example, one professor wrote that "Many people who are already competent writers wish to develop more effective or sophisticated styles. Or they may want to branch out of their usual writing tasks to undertake special projects. In my own case, I am good at writing technical articles in scientific journals, but I would definitely seek instruction before writing an undergraduate textbook." The English department or other writing specialists could provide valuable assistance in defining and responding to these rhetorical situations, he suggested. Another professor, however, stated that "Some connections between the specific requirements of a particular discipline and general writing can only be made in the disciplines." In other words, because the English department has its own disciplinary conventions, it can perhaps offer only limited assistance (as is illustrated by Williams's account of his consulting experiences).

One faculty member demonstrated an especially keen ability to negotiate these issues. While he is aware of the importance of writing in his classes, he also emphasizes to his students that *his* expectations for their writing are *not* universal. His comments in our discussion, we think, are worth recording at length:

> One of the things that I've learned to do is to tell students that I'm not expecting them to take what I require of them in terms of writing, and

change the way they write for everyone all the time. I'm expecting them to try this on for a semester—in fact, I'm demanding it, but I put it to them in terms of expecting—because they're always going to write for a different audience . . . and every audience is going to ask for a different style, a different format. . . . And I don't want to presume to tell them that *this* is the way to write, because there are certain things that I'm looking for in a literature paper or a history paper, or whatever it may be that I'm teaching, that [turning to person sitting next to him] you're not going to want, stylistically speaking [in a paper in your discipline].

Although the Contextual Rhetorician acknowledges that most teachers could probably agree on some standards of good writing, he also believes that "we'd find as many very specific things about which we'd disagree entirely in our courses." It is this distinction that he feels obligated to convey to his own students:

Their high school teachers have told them, "This is the way you write: with five paragraphs, an introductory one that says nothing and a conclusion that repeats everything you've just said and three paragraphs in between." And that's what they tell you: "My high school teacher told me this is how you write so this is what I do." . . . They can do that, but they can only do it mechanically . . . and I can't accept a mechanical five-paragraph essay.

According to the Contextual Rhetorician, students come to college not so much with problems in grammar, but with *problems of rhetorical awareness*. They respond to these problems by falling back upon familiar forms that may have worked for them in the past, and that they assume are universal for all writing tasks. Grammar is just one of many mechanical approaches to writing that presents a major barrier to his students' writing—and it is this "mechanical-ness" that the Contextual Rhetorician tries to disrupt in his teaching.[4]

One way that he does this is to provide what he calls a "Writer's Handbook," which addresses specific problems (sometimes including grammar) that occur in many of his students' papers. In both his upper-division writing-emphasis course and his lower-division lecture course (which carries a general education designation) the Contextual Rhetorician eschews a term paper in favor of lots of short (two- to three-page) papers, "all of which are rewritable." After each assignment all students receive a copy of the handbook, and the class reviews it together. In response to the sample student essays we used in our study, the Contextual Rhetorician sketched out a version of such a handbook. First, he copies the assignment—in this case the exam question—in order to provide a common text and to introduce specific features of this rhetorical task. The next section provides "a paragraph or two from several well-written papers"—those which received a "+" grade. (His grading system includes +, ✓, and, – which are credit-bearing, and **R**, which requires the paper to be rewritten.) He follows these examples with some short comments about what makes these papers good. The next section of the handbook addresses one or two major problems the teacher saw in several of the papers that were turned in. For example, since he thought that the students who wrote the sample essays for our workshop had trouble figuring out what the writing assignment was asking them to do, he said, "Let me suggest a way to start thinking about an assignment and begin organizing your thoughts that should help you toward a better paper the first time around." The handbook then offered five suggestions ranging from "Break the assignment down into its component parts" to "Write down brief ideas as well as specific experiences . . . that speak to each part of the assignment. . . ." Each suggestion is followed by further examples or explanation.

In his Writer's Handbook, the Contextual Rhetorician illustrates general principles with context-specific examples, thus demonstrating to his students a rhetorical approach to the writing process. His, he says, is "*a way* to start thinking" about the assignment—not the way all papers will be written in that class or for every class. Furthermore, by suggesting invention and organization strategies, he provides contextualized models to those students who will be required to rewrite the assignment, and reaffirms his expectations for those who have already completed the assignment successfully.

Several faculty participants agreed on the effectiveness of the Writer's Handbook largely because they saw it as, in the words of one, "a preemptive strike"—that is, attention to potential problems before they arise. However, another pointed out that his department had developed such a handbook—what she referred to as a list of do's and don'ts—"but nobody read it, so it wasn't worth the effort." As we see it, there are two key differences between this professor's efforts to compile a handbook and those of the Contextual Rhetorician: first, the former perceived writing as a matter of static, decontextualized "do's and don'ts," while the latter continually revised his handbook with new examples and strategies that evolved from the context of particular assignments; second, the former expected her students to read (and, presumably, understand) the handbook on their own time, while the latter reviewed it with his students during class time. These practices communicate to the Contextual Rhetorician's students two corresponding "rhetorical values": that while some strategies (e.g., heuristics) can be applied to different writing tasks, rules only apply within contexts; and that writing is important enough for us to spend class time talking about it.

There is much to admire in the Contextual Rhetorician's efforts to make writing an integral part of his class, but there are also drawbacks. While the juniors and seniors "tolerate this system" of rewriting essays, he explains, the first-year students are often taken aback by it: "It takes a lot to get a student to see that [rewriting the papers] is to their advantage. Even though you'd think they'd see the grade advantage right away [after rewriting], they don't. They only see the extra time and extra work it takes." This extra work falls on the teacher's shoulders, too. He admits, "I do find myself—with all of the time that I spend on writing—thinking, 'Why do I have to do this?' I sacrifice time in the content . . . and so I feel put upon by having to do this when they should have learned it in [English] 101 and 102. But if I *don't* do it, they get the sense that the *only* place they write is in English class." It is his conviction that writing is an important tool for learning within his discipline that drives the Contextual Rhetorician to take the time to provide a Writer's Handbook for every paper his students write. Still, his words powerfully evoke a pervasive frustration among faculty that another professor articulated at the beginning of this essay: that departments across campus (including English) have not made clear their expectations regarding writing proficiency.

Sites of Dissonance and Ideas for Improvement

What we have described here may simply confirm what a lot of us already knew or suspected about the attitudes and practices of writing teachers in other disciplines. Nevertheless, we believe that the details are illuminating as we discuss grammar as a shifting rhetorical consideration. The concerns voiced by the participants at our workshop suggest that faculty fully understand the usefulness of writing as a tool for learning, and that they are generally aware that their classes, departments, and disciplines represent different kinds of writing. But for some, the grammar-related problems their students exhibit prove to be too complicated—or, in some instances, too basic—for them to effectively deal with; they wish there was additional developmental support for their students. For others, grammar problems are merely symptomatic of rhetorical problems; these teachers wish they knew how to respond to student writing in a way that made these connections clearer. Until now, our discussion of the UDWPE controversy at the University of Arizona has been cast in local terms, as something significant to *our* educational context, but not necessarily outside of it. However, we see the UDWPE more symbolically, as the embodiment of inconsistent, either/or messages about the goals of academic writing instruction. As such, it represents a site of dissonance between General Rhetoricians, who endorse a notion of general literacy, and Contextual Rhetoricians, who believe that students should achieve proficiency in the specific writing conventions of their disciplines.

This dissonance manifested itself in our study in a number of ways—most profoundly in the written comments of one of our faculty participants. On the sample student essays, he very clearly responded as a General Rhetorician: "Apparently did not grasp point of the essay! No structure or argument! . . . *Very* low on content! . . . Well-stated thesis, though shallow." However, on some additional samples of his own students' writing, this same teacher responded within a rhetorical context specific to his discipline: "This is exactly what I had in mind. You may find yourself doing 2-3 pages when summarizing longer chapters, but this is very good style." What this teacher's comments showed us, others told us in our group discussion. For example, when the Contextual Rhetorician described the connections he saw between audience and writing style, the General Rhetorician passionately disagreed: "[Writing is] not something mysterious and confined to a particular course. . . . This is supposed to be a general skill, which everyone is supposed to be capable of doing." Disagreement on this issue seems widespread among University faculty. In one of the local newspaper stories we mentioned earlier, Michael Hammond, an associate professor of linguistics, was quoted as saying that the UDWPE is "massively inappropriate" because it doesn't promote good professional writing habits: "I don't want my students to sit down and have to express some opinion on something they haven't done any research on" (quoted in Denogean 1B). But Anne Atwater, professor of of Exercise and Sport Sciences, saw many merits in the exam, arguing that it "asks students to develop and clearly express an opinion on a general topic, just as they will have to do in the community" (quoted in Denogean 1B).

We realize the limitations of a timed writing situation like the UDWPE. Most obviously, it contradicts a lot of what we teach about writing as a process and revision as a key component of that process. But as a test of general literacy skills, and as one kind of writing a student encounters at the University, we agree with Professor Atwater that it does serve the important function of determining whether a student is capable of developing and clearly expressing an idea or opinion; the test also brings to the attention of departments on campus which of their majors may need additional writing instruction. Nevertheless, we must make it clear to both students and faculty that the *purpose* of such a writing task is very different from that of the papers they write in their own disciplines. And because the purpose is different, our expectations of that piece of writing must also be different. Consequently, what might be cosidered a "massively inappropriate" writing task to a professor (or student) of linguistics course may hold real benefits for those administering a campus-wide writing program. We can't ignore or dismiss that distinction.

The Contextual Rhetorician in our study realizes this. He admits that the writing he requires of his students may not be appropriate for submission in classes in other fields—in terms of form orauthorial presence, for example—where his colleagues hold different expectations. His Writer's Handbook suggests to students that their purposes for writing may even change from assignment to assignment in his class, and that with changes in purpose will come, in essence, changes in the rules of writing. An example from our own discipline illustrates this point. The sort of prose we expect to see from students in a response journal is likely to be very different from what we expect in the final draft of a research paper. In journals "grammar problems" like fragments and run-ons and abbreviations *aren't* problems—because the main purpose for writing journals has very little to do with a polished, professional presentation and more with the development of thoughts.

By using UDWPEs as writing samples, our study unintentionally perpetuated the dissonance about what kind of writing the University expects, and this posed some problems for our faculty participants. Specifically, we asked them to comment upon the samples "in a way that is faithful to the manner in which you comment on drafts written by undergraduates in your department," even though the samples *did not* represent writing from their disciplines. Of course, the fact that we didn't provide participants with much opportunity to articulate or apply their "rhetorical values" makes it all the more remarkable that so many of them did. Some, for instance, negotiated the general/contextual dissonance by attending to cues that the student writer was writing within a specific set of disciplinary conventions—whether or not they were that professor's own. As one wrote, "Your *credibility* as an Engineering Physicist will depend on your ability to communicate effectively, even in short memos (without the help of your spellchecker)."

The IWC report recognized this dissonance as well, and proposed the following: that instead o having to write a timed test at some point in the future, students be asked to do a significant amount of writing in more of their classes; and that there be a more centralized tutoring facility where faculty could refer writers with the problems they find too difficult to deal with. In this proposal, though, the site of dissonance is simply transferred to writing centers. And as Jean Kiedaisch and Sue Dinitz argue in "Look Back and Say 'So What': The Limitations of the Generalist Tutor," writing center tutors may offer little or no assistance to knowledgeable students in disciplines outside their own. Despite their training in conferencing strategies, the generalist tutors in their study tended to focus on local concerns (e.g., mechanics, transitions) rather than global conerns when confronted with the unfamiliar rhetorical contexts for writing. Kiedaisch and Dinitz conclude that "it doesn't seem fair to place on our tutors' shoulders the responsibility for showing students how to think and write in the disciplines. . . . Isn't this the responsibility of the departments?" (73).

Well, yes, it is. But as writing professionals, we believe that it's *our* responsibility to facilitate this process. One way to do this, we thought, might be to introduce to writing-emphasis instructors Wayne Booth's taxonomy of three types of rhetorics that everyone in the university community should be able to use competently: "frontline" rhetorics, which rely on tacit convictions shared by members of a discipline to construct arguments within the field; "general" rhetoric, which relies on commonsense arguments, "the whole range of plausible or probable beliefs and modes of proof that make the world go round" (319); and "academy" rhetoric, which relies on topics and argument styles shared by everyone in the university, but not necessarily outside of it. An awareness of these distinctions, we reasoned, might be useful to teachers who find themselves caught in the general/contextual dissonance.

Another way to address this might be to open up more discussion with faculty members *as writers*, rather than as writing instructors. Elaine Maimon observes that good writers, like good writing, are a diverse bunch. "Some writers write stories and poems; others write reports, case studies, and proposals. But most experienced writers share certain practices" (95). In other words, writers may not share the same writing conventions or rhetorical contexts, but they are likely to share certain strategies for writing effectively in those contexts—including writing more than they keep, revising frequently, soliciting the opinions of other writers (which they may or may not accept), and so forth. Writing-emphasis teachers, we thought, can foster good student writing by makingclear what the rhetorical context for writing is in their course, including relevant discipline-specific writing conventions; communicating these conventions to their students; and providing class time for the practices that are likely to produce good writing (e.g., freewriting, peer response).

But these, we were told, are "English teacher" suggestions—not exactly what our writing-emphasis intructors had in mind. Repeatedly they emphasized that while they are committed to writing as a mode of learning, they preferred to act as writing resources to students, not writing teachers—and they had several suggestions about how composition specialists might help them do this more effectively. In the follow-up surveys, for example, *every teacher in our study* requested, as one person put it, a "user-friendly list of all resources on campus for students with writing problems (courses, workshops, tutoring, etc.)," and as another said, "the Writing Center's purpose, philosophy, hours, and specific services." Several participants asked for an overview of the content and expectations of first-year composition courses ("so that I can hook into something students have already done when I'm talking to them about writing"), as well as of writing courses that would be appropriate for non-English majors. One teacher commented, "I know . . . that there are courses in Technical Writing, Advanced Scientific Writing, and Business Writing. While the names are descriptive, I don't really know what they teach and how they go about their missions." In addition, two people asked specifically for intensive workshops on grammar, effective assignment-writing, and efficient grading/responding techniques. One inquired about "the possibility of non-English depts. hiring or borrowing English T.A.s for help with writing emphasis courses." Several respondents sought guidance in working with non-native speakers and basic writers.

If these teachers speak for their colleagues across campus, then our first step in meeting the needs of writing-emphasis faculty may not be indoctrination in composition theory, but simply in providing information. With information, writing-emphasis course instructors might feel more self-confident about their ability to deal with their students' writing problems, and better prepared to negotiate the dissonance between general and specific/ disciplinary rhetorics. Ignoring this dissonance, we have shown, results in confusion about what is expected from teachers and students, inconsistency in articulating these expectations, and sometimes, as illustrated by the "crisis headlines" we cited at the beginning of this essay, hostility toward any kind of writing at all.

Notes

1. An example of these pairs of passages is the following:"Set 2: Rhetorical Values: Discipline-oriented Context: As a professor, which sociology paper do you prefer?

A. In effect, it was hypothesized, that certain physical data categories including housing types and densities land use characteristics, and ecological location consttitute a scalable content area. This could be called a continuum of residential desirability. Likewise, it was hypothesized that several social data categories, describing the same census tracts, and referring generally to social stratification system of the city, would be scalable. This scale would be called a continuum of socio-economic status. Thirdly, it was hypothesized that there would be a high positive correlation between the scale types on each continuum.

B. Rich people live big houses farther apart than those of people. By looking at an aerial photograph of any American City, we can distinguish the richer from the poorer neighborhoods. (Lanham, p. 64)

Issues: jargon vs. terminology, clarity vs. accuracy, speculative vs. assertive tone, concise vs. elaborated diction.

Sub-agenda: Does the writer know what he/she is talking about? How important is communicating it to the reader?" (58).

2. Although we consider Mina P. Shaughnessy's *Errors and Expectations* a qualitative study, it differs from ours in its form of evidence. While Shaughnessy draws almost entirely on writing samples from her students and those of her colleagues, we rely primarily on transcribed discussions with faculty about grammar, with little attention to actual students' writing.

3. Our sincere thanks go to the following teachers at the University of Arizona who participated in our study: Bruce Bayly, Ty Bouldin, Ellery Green, Dwaine Greer, Beth Harrison, Elaine Jones, Susan Moody, J. W. Regan, and Rudy Troike. Thanks also to Elena Berman, a writing consultant and instructor at Pima Community College in Tucson. Stephen M. North discusses a similar idea in "The Idea of a Writing Center," through what he calls "a pedagogy of direct intervention." North says that "Rather than being fearful of disturbing the 'ritual' of composing, [writing center tutors] observe it and are charged to change it: to interfere, to get in the way, to participate in ways that will leave the 'ritual' itself forever altered" (439).

11

Grammar and Voice in the Teaching of Creative Writing: A Conversation

Stuart C. Brown, Robert Boswell, and Kevin McIlvoy

The following is an *essai* in the traditional sense of an attempt, an exploration and probing of the role of grammar and its teaching in the creative writing classroom. Attention to the more mundane conventions of writing instruction increasingly occupies class time and distracts readers from the writing itself. As writing teachers in a variety of genres, we are drawn to this discussion out of necessity as well as curiosity.

John Gardner argues in *On Becoming a Novelist* that such attention is necessary for writers: "If the dream is to be *continuous*, we must not be roughly jerked from the dream back to the words on the page by language that's distracting" (6). He points to grammatical problems as an example of such violation of story when "the reader stops thinking about the old lady at the party and looks, instead, at the words on the page, seeing if the sentence really is, as it seems, ungrammatical" (6).

Our chapter is a discussion of the nature of conventions in text and how grammar is perhaps the most fundamental convention students need mastery of to succeed as writers. It is also an argument for imputing value to such attention.

Further, our chapter is a conversation among three very different writers who engage in a wide variety of genres and the teaching of those genres, a conversation that has as its center the common interest in language that all writers share. Among us, we have published novels, short stories, literary essays, poetry, plays, reviews, textbooks, and criticism. We have taught nearly all of these genres to writing students from elementary school through graduate courses. We are returned again and again in our teaching and our own writing to the centrality of which words to put where on the page in what order.

SB: How-to books for "creative" writers abound (Bernays and Painter; Bly; Gardner; Goldberg; Stern; Zinsser). Creative writing classes are now commonplace in university settings, in senior citizen centers, in prisons, in health care settings, on computer networks. While readership and publishing houses decline, writers themselves seem to be everywhere. Yet, increasingly we see student writers lacking the fundamental means of expressing themselves. Students come to class prepared to "express" themselves, yet seem to lack an awareness of the *value* of being able to do so in standard edited English. I suppose I'm more concerned about this lack of awareness, a lack of caring for the language, rather than lack of ability. I could always blame their preparation on television, but that seems too easy—and it's been done to no apparent purpose besides the "self-expression" of whomever happens to make the accusation.

KM: Writers do seem to be everywhere, don't they? I believe that in the U.S. people of varied cultures, subcultures, and economic and educational backgrounds feel more "permission" than ever before to shape their private experiences into public expressions. The writers in creative writing classes represent only a small proportion of this proliferation. I have been fiction editor and editor in chief of *Puerto del Sol* magazine for twelve years, and I've observed a significant increase in submissions each year from *outside* academia and from the academic creative writing programs. It's wonderful to be a writer among so many people hungry to write.

Yet, this new permission has brought with it certain growing pains in the community of writers. I hope I won't seem rigidly judgmental if I state some assumptions I've formed as a writer, an editor, a teacher, and a member of this new "open enrollment" community of writers:

1. Many writers are not readers

2. many have had no direct experience of oral storytelling

3. many are incompletely engaged by their own writing

4. many have no philosophy

5. many have no vocabulary about writing

6. many do not understand the idea of "craft."

My responses to issues of grammar and voice grow from these assumptions.

SB: In a book on learning grammar, Tufte defines grammar as "an account of the formation of words and of the structure for putting them together in sentences" (1–2). She then argues that grammar, narrowed to syntax, is style. From the Latin *stilus*, an instrument for writing, the word originally came into modern English as "way of writing" (2). The *OED* indicates that *grammar* initially denoted the "methodical study of literature," including textual and aesthetic criticism, investigation of literary history and antiquities, explanation of allusions, and the study of the Greek and Latin languages. We've lost that sense of inclusiveness that the old use of these terms conveys. I wonder if we've lost that sense of language as crafted.

Many writers I know would agree with Altenbernd and Lewis in their *A Handbook for the Study of Fiction* that "Ultimately, language is the medium through which literature expresses itself, so that every aspect of fiction ... depends upon the author's words and his way of shaping them into sentences and paragraphs" (73). Yet, that attitude seems to be the least attended to in the books on creative writing that I have. Apparently, the means to impart that sense of language get lost in the larger or more panoramic concerns with plot, shape, character.

KM: Certainly, all around us the whole idea of craft seems to be disappearing. Why should writing be immune? My own most-loved resource for sustaining and developing a sense of craft has been *The Mustard Seed Garden Manual of Painting*. The first edition of this manual appeared in 1679, and it has been republished in countless editions since; the general principles and standards it presents about the craft of painting are the sum of traditions dating back to 3000 B.C. The authors of the manual are master teachers, and it is quite clear that they were unafraid of being prescriptive in teaching craft. Typical subtitles of the manual are "The four elegances of the plum tree phrased for memorizing," "Essentials of plum painting phrased for memorizing," "The Thirty-Six Faults in plum painting phrased for memorizing."

These teachers had made themselves serious students of a tradition of craft, and they tried to sustain this tradition because they believed that in this understanding was the starting place for renewal of the art. Lu Ch'Ai instructed: "You must learn first to observe the rules faithfully; afterwards, modify them according to your intelligence and capacity. The end of all method is to seem to have no method."

A teacher of writing must be hardnosed and humble, teaching what she or he knows about the traditions, the conventions, and yet inviting the student writer to grow beyond that, to move from conscious mastery of tech nique to a personal "style." I agree with Andre Maurois (*The Art of Writing*) that "in anything worth calling style two conditions must be fulfilled: grace and ease in the movement of the prose, and, in the work itself, its visible trace" (16).

The obvious next question is "How does one learn 'grace and ease'?"

RB: I do try to teach that sense of language in creative writing classes; in fact, it's one of my obsessions. In many ways, it's similar to teaching a second language; the goal, after all, is fluency. It surprises and sometimes offends students to be told that they aren't yet adequately fluent in their native tongue to write good fiction. "Translate this into English," I tell them, "and you may be on to something." I have to be smiling when I say this.

I think that language as a topic of study is inadequately addressed in creative writing textbooks for two reasons. First, the books usually focus on the creation of the initial draft of a story at the expense of a discussion of revision. For most writers, early drafts *should* be bulky, messy, and cumbersome. A writer's immediate obligation is to get some words on the screen, and too much attention to the quality of the prose (or the quality of the invention) can be inhibiting. You have to give yourself permission to write bad sentences, express lame ideas, and contrive ridiculous situations. What's called "writer's block" often stems from writers being too critical during the initial stages of composition. Besides, the messier the early drafts, the better the opportunity for the writer to make discoveries beyond his or her original premise—if there is one.

However, this notion has created a false dichotomy, an unfortunate antagonism, in the teaching of writing: that one must choose between nurturing a student's creativity, and teaching the student to write with clarity and elegance. Ideally, one should nurture during the embryonic stages and offer tough criticism during the stages that follow.

Revision is rarely addressed in texts or classrooms with the gravity it deserves. Most of the work of writing is in revision, and the author of the big messy draft has to be prepared to hack away the rubbish later on; otherwise, that student has been poorly served by the teacher who encouraged the mess in the first place.

The second reason that language is inadequately addressed in creative writing texts is because it is the most difficult aspect of craft to teach in the abstract (that is, without a poorly written story in hand). And it's not all that easy to teach even with reams of bad prose readily available. Typically, line editing of the student's story is required, and even that tiresome and time-consuming work is often inadequate. What I frequently do is retype student paragraphs and take them through a number of revisions, editing, combining sentences, adding or altering expression, and so on. I'll typically write five drafts of the paragraph and sometimes as many as ten. This method is usually successful in getting across to the student the degree of scrutiny each paragraph requires.

KM: Precision is a crucial First Principle. I've taped these essential principles from William Blake's *Jerusalem* to my computer:

> Grandeur of ideas is founded on precision of ideas.
> To generalize is to be an idiot. To particularize
>   is the alone distinction of merit.

He who would do good to another
   must do it in Minute Particulars:
General Good is the plea of the
   scoundrel, hypocrite & flatterer,
For Art & Science cannot exist but in minutely
   organized Particulars.

To teach a writer mastery over her or his own vocabulary is essential. To teach precision well is to teach one how to create many "elegances," many "styles," from one brush and one ink.

As a student of literature at the University of Illinois in the 1970s, I do not remember being shown the tensions and the hidden dialectics in the *sentences* of Flaubert, Austen, Joyce, Melville and, then, the sentence-circuses of Woolf, Stein, Beckett, Borges. The emphasis in Lit. classes was—I believe in academia it largely still is—on larger considerations of theme, structure, politics, etc. In other words, I was not shown the trees when I was shown the forest. I know many writers who have expressed the same frustration in formal, academic study of literature.

To grow as a writer, I had to relearn the process of reading, of being completely engaged in each moment of a story. Then I could begin to learn engagement in each moment of my own storytelling.

Virginia Woolf's fiction and nonfiction were important to me during this process of relearning. *To the Lighthouse* and *The Waves* are works that insist on being read sentence by sentence. They teach you as a writer and reader to appreciate the "moments of being." Reading Poe again was important to me. Poe understood about the magic and mathematics of sentence- making so well that in one tightly coiled sentence he could convey the whole complex psychology of a character. Faulkner's *As I Lay Dying* offers writers a similar experience. He said of his process: "Before I ever put pen to paper and set down the first word, I knew what the last word would be and almost where the period would fall" (218–219). Note that he did not say he knew what the themes and the historical and political allusions would be. He did not say he knew the content. He knew the form. He imagined the *words*, the position of the words, even the punctuation of the sentences.

The writer hopes, finally, to learn balance: to understand the traditions of the writing craft and to sustain absolute engagement in every moment of the writing process. A frustration student writers find in academic creative writing programs is that in their literature courses their professors can't see the trees for the forest, and in their creative writing courses their professors can't see the forest for the trees.

There are many good texts to offer student writers who want to see forest *and* tree. The critical writers I most like to recommend to advanced student writers are William Gass, Susan Sontag, Cynthia Ozick, Annie Dillard, Wayne C. Booth, and Roland Barthes, especially *Writing Degree Zero* and *The Pleasure of the Text*.

SB: In most current discussions of composition pedagogy, the "old ways" of teaching grammar (memorization of rules, sentence combining, "skill drills," etc.) are discredited as having very little effect on improving student writing. The emphasis in current theory is on expression. "Get it out" seems to be the maxim. Leave the presentational aspects (spelling, punctuation, sentence structure) until the revision stage.

But that brings to mind a potentially troublesome analogy. In the construction trades, there is an implicit hierarchy—the plumbers and electricians generally occupy the top levels of skill, the carpenters come next, then the sheetrockers and roofers, and at the bottom, getting the least respect, are the painters. But working on a crew, inevitably you'll hear, "the painters'll fix it."

This attitude gets brought to workshop—the surface of the text will be fixed by others. I've seen students bring in a draft and then complain that I haven't noted the spelling and grammatical errors. A teacher or editor or workshop group is supposed to "fix" the language because the story or the evocation or the "message" is what counts.

KM: I too have had the experience of the student writer asking me to "fix" the language in a story. My preference is to react to the work by trying to help the writer first recognize the good passages, the ones in which the narrative voice is extraordinarily engaging. In my margin and end comments the first thing I try to do is to articulate for the student what is right in those extraordinary passages (or, as is sometimes the case, that one passage); I try to encourage the writer to articulate for herself or himself the successful elements of this moment in the work, to understand the process by which this moment was achieved, and to then revise that one passage until it reaches its full potential, in order to critically assess and revise all other moments in the work. In this way of recognizing the good heart of one moment and the good process by which it came to be, a writer discovers in increments what works and what doesn't and how this represents her or his aesthetic philosophy. There are many good processes of revision. I believe one good process is to locate the charged moment, to perfect that one moment, and to work outward from that strong point rather than to locate the weak moments, to "fix" the weaknesses, and to bandage and patch the rest.

RB: This analogy of the painters as fixers only holds if one genuinely thinks of the elements of grammar merely as "presentational aspects." Most of us believe that what a writer has to say is inextricable from how he or she says it. For the fiction writer, the stakes are even higher because the necessary scrutiny of every sentence may lead the writer to alter the structure of a story.

I encourage my students to think of their stories in terms of transitional drafts. No matter how many drafts they've written, the one they are working on is still a transition to the next draft. The idea is to reverse the typical student conception that each draft is a final one, and to suggest that the process of writing is the proper focus, not merely the product at hand. Moreover, this concept permits the student to return to the story and revise in terms of just one aspect of craft, knowing that other aspects may be addressed in later stages. It makes each draft less daunting, and ultimately gives the writer more freedom to explore and discover.

Discovery is crucial to writing fiction, and I suspect it is no different in other kinds of writing. I rarely know where my stories are heading when I begin, and when I do have a sense of direction, it is usually thwarted long before arrival. The fiction writer has to be willing to give up preconceived notions in order to be true to what has emerged; this malleability is what permits stories to be more intelligent than their authors. The complexity of language allows the author a kind of sophistication of expression that he or she might be denied otherwise.

These discoveries are most often made indirectly; that is, while the author is working on aspect A of the story, she discovers something about her characters. Most often, this aspect A will be language (*expression*, *grammar*—pick a term). The writer discovers a slack sentence in the beach flashback: "His father was standing in the sand." This sentence is technically correct, but virtually worthless. The author attempts to make the sentence a stronger image by revising the sentence, which after many drafts ends up as follows: "His father's splayed, white feet glistened obscenely, like the bellies of dead fish." Suddenly, the author realizes that her protagonist was embarrassed by his father. This discovery, in turn, leads her to understand that the protagonist's conflict has a longer history than she'd imagined, which will lead to yet another discovery and another. Eventually, the whole story will be altered by those alabaster feet—feet that stepped into the story in order to correct a mild language problem.

If the first sentence of a story is the classic cliche "It was a dark and stormy night," then the writer will likely begin revising by trying to rescue the idea from the expression. Perhaps, he will first try to eradicate "was," as it is the most generic of verbs. "Dark, the stormy night blew." If he has the good sense to recognize the comedy of this sentence, he will revise again. "The air was filled with lightning." Again he sees "was" and wishes to get rid of it. Finally, he writes, "Lightning struck the fencepost." This sentence is not only much better than the original, he now has a charred fencepost in the story, and that image may well become important to the reader's understanding of the events. It may even alter the events in future drafts of the story.

SB: Joseph Williams suggests in *Style: Ten Lessons in Clarity and Grace* that there are "writers who know the rules, but who also know that not all of them are worth observing and that other rules should be observed only on certain occasions'' (190). The dilemma becomes pedagogic: How does one explain how it's okay to break some of the rules some of the time? And on a different level, what are the ethical implications of this?

I've always tried to follow the truism that to break the rules, one has to know them. In my own writing, when I can get away with it, I seem to operate on the grounds of expediency—whatever works. If that means violating certain conventions, I violate them. I also like to think that I'm usually aware of when I'm doing that, at least at some point. Maybe not when I'm in the early drafting stages, but later when revising.

RB: I try to demonstrate as much as possible what I'm talking about—how the control of sentences affects the power of the story.

Here is the first paragraph of a student story, along with my comments and suggestions for revision:

> When I returned to my parents' house, the home I had lived in since birth until the day I married, my mother's omnipresence and the effects of her death showed in each of the rooms. The kitchen in its swirls of green and yellow, with its restaurant-size stove and rows of spice racks, sat vacant and covered in layers of dust, proof that my father had touched little other than the cereal box, container of milk, and sack of Snickers. Gone were the odors of chili con queso and fresh peeled shrimp. All that was left was a trail of stale tobacco smoke. The rooms looked as she had left them with the English wallpaper, silk flower arrangements now limp at the edges, antique furniture, dying plants in the sun room, and the heat turned up high—she had always complained of being too hot, he of being too cold, and now that she was gone, he kept the thermostat at eighty degrees.

How does one go about revising the language of this? Let's start with the first sentence:

> When I returned to my parents' house, the home I had lived in since birth until the day I married, my mother's omnipresence and the effects of her death showed in each of the rooms.

I notice first that "house" and "home" are both in the sentence, which is practically a repetition, and an unnecessary one. Plus, "mother's omnipresence" and "the effects of her death" are, in this context, pretty much the same thing; I prefer the latter because it is less abstract. Revised: "When I returned to my parents' house, where I had lived from birth until the day I married, the effects of my mother's death showed in each of the rooms."

The revision then allows me to ask "How much of this is really important?" in the following sentences.

> The kitchen in its swirls of green and yellow, with its restaurant-size stove and rows of spice racks, sat vacant and covered in layers of dust, proof that

my father had touched little other than the cereal box, container of milk, and sack of Snickers. Gone were the odors of chili con queso and fresh peeled shrimp. All that was left was a trail of stale tobacco smoke.

The writer wishes to convey the mother's continuing presence, the father's inability to cope with her death. How can this be shown without making it sentimental? Some of the details don't really accomplish as much as they could. For example, the swirls of color may be meant to characterize the mother, but they don't convey very much, and the reader isn't even certain that she's responsible for them. The stove doesn't reveal much either, and who doesn't have spices and cook chili? Look at the sentence that emerges from making some tough-minded cuts: "The kitchen sat vacant, covered in dust, the only odor a trail of stale tobacco smoke."

Why is this better than the above? Because it *shows* what is important—the vacant room, the dust, and most important, the trail of smoke—without the interference of the other, less important stuff. Here's the remainder of the paragraph:

The rooms looked as she had left them with the English wallpaper, silk flower arrangements now limp at the edges, antique furniture, dying plants in the sun room, and the heat turned up high—she had always complained of being too hot, he of being too cold, and now that she was gone, he kept the thermostat at eighty degrees.

What strikes me is that two of the elements have changed a little (the silk flowers are limp and the plants are dying), while the rest have not.

The silk flower arrangements were now limp at the edges and the plants in the sun room had yellowed; otherwise, the rooms were as she had left them—English wallpaper and antique furniture. Even the heat was kept at eighty degrees, as she had liked it.

Note that I've changed the last sentence, making the mother the one to prefer the heat at eighty degrees because it makes more sense in the context of the paragraph; that is, I alter the facts of the story to better suit the logic (and style) of the paragraph.

After one revision, the paragraph reads as follows:

When I returned to my parents' house, where I had lived from birth until the day I married, the effects of my mother's death showed in each of the rooms. The kitchen sat vacant, covered in dust, the only odor a trail of stale tobacco smoke. The silk flower arrangements were now limp at the edges and the plants in the sun room had yellowed; otherwise, the rooms were as she had left them– English wallpaper and antique furniture. Even the heat was kept at eighty degrees, as she had liked it.

I can cut "my parents' house" from the first sentence, as it becomes quickly clear whose house it is. The flower arrangements need to be located, and the wallpaper and furniture are awkwardly introduced.

And now it's not a bad paragraph, except that there's a logical problem. The house is supposed to show the effects of her death, but the unchanged rooms do not convey any change (they did show her omnipresence, but that's been cut and I still think that it's a good cut). From the word *otherwise* on, the paragraph contradicts itself. Also, the verb *to be* is a little overused (twice in one sentence). And because the emphasis in the first sentence is on the rooms, I make the second example begin with the room it's in ("In the hall . . ."). But how do we fix the logical contradiction? Here's a first attempt.

> When I returned to the house where I had lived from birth until the day I
> married, the effects of my mother's death showed in each of the rooms. The
> kitchen sat vacant, covered in dust, the only odor a trail of stale tobacco
> smoke. In the hall, the silk flower arrangements turned limp at the edges.
> The plants in the sun room had yellowed, as had the English wallpaper in
> the living room. The antique furniture crowded the corners of the rooms
> impractically. Only the house's heat, kept as she had liked it at eighty
> degrees, was unaffected.

The sentence about antiques is weak, especially with the hanging adverb, and I think it can just go as it adds little to the scene. I don't like the repetition of *room*, so I move the wallpaper to the den. I also dislike the sound of the last word here (*unaffected*) because it repeats the sound of the above *effects*, so I change that too.

> When I returned to the house where I had lived from birth until the day I
> married, the effects of my mother's death showed in each of the rooms. The
> kitchen sat vacant, covered in dust, the only odor a trail of stale tobacco
> smoke. In the hall, the silk flower arrangements turned limp at the edges.
> The plants in the sun room had yellowed, as had the English wallpaper in
> the den. Only the house's heat, kept as she had liked it at eighty degrees,
> was unchanged.

The paragraph is now eighty-eight words long, almost half the length of the original, and it's clearer. My end comment to the student:

> The meaning of the paragraph has changed, but for the better. It has been
> sharpened and the reader is more guided. Close attention to language makes
> writing stronger in unanticipated ways. One must give this sort of attention
> to every paragraph, cutting all that doesn't earn its space, sharpening the
> language, honing the meaning, guiding the reader. It is by paying attention
> to every word that one makes discoveries.

These language concerns may not fall under a traditional view of "grammar," but I think that the primary point of grammatical revision is to insure clarity, and often the writer, once he sees his work with greater clarity, discovers just what it is he meant to say. Such a discovery at the sentence-level has the power to change everything else in the story.

SB: When I talk with students about "voice" and style, I often get into a muddle. How does a student accomplish clarity, much less a distinctive voice, without serious attention to grammatical concerns? At the same time, however, that attention to grammar seems to bog them down.

The problem with close attention to grammar is that grammar in the abstract or out of context cannot be intuitively understood. As Williams notes, "these rules have been hoarded up less on the basis of their intrinsic logical force or on principles of inherent clarity and precision, than on grounds that have been largely idiosyncratic, historically accidental" (190). A further problem is that "as one consequence of this largely random accumulation, not all rules of usage have equal standing with all writers of English, even careful writers of English" (190). Not only does the beginning writer need to be able to handle the higher cognitive functions at play in determining the structure of a story or the evocative potential of sound in a poem, but the writer must also have at hand the conventions of language use that the writer shares with the reader, that make "conveyance" possible. It's hard work.

I was on a master's thesis defense recently where a young poet was discussing his approach to punctuation. He indicated that he punctuated according to breath pauses—this seemed to work when he read his work aloud. It was quite effective. His introduction, in prose, however, was punctuated the same way. He wanted the prose, his discussion of what his poetry was attempting, to mirror the poetry itself. It was impenetrable.

That raises some questions for me. Is there a conflict between the correct use of language conventions and personal voice? Is it possible to reconcile that most great literature (however generously defined) toys with the strictures of grammatical convention and by doing so, establishes its distinctiveness?

Standard edited English as a convention seems to raise the hackles of many writing teachers, at least if the literature in some composition journals is an accurate portrayal of the profession. This aversion is even more pronounced among language acquisition scholars. Yet the scholarly approaches to the topic all appear to be written in standard edited English. And aside from some poetry or work that intentionally brings in dialect, so is the contemporary fiction I read.

Joseph William notes "For better or worse, all parts of the English-speaking world have tacitly agreed on most of the conventions that define careful standard written English" (190). The implications of this agreement, however, don't appear to be getting across to writing students. Is it a matter of emphasis? A matter of the teachers themselves not having an adequate grasp of the conventions?

I remember reading somewhere that a Roman emperor proclaimed being above grammar, but then he was emperor, a deity of sorts. I've been known to suggest to certain students that I'd be willing to overlook egregious errors if they could demonstrate this shade of omnipotence. So far I've not had any that could, so I usually follow with E. B. White quoting Strunk in *The Elements of Style*: " 'It is an old observation,' he wrote, 'that the best writers sometimes disregard the rules of rhetoric. When they do so, however, the reader will usually find in the sentence some compensating merit, attained at the cost of the violation. Unless he is certain of doing as well, he will probably do best to follow the rules' ' (xi–xii).

RB: Recently, I read "The Spandrels of San Marcos," an essay in which Stephen Jay Gould argues against the strict adaptationist interpretation of evolution. The strict adaptationist looks at some aspect of a creature's being and suggests how the trait affects survival. Adaptationists acknowledge that there are other (rare) possible explanations for traits, but Gould and his coauthor suggest another probability, that adaptations may have side effects that are not necessarily adaptive but are nonetheless productive. Gould supplies an architectural metaphor.

In domed buildings supported by arches there are small elongated triangular spaces between the tops of the arches. These triangles are called spandrels, and clearly they are a secondary product of the making of arches since the arches are what support the weight of the dome. This makes the arches primary adaptations and the spandrels byproducts. However, Gould points out that the spandrels have been incorporated as prominent features in the ornamentation of the domes; an observer looking at the spandrels and analyzing the part outside of the context of the whole might see how they serve the larger pattern and suggest that the spandrels were adaptive. That is, if the building were a living organism, an adaptationist viewing it would likely think that the spandrels were the product of natural selection, rather than a byproduct of an adaptive trait.

Gould's argument is complex, but the two main points are that an organism must be considered as a whole and not as a collection of traits or "things." And that some characteristics, even ones that are at present adaptive, may have come about as byproducts. For example, it is quite likely that larger brain capacity in humans was adaptive, but the powers of advanced abstract reasoning that came with it (that permit, say, higher mathematics or jazz) were not adaptive but byproducts.

These ideas interest me in a number of ways. First of all, I have always resisted that adaptationist kind of reasoning—without knowing exactly what it was that I was resisting. It's that notion that if it exists then there must be a good reason for its existence. I've always tried to buck off that particular rider.

Second, I am a great believer that one should evaluate the whole and not merely certain aspects. I'm not advocating the elimination of analysis, but *nothing* is merely the sum of its parts.

Third, the central metaphor of the essay interests me because I feel that it has application to creative acts as well as evolutionary ones. It seems to me that in the process of writing stories, we work to create the necessary structures to support the story—the arches, to borrow Gould's metaphor—but we also inadvertently create spandrels along with them. And I honestly believe that it is often these spandrels that become the organizing principles of many stories. This is why I'm often suggesting to a student to "listen" to her stories and see if the details can guide her in its revision.

A student who feels his voice is limited by the conventions of grammar is probably rationalizing, is probably merely unwilling to admit a lack of understanding of grammar. But his larger mistake is in separating grammar from voice—something like separating the desire for respiration from the necessity of lungs. Good writers often work against the conventions of grammar, but they never ignore them. Nothing in the ungrammatical passages in Joyce or Faulkner is random.

Moreover, the student who wishes to ignore grammatical responsibilities is missing out on the imaginative spandrels that are the byproducts of clarity, and that may well become the ultimate principles of the story's organization. The writer who abjures these spandrels had best be a genius because the story will be limited to abstract intelligence.

KM: Maurois wrote, "Art is different from life but cannot exist without it." I've read that same philosophy in many incarnations. People bring different kinds and depths of life experiences to their writing. I hope that the other creative writing programs, like our own, welcome writers other than English majors. Some of the best novelists, after all, have come from the ranks of biologists, physicians, politicians, and bankers.

Writers from such varied ranks have varied kinds and scopes of vocabularies. The teacher of writing must make the writer realistically assess her or his vocabulary and reckon with the potentials—or limitations—of that palette. I know of no better way for one writer to help another than to closely examine and comment on many pages of writing in different narrative voices. In this way, patterns of usage and meaning become apparent and, according to the subject matter that is the particular obsession of the individual writer, certain paths of learning can be chosen.

For example, less experienced writers often need to reconsider how to present dialogue. In the manuscripts I read as an editor and teacher, I find a constant problem is that a writer will often depend heavily on dialogue and that all of the dialogue is similar in tone, syntax, even length—the characters express themselves in equivalences. As a teacher of writing, I insist on the principle that the most important part of dialogue is what is left *unspoken*. No matter how verbal an individual character might be, much must be left unsaid. I ask student writers to be less generous with their own vocabularies and let the characters speak for themselves.

SB: I sometimes have to establish "vocabulary" lists to talk about writing. style sheets, editorial marks, summaries of common usage errors. Then that gets us into discussions of the value of grammar. George Steiner's essay "Understanding as Translation" in *After Babel* captures some of the complexity, especially on historical and aesthetic levels. He notes that language is always in flux—at times, radically being altered; at other times, highly conservative.

I usually insist that we follow E. B. White's advice that students of creative writing "err on the side of conservatism" (76).

RB: One of the most common responses I hear from students studying the red ink on their manuscripts is the following: "But you know what I mean." While I may know more or less what they mean, I let *them* know that their approximations are insufficient. I firmly believe that the students who work to clarify the vagueness in their expression also sharpen their reasoning abilities. Isn't this movement toward clarity, after all, the fundamental movement of intellectual maturation? We make finer and finer distinctions while simultaneously considering more and more complex issues.

To solve a mathematical equation, the student must first discover the requisite quantities and then arrange them in a specific order; this requires an understanding of certain principles, as well as the ability to apply those principles. To solve a grammatical equation, the writer must find the precise words and put them in the ideal order; this requires an understanding of certain principles, as well as the ability to apply those principles. Each process inevitably requires scrutiny of beliefs.

SB: I know that having to justify grades has made me more conscious of the conventions in written language. I even have to confess to having made rules up when backed into a corner about why I've flagged a passage or noted "awk" or "s/s" (often taken to mean "stupid sentence" when I've meant difficulty in sentence structure). Or I point to a shelf full of handbooks on correct usage and grammar, some dating back to the middle 1800s. Rule books. Regulations. *Dicta*. All are densely packed in alphabetical arrangement with a minutiae that seems terribly removed from what writing is.

The better ones, especially the current ones, emphasize the rhetorical nature of grammatical decision making—clarity and effectiveness of the expression take priority. However, short of devoting large amounts of class time to exercises that may or may not "take," how does one get students to use these? How does one even get the students to realize they need help with certain problems? That each student often has a different set of problems makes this even more daunting.

RB: I assigned Strunk and White's *Elements of Style* to a graduate creative writing class, and I tried to open each class with an exercise I'd invent based on some grammatical problem presented in the book. However, the students became restless, desiring to get to the stories or novel we were to discuss that day. I decided to integrate the study of grammar more thoroughly into the study of fiction writing, and I came up with a new assignment.

Like every fiction writer, I have files of lousy stories: some I'd written as an undergraduate, some that had come from exercises, some whose plot meanders around and then peters sadly out. I selected one particularly lively but egregiously bad story from my files, and I went through the text and messed up the grammar, making various errors. Each student was given a copy of standard proofreader marks and a copy of the story, along with the following instructions:

> You are the new fiction editor of a major magazine that publishes one story per issue. This story was accepted by a previous fiction editor (since fired). The magazine has put off publishing it, but the author has a contract and the magazine's lawyers say it must be published; however, it may be significantly edited. The editor in chief doesn't think it's such a bad story that it can't be saved. The writer is agreeable to heavy editing but is also miffed about the delay and wants you to do all the work; in fact, the author is open to major rewriting, as long as it is done by the editorial staff. Your first step should be to go through the story and make editorial marks, line-by-line suggestions and corrections, and margin comments about what should be changed overall. The basic integrity of the story should be kept intact. The editor in chief is a tough bastard—me. This first revision is due next week.

After receiving their first revisions, I divided the class into four groups and had them work as editorial teams to come up with final edited copies. I then typed up their four very different drafts and returned the clean copies, along with queries and suggestions. Grammatical errors that they'd missed were circled but not explained; however, very few had been missed.

The groups worked through a number of drafts. Basic elements of grammar were generally agreed upon, but many of the more complex elements of grammar (clarity, sentence structure, precision of expression) were heavily debated. Ultimately, each group was asked to write a cover letter (which also was submitted and revised) and to target literary magazines for the story. Within a month, one version of the story was accepted for publication by a respectable literary magazine (other versions were withdrawn) and published under a pseudonym. The author's note credited members of the group as the author's teachers.

SB: But was this teaching or learning? Learned, but not taught in any formal sense. I hear rumblings that teaching writing is not possible, that students can be given opportunities to write, but actually teaching them to write, especially in college isn't effective. In an odd way, this sort of brings us back to the rejection of grammar training now in vogue—grammar can't be taught.

RB: Do people also suggest that the ability to play a musical instrument cannot be taught? If you can't simply grab a trumpet and blow tunes, then you ought to quit? Do they say that mathematics cannot be taught? Are we to believe that math prowess lingers like a disease of the brain, showing itself at odd moments until, at some point, it becomes pervasive?

Most people who say that writing cannot be taught are really saying that greatness cannot be taught. You can't teach someone to become Alice Munro or Charlie Parker or Barry Mazur, but you can give them the opportunity to fail in that quest. That's a great thing to offer. There are a whole lot of sax players who aren't as good as Charlie Parker.

Others who say that writing cannot be taught believe that *they* do not need to learn anything. These people think they are great writers and prove it not by writing but by holding virtually all literature in contempt. If they had the time (if it were worthy of their time), they could crank out a '90's *Anna Karenina*, no sweat. It's just words, after all, and they've been yakking all their lives. Each owns a dictionary and knows somebody who has a thesaurus to borrow. These folks think that to act on a desire is to degrade it.

Finally, a percentage or two of the people who believe writing cannot be taught are writing teachers who, at present, have students who can't seem to learn. These students are statistically irrelevant; do well by them, but don't quit teaching and get an MBA because some yahoo continues to split infinitives. Get on with your work. Things well taught, may not be well learned.

A final note: Roy Hargrove studied formally, and he's one of the best young horn players around.

KM: A writer can be rigorously initiated into the idea of craft.

A writer can be taught to reckon with her or his own vocabulary and can be shown its potentials and limitations.

A writer can learn processes of revision which might lead to artistic recognition and, so, might lead to the forming of individual philosophy.

A writer can relearn the reading process and, so, rediscover moment-by-moment engagement with her or his own work.

A writer can be educated in the traditions (even the lost traditions, such as certain oral forms of storytelling) in order to continuously reenergize the traditions—and herself or himself.

This much is possible, and we should honor the writer who attempts it. "In literature, the lower ranks are as necessary as in the army," wrote Chekhov in "Dunghills As Artistic Materials," "—so says the mind, and the heart ought to confirm this most thoroughly" (244–245).

Coda

Any conversation must necessarily stop, although few reach any sort of closure. Our comments and observations above are far from complete nor fixed in our own minds as we continue to mull over, to puzzle the implications and connections that grammar and voice have in the teaching of writing, in writing itself. Our own explorations of this theme are hardly over as we will return again and again to the intricacies of composing and revising. Our only certainties are in recognizing the value of struggling to achieve clarity and to teach the value of clarity to our writing students. But, and this is an invitation, now it's your turn—as reader, as writer, as teacher—to pick up the conversation.

12

Teaching Grammar for Writers in a Process Workshop Classroom

Wendy Bishop

We all know the problem with false dichotomies—hot and cold, good and bad, old and young cannot comingle—although they do as warm, complex, or midlife. So too, we think, process never includes product, or so it would seem, since products would short-circuit the recursive, non-linear, reiterative, exploratory and therefore open-ended flow of a pedagogy meant to encourage further and deeper thinking about and through writing.

But we don't live in a kinetic universe; it's not simply that we get the fly-wheel of process started and, like a perpetual motion machine, it keeps on moving, always. Process writing workshops, contrary to labeling, continuously result in products. Writers start again, explore, push, examine. Texts are produced, published, stopped, conflated, interwoven, reshaped. In the same way, writers' themes and topics are investigated and avoided, rewoven and never discarded, borrowed and begged and rebraided into new understandings. We assume far too easily, it seems to me, that process classrooms have abandoned instruction, activities, or writing opportunities that would result in well-edited, well-written products. When we teach writing as writers, it is inevitable that we include instruction in grammar for writers, for we must examine content, structure, linguistic, and cognitive choices that form the congeries of style(s), usage(s), and grammar(s) that are available to all authors and from which professional writers constantly draw. In addition, this choice-making and analysis takes place in an examined matrix of ongoing writing activity as writers use classrooms, and their out-of-classroom time, to read and write their own and others' writing more fluently and accurately.

When "process" is viewed as a mindless perpetual motion machine, as if we kick-start student writers and let them generate words for a long fifteen weeks, then process instructors are ethically remiss: they are not teaching and they are not teaching writing as the process we know it to be. When we examine writers' processes in our classrooms, we teach better, for we look at the product payoffs that all invested writers strive for: texts that go out into the world and make meaning when read by ourselves and others.

Product is Part of Process: Examined Process Classrooms

Let's look at some of the benefits of process theory writing classrooms. Why did compositionists jump on the process bandwagon in the 1970s and 1980s, seemingly leaving issues of grammar and style and producing final products in the classroom dust? A writing process, workshop classroom—what I've termed a transactional workshop (*Released*) and what Robert Brooke describes as a response workshop—situates students as writers in writing communities, either drafting teacher-assigned essay sequences or, more often, generating their own topics, often through drafting. Idea and topic generation quickly became a focus of this type of classroom, resulting in a great number of exploratory invention heuristics like looping and cubing and asking reporter's questions. Invention *was* important since students were often enrolled in compulsory first-year writing courses and teachers noted a not unreasonable lack of investment from students when they were so assigned. Students, asked to write canned themes in strict forms, could sometimes do so, but little learning beyond canning and forming seemed to be taking place, and teachers who were sometimes teaching five sections of twenty-five writing students were overwhelmed with, basically, bad writing. While it was easy to translate this scenario into a disdain for college students, it was more reasonable to see the problem as one of curriculum and context.

> Our texts are "safe" when we do what we know we've gotta do to get a good grade, rather than approaching a paper creatively. Regardless, you must make your point, but a safe paper is one you write, stylistically, for others, not yourself. I hate safe. Freshman English teachers try to "unteach" this style, yet freshmen must stick to it in history classes and humanities (sometimes).

Writing researchers in the 1980s started to understand the nature of professional writers' processes and the nature of basic writers' lack of progress when given traditional writing instruction. Traditional instruction relied on reading and examining model essays that were often culturally inaccessible to these students; class consisted of discussion of an essayist's exemplary text, and a command to emulate that text outside of class, and to submit student-written imitations for a close reading by the teacher who gave a one-time grade. During this period, we began to understand that expert writers undertake multiple drafts and have an ability to plan, generate, revise, and refine at both the global and local level. Students did not become more fluent, however, from grading. They did not transfer corrections from an initial, graded paper to the next graded paper, and, when faced with a daunting writing task, many students simply did not write at all, or wrote in a mad rush, just hours or minutes before class.

> Just before the deadline, I would type those words out. I still do this style of pre-editing, making sure that when I type the words, they are the words that I want on the page. However, now [after a process workshop class] I allow at least a day or two to look at a hard copy for editing.

Even as we began to gain a more sophisticated view of professional writers' revision processes and basic writers' underdeveloped revision strategies, we found also that simply assigning "a revision" or multiple drafts did not clarify the process for students. In fact, assigned process sequences too often produced a "clunk" curriculum, with invention on Monday, drafting on Wednesday, and editing on Friday, inculcating still a linear and unitary sense of writing. Second drafts, then, were seen by students as nothing more than a call for implementing a teachers' red-inked corrections, again with learning about writers' grammars and choices seemingly never transferring from one paper to the next.

In studies of revision processes, less expert writers would usually draft less and hesitate more. They instituted fewer global changes and often chose safe subjects and simple syntax rather than push their learning through exploration and questioning and language play. We have learned that years of assimilating competing and conflicting writing rules in school can block or stymie a writer: one teacher insisting first person voice is never appropriate and another plaintively asking for it. One teacher pushing for correctness and another for complexity.

> My past writing classes had not developed too much of me. I've either analyzed texts without really including personal views, or I've written stories that sounded pretty but had no depth.

Writing process classrooms attempt to foreground all these issues by setting up communication between the writer and her readers. Audience is broadened from the teacher only to, at a minimum, the teacher and class peers. Often previous writing issues and histories are examined as students write literacy autobiographies or voice analyses. Knowledge about writers' writing processes is shared as each writer examines her own processes, through the use of cover sheets on essays or letters of writing self-analysis at the end of the term.

When we moved to classrooms emphasizing the recursive nature of the drafting process, by asking students to draft and re-draft an essay, we also had to develop methods of response and evaluation that rewarded and complemented such a movement. If a text is viewed as revisable, then a student should not be encouraged to edit at the local, sentence level while pushing to develop ideas because those very sentences may disappear in a future draft. If a student spends too much time at this initial thinking-through stage on local issues, he's much less willing to discard an ineffective sentence or paragraph in the interest of improving the global effect of the paper. After all, like us, students are pressed for time in every facet of their lives, and writing classes represent just a small portion of their lives; they can't be expected to explore and take risks unless exploration and risk are valued, tangibly, through revision instruction and credit for such work in course grades.

Evaluating workshop products in a final course portfolio assures students that their processes and journey through the class were valuable. It also offers a chance to highlight products, since well-written, well-edited texts are always included, and to teach grammar for writers. By examining all work done in a term and then choosing to refine the best texts, a student puts her products firmly at the center of the writing workshop experience. The writer's past is explored, drafting process valued, peers and teacher offer response on workshop drafts, and then the writer is allowed time to reflect on and improve work he has become invested in.

> I've very proud of the material I've produced in here [portfolio]. Writing, revising, editing, workshopping, revising again—these all motivated me to rework my texts (or at least think about different ways to revise as I showered, walked to class, brushed my teeth, and ate lunch).

In this sense, grammar for writers has never been absent from the writing process workshop, but it has certainly been under-discussed and, I'd argue, under-taught. Most composition textbooks and teachers speed dizzily through revision discussions, assuming assigning drafts and allowing for peer response will do the work that needs to be done. It doesn't. We need to be teaching grammar(s) for writers. We need then to be paying much more attention to how we teach drafting, to examine what we mean by and how we teach revision; ditto for style and editing. We need to do this as frequently and as well as we've learned to teach topic generation through invention strategies. In the rest of this chapter, I'll address just how we might.

Grammar(s) for Writers

Near the end of her book *Grammar for Teachers*, written in 1979, Constance Weaver ends her considerations of the pro-grammar and anti-grammar instruction arguments this way:

> Indeed, formal instruction in grammar may have a harmful effect, partly
> because it tends to alienate students, and partly because it takes time that
> might more profitably be used in helping students read, write, listen, and
> speak more effectively. (89)

An underlying assumption of examined process classrooms has been similar
to the point Weaver makes: writers need time to explore their ideas, to push
and challenge received thinking, to experience the many frustrations *and*
rewards that professional writers experience. They need to write, *often*, with
support and feedback, in a variety of genres and styles. Given the artificial
constraints of the writing classroom and the school calendar, it is not surprising that the many studies referenced in this book have shown that time spent
on decontextualized grammar instruction provides little-to-no support for the
developing writer. Weaver does argue that teachers may benefit from a good
knowledge of language history and understanding of grammatical terms and
vocabulary. And certainly language use is the central discussion in all writing classrooms. Each teacher needs to find his best terms for discussing language use and rhetorical choices with writing students. However, many of us
function very well with our personal amalgam of traditional terms, journalists' vocabulary, class-generated or -invented terms. Our technical talk and
discussion focus has to be relevant to our developing community of writers,
even if that community is artificially convened.

In *Grammar and the Teaching of Writing*, written in 1991, Rei R. Noguchi comes to similar conclusions though he pushes them one step farther:

> While formal grammar instruction seems to offer little in the area of essay
> organization, it does seem more potentially beneficial in the area of style.
> "Style" here is used broadly to encompass characteristic or recurrent lin-
> guistic features. Style includes not only syntactic and morphological forms
> but also salient features of punctuation and spelling. (11)

I intend to use a definition of "grammar as style" for the remainder of this
chapter. In teaching grammar for writers I am advocating teaching characteristic or recurrent linguistic features of writing within "recognized" forms *and*
"alternate" forms. Certainly, it's easy to "name" those broadly repeating
features in conventional forms like the compare/contrast essay or the *bildung-
sroman*. However, it's less easy to tell what is recurring or characteristic when
a conventional form is being challenged: say when we write a prose poem
which partakes of fiction and poetry writing conventions, or when we choose
to use fragments for effect in the manner of the new journalists or literary
authors. Still, even alternate forms recur, internally within the text, or exter-
nally, due to an author's repeated attempts to map her "new" territory by
trying the form several times and creating "comparability."

I find it interesting that neither Weaver nor Noguchi mention what for me
has been an influential work: Winston Weathers' *An Alternate Style: Options*

in Composition (first published in essay form in 1976 and expanded to a book-length study in 1980). Weathers argues for the expansion of the tools of a writers' trade. He argues that by neglecting to teach grammar(s) of style we are teaching students to play only Bridge with a deck of fifty-two cards when many other games (options, alternatives) actually exist. He claims:

> Any number of such "grammars" or "stylistic families" may theoretically exist and be available to a writer at any one time. Yet on a practical level, in today's classroom we keep all our stylistic options within the confines of one grammar only—a grammar that has no particular name (we can call it the "traditional" grammar of style/or for my purposes Grammar A) but has the characteristics of continuity, order, reasonable progression and sequence, consistency, unity, etc. We are all familiar with these character-istics, for they are promoted in nearly every English textbook and taught by nearly every English teacher. (6)

Essentially, we do not make this diversity of grammars available because we are busy inculcating the dominant grammar, what Weathers terms Grammar A, and we do this because "what is socially prestigious, or 'correct,' in (for-mal) writing depends on which social variety of language, officially or unof-ficially, gains acceptance within public institutions" (Noguchi 115).

There are two problems here. We may severely limit grammars for writ-ers in order that their formal writing approaches the official norm. We also tend to do this when we ignore the options and grammars of informal and exploratory writing that researchers like James Britton and his colleagues have argued are essential for thinking through writing. And, we decontextu-alize grammar instruction—foregrounding the dominant grammar and mut-ing or silencing alternate grammars—so a writer has no sense of the "whys" or "hows" of textual choices.

Weathers' work helped me begin to reconceptualize how I taught gram-mar for writers. Although he borrows heavily from literary writers, he argues that these techniques should not ever be limited to literary texts; indeed, he advocates for Grammar B in composition classrooms. Grammar B techniques include crots (prose bits or fragments that are strung together, though each terminates abruptly), labyrinthine sentences and fragments, lists, double voice, repetition and refrain, orthographic schemes, synchronous time, and collage/montage.

Feminist theorists have done much to revolutionize academic writing in the last twenty years by using Grammar B techniques in their own writing and by attempting to define and advocate non-patriarchal forms of discourse. Composition as a marginalized, many argue feminized, field in English Stud-ies now allows alternate styles in its professional journals although it's unclear to what degree the students of these authors are encouraged to under-take similar explorations. For instance, the February 1992 issue of *College*

Composition and Communication has Donald McQuade in his 4Cs Chair's address presenting an impassioned personal narrative and Nancy Sommers exploring the relationship between her writing and family life in a text that is full of alternate expression, including orthographic schemes! and stories that have crot-like pungency. Terry Myers Zawacki presents a single-authored, multi-voiced text while Beverly Lyon Clark and Sonja Wieden-haupt present their research in bold- and regular-type dialogue.

In "Rendering the 'Text' of Composition" Sheryl Fontaine and Susan Hunter invited a reader's active participation in text-making when they assembled together many prominent "voices of composition," in order to "render" instead of analyze the field, in order to challenge and disrupt textual boundaries. The reader plays a game with this collaged text, identifying authors and documents and then listening to the way those voices amplify and echo and invoke meaning by juxtaposition and association, each text voice altering the text voice it is placed near. This fall 1992 *Journal of Advanced Composition* essay, which is as much the text of others as it is the text of authors, seems exciting but not surprising since the range of grammar(s) of style in composition publications continues to broaden rapidly.

In October of 1992, Lillian Bridwell-Bowles published an essay in *CCC*, urging just such stylistic diversity; this essay can be read as a summation of the new directions we've taken since Weathers's work and may serve as a lens for understanding what was being practiced in the February *CCC* and Fall *JAC* issues I've just mentioned. She suggests that alternatives allow us to include other worldviews: "Our language and our written texts represent our visions of our culture, and we need new processes and forms if we are to express ways of thinking that have been outside the dominant culture" (349). Like many feminists, she challenges traditional models of argumentative writing (see also Frey), and advocates what she calls "diverse discourse"—we may posit this, perhaps, as Grammar C?

Personal/Emotional Writing

Breaking the Boundaries of Textual Space

Language Play

[Writing] Not [as] the Mythic White Woman

Breaking out of Linguistic Prejudice

[Writing that Challenges] Class Barriers, Sexual Orientations

[And Acknowledges or Encourages] Different Composing Process

These stylistic suggestions are Bridwell-Bowles's essay's subtitles. More or less.

How to Teach Grammar for Writers and/or What's In It For Me and My Students?

Warning: More serious attempts at Grammar B follow. Reading farther should challenge your textual expectations.

Questions:

- At what point in their writing are writers (usefully) (actively) revising?
- When do they need to obey conventions? (Do they? Can they know them all first?)
- When do they need to break with convention? (Can they? Do they have ideas about how to?).
- When should grammar(s) of style be introduced?
- Which grammar(s)?

Ideas:

- A planned drafting sequence that introduces and incorporates revision (Fulwiler "A Lesson" and "Provocative").
- A term plan that includes an intensive period of revision (*portfolio preparation can function this way in any class*) or a time when a single paper is revised (Bishop "Risk-Taking and Radical Revision").
- A term of intense drafting where ideas are explored and followed in informal and exploratory writing (Elbow suggests setting up "evaluation-free" zones) and near the end of term, ideas from this matrix are shaped into formal texts; (*hey!*) use journals in the same way.
- Students revising the same paper all term long (*sounds a bit rough for the many but possibly profoundly useful for certain writers*).
- Analysis of the grammar (*style, rhetorical*) choices of student writers at any point in the term.
- An examination of exemplary texts (*on overhead projectors, in published class books*) during the *revision* rather than the invention stage (*it strikes me that we might begin prompting writers with media other than the overwhelmingly awe inspiring professional text–use movies or ads or MTV or music to provoke spoken/written discussion, inner/outer voices–and then later when the writer is jogging along, but a bit out of energy and breath, offer the pick-me-up of written texts from writers who are exhibiting provocative*

moves so the writer [runner] can imitate, find the new spark that leads her on).

A few more ideas:

• Discuss writers' options, ask for suggestions about how texts can be made riskier and more conventional, how style can be altered.

• Ask what it means to write into one's own strengths and weaknesses—what is learned when drafting or revising in this manner? (*that is, don't we learn different important writing things when we push on where we're already good* **and** *when we push into the difficult, sore, raw, hard to do part of our work?*)

Don't you think certain of these ideas need more flesh?

Let's go global.

In "Provocative Revision" Toby Fulwiler suggests four assigned provocations that will teach writers needed revision vision. They can be asked (when completing multiple drafts) to limit their writing (time, place, action, scope, focus); they can add to their text (dialogs, interviews); they can switch (point of view or voice) in their work; they can transform their writing (recast into a different genre entirely, essay to letters or diary, journals to research reports, and so on). (*If you want to see student samples and a three draft version of "taught revision," look at his "A Lesson in Revision."*)

Q(Question): He says students should be *assigned* revision—but we know writer doesn't really need to go through multiple drafts while others need to go through countless drafts. Isn't this draconian?

PA(Possible Answer): But how do you know revision options, grammars other than the ones you've been introduced to, what you can do well (what you need to practice more) unless you try a canny and well-designed sequence to show you? Unless you try this or other sequences several times, in fact (who ever learns anything the first time)?

In my classes: I work with semester long writing contracts—asking students to decide on a plan for drafting five papers a term. The fifth paper is automatically designated a "radical revision" of papers 1, 2 or 3. Four is not up for radical revision—initial writing of that paper takes place too close to the revision assignment for writers to have either the glow or weariness of initial drafting diminished. The radical revision must represent a risk for the writer—this leads us to class discussions of

a. conventions;

b. how writers know and understand their strengths and weaknesses, and

c. what is radical?

We brainstorm on the chalkboard all the ways we think a paper can be revised:

- time changes
- genre changes
- style/voice changes
- topic deviations
- experiments with the physicality of texts
- being conservative when you're normally flamboyant (vice versa)
- multi-media
- multi-voice
- borrowing

and so on (other "revision" grammars have been reviewed above)—resulting in

> essays turned into crots with photographs woven through, into songs that are performed, into T- shirts that must be read, into collaged paintings, into applications to graduate school, into poems, into bumper stickers, into multi-voiced arguments of self and soul, into harangues, into papers that cannot be graded or they would not be written.

So . . . I ask for process narratives of what was learned about revision and grade on the exploration that was undertaken (in good faith) and how well it was narrated (in fact, writers may need to fail to produce learning through radical revision). Here's an example:

> I launched on my radical revision, which attempts to bring the piece "out" from the constrictions of a straight essay. Instead of using italicized motifs to represent the letters, I decided to reconstruct the letters themselves. With assorted pieces of stationary I rewrote these letters with as much authenticity as I could (using an old typewriter, *intentional* misspellings, smudges, and my own handwriting). [Here indeed is a way to teach local concerns, traditional grammar, this student must know how to spell to misspell **intentionally.**] To further bring the piece out, I included the photographs of which I spoke and cut them up as to represent which segments of the essay were "mine" (the things I recall) or simply my parents'. What results is radical in that it accomplishes what I only spoke of accomplishing in past drafts, making the text more clear, more visual. More accessible.

One problem: we have to learn to read radical revisions, to honor the learning in the exploration, to value grammars of style, to understand the alternate ways they show us how much has been mastered and mistressed of the dominant grammar:

LIGHTS OFF. SITTING DOWN IN
FRONT OF THE GLOWING GREEN
PHOSPHOR LETTERS ON THE SCREEN.
FINGERS
WANTING TO MOVE RAPIDLY.
TWITCHING
TO MAKE THE KEYS RATTLE.
STRAINING
THROUGH THOUGHTS.
SIFTING.
NO. YES. MAYBE. WHAT ABOUT THE
LADY ON THE SUBWAY TODAY?
TOO CLICHE.

THE TRICK WAS TO PICK THE
RIGHT HOLE. HE HAD OFTEN
SPENT DAYS WORKING ON AN IDEA,
JUST TO FINALLY REEL IN AND
FACE THE FACT THAT THINGS
WEREN'T BITING ON THAT HOOK.
NORMALLY THAT WOULD HAVE BEEN
FINE, JUST CHANGE THE TACKLE
AND THROW IT OUT AGAIN, MAKING
SURE TO KEEP THE LINE TAUT.
BUT HE HAD TO FACE HER EACH
TIME.

IT'S HARD, ISN'T IT, TO STOP FLESHING OUT THESE IDEAS BECAUSE REVISION IS ITSELF GENERATIVE.

Time's running short, let's go local.

- Examining writer's productive and nonproductive writing rules may aid revision. If a writer believes his first paragraph has to be perfect before he moves to the next, revision has too high a price. So beliefs must be examined and contradictory rules must be defused.

- Writers change their writing habits and rituals lifelong—that is, they keep many—but abandon some—due to external pressures. When I have this draft due, as it is, I'm writing late at night (*normally, I can't*) with a glass of white wine that should make me sleepy (*but it's not, because I'm not used to drafting at night, so I forget to sip from the glass as I find an idea and follow it to earn the end to my evening*). Students may more easily explore alternate grammars and attempt drafting if they change their physical writing conditions and experiment with altered processes–not forever, just to try new muscles, flex new wings.

- Introduce just a few new ideas (grammars, terms, encouragements, freedoms) concerning style. Although my students always critique Weathers's own writing style—a bit dry when advocating innovation—they take to his terms—crots is a particular favorite—and understand his concepts readily. Grammar B allows them to name what they have often, already, been attempting in their texts; it is a great relief for them to have terms for discussing alternate ways of writing and this fluency leads to more expert class discussions.

- Publish writing—there is nothing like performance to make us try to make ourselves and our writing presentable. Publish class anthologies for writing workshops even if only five essays are to be discussed that cycle, everyone (*cleans house*) straightens his or her prose when they know it will be inspected. Emphasize final portfolios as a site of publication; insist that students spend time preparing final copies by offering:

- Editing sessions. These can occur at various points in the classroom and range from tapping group members' skills as copy editors, fine spellers, comma squad participants, and so on. My favorite editing device is what I call *wall editing*. The first time a "product" is due, I ask how many class members have read their papers aloud. In a class of twenty-five, usually only two to five have done so. I ask each writer (and I participate) to find a blank piece of classroom wall and read aloud to check for errors before publication. I offer myself as a resource for advice and I've already asked writers to come prepared with white- out and black pens to make corrections. Soft and loud, a manic murmuring of written texts takes place. Inevitably, I see nearly every class member return to his/her desk to make a grammar level improvement in the text being prepared to represent him/her to the world of readers.

Haven't you really already added to this list of items yourself, though? All your editing and grammar tricks and wisdoms and advice and tools don't have to be abandoned in the process classroom. We just need to find the right balance and the right places for this essential type of instruction. Teaching grammar for writers is nothing more (and nothing less) than teaching writing itself.

III

Future Places of Grammar
in Writing Instruction

David Blakesley turns our eyes toward the future relationship of grammar and writing by drawing on past rhetorical and linguistic theories from Cicero to Kenneth Burke. He advocates "Reconceptualizing Grammar as an Aspect of Rhetorical Invention" using Francis Christensen's "A Generative Rhetoric of the Sentence" and Winston Weathers' Grammar B as heuristics that can realign grammar and invention—a pedagogical goal related to Wendy Bishop's contemporary practice in her college writing classroom. For Blakesley, the future of grammar is secure: writers need its power from the first moments of invention to formulate and shape their intentions. Irene Brosnahan and Janice Neuleib also seek to secure the future place of grammar in writing classrooms by changing the nature of grammar instruction itself. In "Teaching Grammar Affectively: Learning to Like Grammar," their research about the relationship between learning preferences and the teaching and learning of grammar leads Brosnahan and Neuleib to a new affective methodology for preparing future teachers of grammar.

Directing our gaze away from future pedagogies to virtual reality, Eric H. Hobson speculates that as more and more writing in the future occurs and remains in a virtual space created by systems of interconnected computers, attitudes toward grammar will change in as yet unforeseen ways. And he urges college writing teachers to be at the forefront in "Taking Computer-Assisted Grammar Instruction to New Frontiers." In the closing look toward the future place of grammar, "Correctness or Clarity? Finding Answers in the Classroom and the Professional World," Neil Daniel and Christina Murphy draw on extensive experience in writing classrooms, writing centers, and corporate writing workshops to suggest radical changes in the way academic institutions support the teaching of writing. These college writing teachers recommend that in the future we eliminate the first-year composition course and look toward writing across the curriculum efforts and writing center pedagogy for models of the apprenticeship learning that occurs in professional contexts.

13

Reconceptualizing Grammar as an Aspect of Rhetorical Invention

David Blakesley

> I hear some making excuses for not being able to express them-
> selves, and pretending to have their heads full of many fine things,
> but to be unable to express them for lack of eloquence. This is all
> a bluff. Do you know what I think those things are? They are shad-
> ows that come to them of some shapeless conceptions, which they
> cannot untangle and clear up within and consequently cannot set
> forth without: they do not understand themselves yet.
>
> —Montaigne[1]

Never one to make excuses, Montaigne quite emphatically answers a question that in various forms has long puzzled rhetoricians: whether thought is
temporally and causally prior to its expression in language or whether language is the agency for generating thought itself. Is it possible to have one's
head "full of many fine things" without the linguistic resources to express
them, without knowing how to use the relational principles of the language
that would make them meaningful? For Montaigne, the chief barrier to meaningful communication is not lack of eloquence, or an inability to stylize
thought. Inarticulate people, rather, lack skill in using the resources of language to "shape" concepts themselves, to "untangle" and "clear up"
thought at its inception. Watch those who use lack of eloquence as an excuse,
says Montaigne, and "you will conclude that they are laboring not for delivery, but for conception" (125).

At issue here is the always perplexing interrelation of thought and language. Explanations of this interrelation range from those that see language and thought as fused or coexistent (i.e., when we think, we think with/in words and language patterns), to those that see a metaphysical disjunction or segregation of thought and language (i.e., we think, then we translate thought into words and language patterns) (Vygotsky 2). Ultimately, our understanding of the interrelation of thought and language affects all that we say about language and language use, especially so when we make claims for how best to teach people to improve their writing. Vygotsky never settled this complex issue, but he did provide what I'll use as my major premise. The relation of thought to word is not a thing, but a living process: "Every thought tends to connect something with something else, to establish a relation between things" (125). I'll use the term *grammar* to name the relational principles that direct this "living process" of the mind forming connections.

To provide sound theoretical and historical justification for this new role of grammar as an aspect of rhetorical invention, I'll reexamine the received views of rhetorical invention and grammar to show how texts of "recipe-rhetoric"—to use William A Covino's phrase (34)— succeeded in fragmenting what had been in Aristotle and the mature Cicero a holistic view of invention. I'll argue first that rhetorical invention is the conceptualization and elaboration of meaning, an act of cognition mediated by the writer's formal, stylistic, and grammatical fluency in the strategies needed to generate as well as express this meaning. (From such a perspective, the "labor for delivery" and "conception" would be seen as mutually dependent acts.) Conceiving of grammar as a set of relational, generative principles, I'll identify its two primary roles in the composing process: (1) cognitively, as the means of articulating formal relationships among ideas, and (2) rhetorically, as the set of structural principles that help writers convey these relationships to readers effectively. The remainder of the chapter will explore the practical implications of this realignment for writing instruction and point to already extant pedagogies—e.g., Francis Christensen's "generative rhetoric" and Winston Weathers's "Grammar B"—that enact but do not fully articulate the idea that grammar is an aspect of rhetorical invention. Grammar will have a legitimate place in the future of writing instruction if we can learn to exploit its "rhetorically generative" potential.

Rhetorical Invention

Reconceptualizing grammar as an aspect of rhetorical invention labors against the classical division of rhetoric into five distinct faculties: Invention (*inventio*), Arrangement (*dispositio*), Style (*elocutio*), Memory (*memoria*), and Delivery (*pronuntiatio*). Hegemonic by the time of their appearance in Cicero's *De Inventione* (ca. 87 BCE) and the anonymous *Rhetorica ad Herennium* (ca. 84 BCE), these were the parts "as most authorities have stated" (*De Inventione* 1.7.9). Invention was "the discovery of valid or seemingly valid arguments to render one's cause plausible" (*De Inventione* 1.7.9). Style was "the fitting of the proper language to the invented matter" (*De Inventione* I.vii.9). Although it received only limited treatment in these rhetorical handbooks, the subject of grammar (here, the traditional "parts of speech") fell under the province of style.

Classically, invention and style were separate faculties (both temporally and cognitively): Invention involved the systematic discovery of proofs suited to the occasion and purpose of the speech; style, the subsequent rendering of this content in suitable words and sentences. In such a scheme, content is "discovered" (not "created") independently of the forms in which it is ultimately expressed. Content is "found" in either the facts surrounding a particular case or in the more general knowledge produced by particular sciences (politics, history, medicine, ethics, etc.). Style is primarily thought of as a collection of strategies for embellishing arguments (or ideas). Our contemporary conception of grammar and style as discrete features of writing that play little if any role in the invention of content are traceable to this classical scheme. The organizing metaphor of this conception is that form is a container. Effective writers simply choose the right containers in which to pour their thoughts. As I. A. Richards notes, however, this form/content distinction is "wretchedly inconvenient" because it "makes language a dress which thoughts put on" (12).[2]

Even though Cicero himself later admitted that schematizations of rhetoric like that in *De Inventione* relied on "precepts drawn from the infancy of our old and boyish learning" (*De Oratore* I.6), they became for later rhetoricians "the major authority for all later knowledge of rhetorical invention" (Kennedy 90-91). Works like Cicero's *De Oratore* and *Oratore* confounded the view of invention as distinct from memory and style, but the ease with which the ready-made rhetoric of the handbooks could be digested and disseminated made such qualifications superfluous.[3] Many modern textbooks maintain these distinctions in their tendency to treat style and arrangement as strategies clearly distinguishable from invention and enacted at different stages of the composing process.

To counteract the influence of recipe-rhetoric and its linear model of the composing process, we need to begin reassociating style, grammar, and invention. In his *Rhetoric*, Aristotle provides a more holistic model of rhetorical invention than was later advocated in the handbooks of Roman rhetoric. He devotes the first two books of the *Rhetoric* primarily to invention, relegating stylistic issues to Book III and paying them considerably less attention than we might expect given his penchant for detail.

In Book I of the *Rhetoric*, Aristotle provides two crucial definitions of the function of rhetoric that reveal some inclination to collapse artificial distinctions between the faculties of invention and style. In the first instance, rhetoric's function "is not so much to persuade as to find out in each case the *existing* means of persuasion'' (1.1.14; emphasis added).[4] In the second, rhetoric is "the faculty of discovering the *possible* means of persuasion in reference to any subject whatever" (1.2.1; emphasis added). Various commentators amplify these definitions by adding "through speech," but as Kennedy notes, Aristotle's use of *rhetoric* already denotes language's role in the process (*On Rhetoric* 36). In both definitions, rhetoric is a *dynamis*, an ability or capacity to find out or discover means of persuasion. The primary difference is that in the first, Aristotle describes the "means" as "existing" (or "available") and in the second, as "possible." "Existing" (*hyparchonta*) implies that the arguments exist independently of the act of invention, that persuasive arguments are not "invented" so much as they are "found." The use of "possible" (*endekhomenon*) in the second definition implies that new arguments may be generated through the process of invention, there being possible arguments heretofore "unavailable" because no art had conceptualized them or because the circumstances of the particular case are unique. The "means of persuasion" may exist in the culture's storehouse of shared knowledge, or they may be principles for reformulating this knowledge.

These latter means, or principles, take many forms, and in Aristotle, include *topoi*, patterns of arrangement, and the many techniques of style. The *topoi*, for example, are either special (*idia*) or common (*koina*). Special topics are the paradigmatic arguments of a particular subject, such as politics. The common topics are essentially the grammatical principles of rational (enthymatic) argument, and enable rhetoricians to generate using this grammar an infinite variety of "possible" means of persuasion. As Ellen Quandahl has noted, the Aristotelian topics are "ways of putting sentences together in order to make inferences. We might say that they are conceptual structures, ways of relating concepts to one another to produce new insights about these concepts" (134). Because particular cases and contexts ambiguate general truths, the rhetorician must know both how to use existing arguments and how to generate new ones from them using these principles, which are in the most general sense the formal patterns of the language used to convey meaning.

When the role of invention is limited to the discovery of "available" arguments, as in the rhetorical handbooks described above, the ability to use the resources of the language to generate meaning atrophies. Conceptions of style and arrangement as the means of manipulating received or extant knowledge lead to writing pedagogies that stress, first, the acquisition of knowledge, then its formulaic re-presentation or embellishment—what Kennedy calls "technical rhetoric" (*Classical* 18–24). Throughout the history of rhetoric, many persuasive arguments have been levelled against technical rhetoric and the pedagogies that validate it. Nevertheless, grammar and style continue to be taught as concerns relevant only at the revision and editing stages of the writing process. Their role in the production of content itself has been disregarded in spite of rhetorics that argue for their alignment with invention.

Works like Cicero's *De Oratore*, for instance, stress that knowledge is not simply a commodity to be acquired and then redistributed. It is, rather, produced by and through the activity of rhetorical inquiry itself and always involves the confluence of the writer's experience with and recognition of the complexity of the subject, awareness of the audience's preconceptions, the demands of the immediate rhetorical situation, *and* the ways in which the means of presenting such knowledge (style, grammar, and arrangement) determine its ultimate form. In spite of such holistic, philosophical models of rhetoric and rhetorical invention, the model of rhetorical invention posited by the technical rhetorics of antiquity even now guides our thinking about what writers need: they need to know what to say and how to say it, which sounds fine, at first. The problem is this: Knowing and saying, conception and delivery, thought and language—each opposition describes what in reality is a unified, living process. Saying is coming to know; knowing is having said. So writers need to learn *how to know* by knowing *how to say*, then to say what they know by saying it so that others know it. We know the world through language; a writer's world has more texture, more "reality," more persuasiveness, when the perspectives from which he or she knows it and communicates it to an audience are many and varied.

Grammar as an Aspect of Rhetorical Invention

Thus far my use of the term *grammar* has been primarily as a description of the formal means of relating ideas, and this usage I realize needs more justification and qualification. In "Grammar, Grammars, and the Teaching of Grammar," Patrick Hartwell identifies five operative meanings of *grammar*: (1) the set of formal patterns in which the words of a language are arranged in order to convey larger meanings; (2) linguistic grammar, which studies these formal patterns; (3) linguistic etiquette (usage, which Hartwell says is not grammar, *per se*); (4) school grammar (the grammar of textbooks); and (5) stylistic grammar (grammatical terms used to teach style) (109–110). There is, I believe, ample justification for adding a sixth meaning that will help place my usage of the term in proper perspective. Sometimes *grammar* is used to designate formal patterns themselves as grammars, forms bounded by relational principles that people use to convey meaning, as in #1 above, but with the qualification that such grammars aren't limited to words/ sentences, but also include larger units of meaning—paragraphs, passages, even philosophies.

The idea that a grammar of relational principles regulates and enables rhetorical invention is hardly new, or even controversial. Heuristics are, after all, simply ways of discovering and relating available information, and they have long had an important role in writing instruction. However, whether such a grammar *generates* content (rather than manipulates it), has been a controversial issue, at least since Socrates's argument in Plato's *Phaedrus* that a "man must first know the truth about every single subject on which he speaks or writes" (276). The idea here is that a person first must "possess" the essential content; rhetorical invention would then be the act of choosing the best means of conveying this content to another. The principles for generating this content are independent of the means of representing it.

Kenneth Burke counters this view of grammar in *A Grammar of Motives*, as does Richard Coe in *Toward a Grammar of Passages*. In Burke's formulation, a "grammar" of motives should be "concerned with the basic forms of thought which, in accordance with the nature of the world as all men necessarily experience it, are exemplified in the attributing of motives" (xv). Here, grammar refers to the "basic forms of thought" people use when they "say what people are doing and why they are doing it" (xv). These forms of thought, Burke argues, "are equally present in systematically elaborated metaphysical structures, in legal judgments, in poetry and fiction, in political and scientific works, in news and in bits of gossip offered at random" (xv).

Burke conceives of this grammar as a set of principles (whether articulated or not) that people use to produce meaningful statements about human motives. Philosophies of human motivation are thus "*casuistries* which apply these principles to temporal situations" (xvi). As a set of forms, this grammar generates, organizes, even delimits the possible statements one can make about motives. Whether the forms are "basic" is debatable (Burke here limits them to five—act, scene, agent, agency, purpose); I've cited Burke's use of "grammar" only to relay his insight that a grammar is a set of structural principles that aid, or direct, invention—generative principles for producing speech or writing. The principles themselves may not be innate, or "basic," but the symbolic motive underlying them may be. While grammars may vary from language to language, culture to culture, *some* type of grammar is needed for producing statements that people who use the same language can understand (that are "acceptable"). And, as Burke would have it, these grammars may generate whole discourses, or "philosophies," as well as individual sentences. Conceived as the relational principles of a language, grammar has a fundamental role in making meaning.

The Linguistic Basis of Grammar as Rhetorical Invention

Persuasive theoretical justification for viewing grammar as an aspect of rhetorical invention is provided by Chomskyan and post-Chomskyan models of language acquisition and performance.[5] In brief, Chomsky's model, elaborated most fully in *Aspects of the Theory of Syntax* (1965), rests on the basic premise that all languages have in common a creative aspect, a set of rules (a "generative grammar") for producing an infinite range of well-formed sentences (3–9, *passim*). At a relatively early age (four- to five-years-old), people acquire an intrinsic *competence* (knowledge of the language) that they can use to produce or interpret meaningful statements. Chomsky distinguishes competence from *performance*, which is the actual use of the language in concrete situations (4). Every well-formed utterance has both a deep structure and a surface structure. Deep structure is an abstract concept referring to a unit of meaning or form of thought that is transformed into surface structure, which is the concrete manifestation of the deep structure. As Chomsky puts it, "The central idea of transformational grammar is that they [deep and surface structures] are, in general, distinct and that the surface structure is determined by repeated application of certain formal operations called 'grammatical transformations' to objects of a more elementary sort" (16–17). The "elementary object" is the deep structure, the unit of meaning or form of thought that may potentially generate numerous surface representations. To clarify by way of example, the sentences (1) "The truck hit John" and (2) "John was hit by the truck" have different surface structures (#1 being active; #2, passive) but share the same deep structure, which might be stated as an agent (the truck) performed an action (hitting) upon an object (John). In this example, the deep and surface structures of #1 are closely related. Sentence #2 demonstrates a passive transformation of deep structure.

Chomskyan linguistics says, basically, that deep structures are reflections of basic forms of thought enabled by language that all users of the language possess as competence. Because speakers possess varying resources for making these linguistic transformations, in performance these deep structures may assume widely variant syntactic forms. While the innate competence of the language user is static, performance will change as the user acquires fluency, which can be thought of as familiarity with the wide range of possible transformations.

The most obvious lessons to learn from Chomsky's model are simply that the relational patterns (or deep structures) of a language can generate an infinite variety of understandable statements, that meaning has both formal and semantic aspects, and that people learn to utilize both naturally. Like many linguists, Chomsky limited his claims to sentence-level phenomena, but there are good reasons to believe that grammars of form and style are equally generative and "natural."[6] Aristotle's common topics can be thought of as the deep structure of enthymatic reasoning. As abstract principles, the common topics are static but when performed generate a wide array of possible arguments. As forms of thought, they are subject to a variety of semantic and syntactic transformations.

One problem with viewing the relational principles of a language as the basic constituents of rhetorical competence could be that people may be naturally predisposed to learn only the most elementary patterns of syntax, but not those principles that govern units of meaning larger than the sentence. The Chomskyan model says that people possess at an early age basic linguistic competence (the deep structures of the language needed to produce and judge grammatical sentences), and that this competence is relatively static. Only performance varies from person to person. However, John Mills and Gordon Hemsley (1976) have shown that levels of education do affect peoples' judgment of sentence grammaticality, suggesting that competence is more fluctuant, more a result of literacy learning and socialization than previously thought. If learning changes the deep structure of the internal grammar used to produce sentences, then it may also be that other types of grammars, though they may be learned at different rates and stages of development because of their complexity and restricted opportunities for use, undergo similar revision. In other words, grammar may be a set of relational principles that people internalize as the circumstances for using them to produce meaningful discourse become more urgent. What may be constant is the mind's predisposition to learn formal principles themselves, whether they be ones used to construct sentences or larger units of meaning. Conceivably, people can develop rhetorical competence (stylistic and formal fluency) just as they can have sentence-level competence (competence here referring to the ability to use structural principles to produce and evaluate meaning). There are grammars of form and style just as there is a grammar of sentences.

Stylistic Grammars as Rhetorical Invention

I want to turn now to a survey of pedagogies that articulate grammars of style and demonstrate their heuristic potential. Oddly enough, however, while these pedagogies claim to offer writers ways to "find things to say," their general focus, and the concern of those who critique them, has been on their capacity for either improving the surface structure of sentences or increasing the number of stylistic options available to the writer. The purpose of manipulating surface structure is reader-based and whatever consequences these skills have for the writer's competence (potential for generating deep structure) remain unarticulated. I'll concentrate on those approaches that were designed to improve style—what Hartwell calls "stylistic grammar" (110)—and will only note here that much useful work has already been produced identifying the heuristic possibilities of form, including W. Ross Winterowd's "*Dispositio*: The Concept of Form in Discourse" (1971), Ann Berthoff's *forming/ thinking/writing* (1982), Richard Coe's "An Apology for Form" (1987) and *Toward a Grammar of Passages* (1988). The purpose of teaching style and form should not be simply to create writers who can write effective or "correct" sentences or essays, but to help writers both use the available resources of the language at the moment of conception itself and understand how these means of representation in effect determine what can be known (expressed) about anything, the epistemological basis of form.

The two stylistic grammars I'll discuss—Christensen's "A Generative Rhetoric of the Sentence" and Weathers's "Grammar B"—share the general premise that stylistic form helps one generate content and that stylistic options are structural devices that are themselves "an aid to discovery" (Christensen 24). (Some stylistic grammars, such as Joseph Williams's *Style: Ten Lessons in Clarity and Grace* and Richard Lanham's *Revising Prose*, make few, if any, claims for grammar's heuristic potential.) After briefly summarizing Christensen's and Weathers's approaches, I'll discuss the central aims and methods of each, then argue that both recognize the generative capacity of imitating particular relational principles. While neither adequately addresses the critique that such exercises when removed from "the living context of the rhetorical situation" are hardly more than "dry runs" (Winterowd, 1975, 338), Christensen and Weathers recognize that technique needs to be exercised in real communicative situations. By contextualizing imitation in the immediate experience and rhetorical purposes of individual writers, these "exercises" initiate the same language learning process that characterizes the more elementary (though no less complicated) process of rendering thought grammatically. Imitating the syntactic forms in the "living context" of their rhetorical situation, writers learn new ways to structure meaning, a necessary and critical step in the invention process. As Vygotsky points out—citing Piaget—"the child uses subordinate clauses with *because*, *although*, etc. long before he grasps the structures of meaning corresponding to these syntactic forms" (127).

The four principles of Christensen's generative rhetoric are "addition," "direction of modification," "levels of abstraction," and "texture" (26–30).[7] Christensen sees these principles as ways for writers to "work for greater density and variety in texture and greater concreteness and particularity in what is added" (30). The bulk of his essay consists of cumulative sentences in which free modifiers are separated from the main clause and the grammatical character of each addition is cued (NC=noun cluster, Abs=absolute, PP=prepositional phrase), as in the following written by Sinclair Lewis:

1. He dipped his hands in the bichloride solution and shook them,

2. a quick shake (NC)

3. fingers down (Abs)

4. like the fingers of a pianist above the keys.(PP) (31)

Christensen encourages writers to imitate these structures, providing their own content, in the interest of gradually improving the stylistic maturity and texture of their writing. He describes what I'd call the "grammar" of the cumulative sentence as follows:

> [The cumulative sentence] is dynamic rather than static, representing the mind thinking. The main clause . . . exhausts the mere fact of the idea; logically, there is nothing more to say. The additions stay with the idea,

probing its bearings and implications, exemplifying it or seeking an analogy
or metaphor for it, or reducing it to details. Thus the mere form of the
sentence generates ideas. (28)

Commentators on Christensen's generative rhetoric have criticized its tendency to equate a mature style with the sort of texture enabled by cumulative sentences, which seems to ignore other equally important criteria, such
as whether the writing achieves its purpose, whether the style is suited to the
content, and so on (Johnson 360–364). As with sentence-combining, students
who practice writing cumulative sentences seem to improve their style, but
the effects are short-lived unless the skills are reinforced over time.[8]

Christensen's contention that the cumulative sentence "represents the
mind thinking" and that imitating structure helps one generate ideas has also
been challenged. Sabina Thorne Johnson, for instance, argues that neither "the
cumulative nor the periodic sentence imitates thought, which by its nature is
usually chaotic and inchoate" (357). The disagreement here is illustrative
because it focuses on the issue of whether any formal patterns can represent
thought, or, as I've been arguing in this chapter, whether formal patterns
themselves are constitutive of thought. Christensen perhaps misstates the relationship between the structure of the cumulative sentence and thinking. The
pattern of making a proposition then amplifying it with free modifiers *directs*
thought. Prior to the imposition of *some* formal pattern, thought is not thought
per se, but some inchoate feeling or inclination. As Richard Coe notes, "There
is not meaning without form: information is *formed* matter (which become
meaningful in relation to contexts)" (1987, 16).

Having observed students producing cumulative sentences and having
imitated the forms myself, I'm certain that people do generate ideas that
would not have been formulated without the imposition of these structural
principles. (Whether the ideas generated in this way are good ones is another
matter.) Johnson questions whether students can "know how one wants to
say something unless one first knows what one wants to say" (357). But her
question rests, again, on the faulty premise that "knowing" is temporally
prior to linguistic formulation. The "grammar" of the cumulative sentence
helps one "untangle and clear up within" the "shapeless conceptions" of
which Montaigne spoke.

In practice, students can learn from Christensen's generative rhetoric of
the sentence useful ways to amplify simple propositions. The major problem
most inexperienced writers suffer from is not merely paucity of ideas, but
insufficient means of elaborating ideas, so any form of rhetorical invention that
would initiate the process of amplifying, relating, reformulating, or contextualizing the ideas they do have is helpful. It's also important to realize that
while imitation for its own sake can make students aware of stylistic options,
it needs to be directed by the exigencies of the individual writer's rhetorical
situation. Invention, in other words, must be *rhetorical* invention. I ask students to imitate these forms in the context of producing larger discourses, the

aims of which ultimately determine whether particular stylistic choices are good ones. (As a form or grammar, the cumulative sentence helps students more in generating narrative than it does argument, since one of the primary purposes of argument is not to create texture, but chains of evidence.)

One interesting consequence of conceiving of stylistic imitation as rhetorical invention is that students learn conventional grammar and punctuation implicitly. Producing cumulative sentences, for instance, teaches students that commas are used to separate grammatical clauses from modifying phrases or other clauses (to put it simply). And, finally, teachers don't have to spend much time discussing traditional grammar to teach generative style. As Rei R. Noguchi has argued, for the purposes of improving writing, we need only identify "the basics": sentence, subject, verb, and modifier (17).

Winston Weathers's *An Alternate Style: Options in Composing* (1980) is a provocative (and playful) book whose central premise is that contemporary modes of composition, including academic themes as well as conventional grammar, teach writers to construct "the well-made box" (1). There's nothing implicitly "wrong" about the well-made box (what Weathers calls Grammar A), but as the singular option available to writers, it prohibits certain ways of thinking about a subject, when the real task of writing teachers should be to "identify compositional options and teach students the mastery of the options and the liberating use of them" (5). Some of the stylistic options of Grammar B Weathers identifies are crots, labyrinthine sentences, sentence fragments, lists, double-voicing, repetition, refrains, repetends, and language variegation (including typography). He finds such options exercised by many competent writers yet excluded from the range of options made available to students in the writing classroom, partly on the premise that students need to know how to write a correct sentence *before* they earn the right to take liberties with conventional style.

What Weathers realizes is that structure (formal, stylistic, or grammatical) helps writers shape ideas both at the moment of conception and at the stage of delivery. Confronted with having to produce the well-made box, he writes,

> I begin to wonder if there isn't some sort of container (1) that will allow me to package 'what I have to say' without trimming my 'content' to fit into a particular compositional mode, (2) that will actually encourage me to discover new things to say because of the very opportunity a newly-shaped container gives me (even though I can never escape containers—e.g., syntax—altogether), (3) that will be more suitable to my own mental processes, and (4) that will provide me with greater rhetorical flexibility. (2)

Of note here is the contention that "containers" encourage invention; how we decide to "package" ideas generates, at least to some degree, the very ideas packaged. And, as suggested by (3), particular forms reflect, even deflect, mental processes.

In teaching students the stylistic options Weathers enumerates, I've found that many of them relish the opportunity to experiment with style.

Students who already know how to construct the well-made box quickly learn to use the options of Grammar B in purposeful and provocative ways, even though many of the options are new to them. Less competent writers, while they seem able to imitate the structural principles of Grammar B, have difficulty using them to pursue some larger rhetorical purpose. This discrepancy suggests that advanced writers know how to use the relational principles of style and form to advance meaningful intention, to make a point, or to create an effect. Whatever the grammar, good writers know how to exploit it. Inexperienced writers, however, see form as a container for meaning (*any* content that will fit into the prescribed form will do). I've had many writers tell me after having written formulaic but meaningless Grammar B essays that they didn't realize they "had to say something." When I tell them, "Okay, now use Grammar B to say something," some realize a very important point about writing: that writers select particular strategies in order to accomplish some purpose grander than merely demonstrating technical competence. Grammar B breaks the molds of the well-made box that many students have never thought of as a box in the first place. It defamiliarizes the opposition between form and content that subtly communicates to students that what they say (and what they know) bears no relation to their means of expressing it. And perhaps most important, Grammar B helps students realize the extent to which more familiar ways of relating and expressing their ideas have directed their thinking in the past.

A Future Place of Grammar in Writing Instruction

There are legitimate reasons for viewing grammar as an aspect of rhetorical invention. But this realignment of grammar and invention will only have a significant impact on writing instruction when teachers and researchers understand its historical and theoretical precedents. I have presented some of them here, but there are more. In the history of rhetoric, for instance, Giambattista Vico presents in his *On the Study Methods of Our Times* (1708) a view of the *topoi* as figures of thought, as the relational principles of language that help one be "copious." Thomas DeQuincey sees style as the "great organ of the advancing intellect" itself (261; also quoted in Covino, 111). In addition to mining the history of rhetoric, we need to study more rigorously how, why, and to what extent the stylistic and generative grammars I have described affect writers' abilities to conceptualize and articulate subject matter.

In reconceptualizing grammar as an aspect of rhetorical invention, I don't intend to advocate the empty and monotonous routine of practicing technique for the sake of technique, which has been the fate of many stylistic grammars in the past. If, however, we understand grammar as the primary means of relating ideas in language—at the level of the sentence and beyond—then it seems useful to encourage students to see grammar not as a system for expressing ideas "correctly" (at the sentence level) but for generating ideas dialectically, through the many relations a grammar makes possible. Ultimately, the usefulness of a grammar of style, form, motives, argument, etc. depends upon the individual writer's ability to use it to achieve some intention—whether it be to persuade, teach, delight, critique, or analyze—in an exigent rhetorical situation.

Notes

1. "Of the Education of Children," 125.

2. Quoted also in Coe, "An Apology for Form" (16).

3. See Covino, *The Art of Wondering* (33–44), for a provocative discussion of memory as a "faculty for the invention of narrative and argument, not for the storing and retrieval of facts" (40).

4. In this instance, I'm using the 1926 Freese translation for both definitions because Kennedy's 1991 translation makes no distinction between them, in spite of the fact that in the first definition Aristotle uses the phrase *ta hyparchonta pithana* (which Freese translates as "existing means of persuasion"), while in the second he uses *to endekhomenon pithanon* (which Freese translates as "possible means of persuasion"). Kennedy translates both phrases as "available means of persuasion" but notes that *endekhomenon* often means "possible." Henceforth, all citations of the *Rhetoric* will be from the Kennedy translation.

5. For a more detailed discussion of Chomskyan linguistics, see Terence Moore and Christine Carling, *Understanding Language: Toward a Post-Chomskyan Linguistics*, and Frederick Newmeyer, *Linguistic Theory in America.*

6. See, for instance, Winterowd's "The Grammar of Coherence."

7. For more detailed explanations, extensions, and critiques of Christensen's program, see Johnson's "Some Tentative Strictures on Generative Rhetoric," Stull's "Sentence Combining, Generative Rhetoric, and Concepts of Style," and Berlin and Broadhead's "Twelve Steps to Using Generative Sentences and Sentence Combining in the Composition Classroom."

8. See, for instance, Crowhurst's "Sentence-Combining: Maintaining Realistic Expectations."

14

Teaching Grammar Affectively: Learning to Like Grammar

Irene Brosnahan and
Janice Neuleib

Future teachers of English and language arts need a new way of viewing grammar, but until professors who instruct those future teachers improve their instructional methodology, classroom teaching will not change. For new teachers to find a meaningful, experiential way to instruct their students, they must first experience new learning patterns themselves. We have, for the past two years, implemented an experiential, creative approach to grammar instruction, resulting in changed attitudes about and increased interest in grammar, as reported in student journals. The theoretical underpinnings for this new approach are grounded in our research in learning styles as dictated by personal preferences for both classroom interaction and information processing. This chapter investigates both the connections between positive affect and learning, as well as methods of producing that positive affect in future teachers.

For the past five years we have researched the relationships between learning preferences and the teaching and learning of grammar. We have discovered that the students who most often major in English prefer to learn affectively and therefore cannot or will not learn grammar unless they like it, and for the most part their experiences in school have taught them not to like it. They therefore often begin grammar classes with resistance and antagonism. Given at the same time their inability to learn without an affective commitment, it should come as no surprise that they do not learn grammar, do not like to teach it when they enter the schools, and in turn teach their students to dislike it as well.

We have dealt extensively in other publications with issues of the desirability of teaching grammar at all and with writing, tutoring, and personality type (Neuleib and Brosnahan, Scharton and Neuleib), but a brief review will clarify issues as our discussion develops. Research into writing and grammar instruction has shown that students make almost no connection between traditional grammar instruction and the editing of their texts, and they make no connection at all between grammar instruction and the production of text (Hillocks). Research has not investigated, however, differing methods of teaching grammar and their effects on grammar learning, nor has it investigated what approaches to writing do help students improve their editing skills. Nor has research investigated the reasons for the schools' continuing insistence on traditional grammar instruction in spite of professional organizations' objections and teachers' distaste. Finally, research has not acknowledged the steady stream of commentary in the English teaching publications by teachers who must deal with the issues in the teaching of grammar (Coats, Cramer, Davis, DeBeaugrande, Sanborn, Sanford, Streed, Tabbert, Taylor, Warner, Vavra). These discrepancies in expert opinion have created a teaching-learning context that confuses teachers. The teachers then approach language literacy classes with hesitation and resistance that leave students bored and uninterested in their English language classes, especially junior high students who most need variety and stimulation and who are most likely to experience drill and kill in grammar class.

Even were composing researchers to discover that some specific methods for teaching grammar do improve style and editing skills, students with differing talents and abilities would still write and edit differently. Studies investigating personality type preference and writing processes have shown that individuals with differing preferences for learning and working find different stages of the development of a text more or less pleasurable or tension-producing (Jensen and DiTiberio). Thus a person who enjoys linear work that has a clear goal and specifically defined rules will prefer perfecting the technical aspects of her own or another's text. On the other hand, a writer who enjoys discovery stages of composing may find the final polishing stage boring and frustrating. Thus persons with differing preferences will find themselves engaged at more or less intense levels as they work through the stages of composing any particular text.

Our research studies (Neuleib and Brosnahan) show that the same discrepancies exist for grammar learners. Those who prefer to learn in global associative patterns (described as intuitive in personality type terminology) are more interested in and have more aptitude for the theoretical aspects of grammar. On the other hand, those who prefer to learn in specific linear patterns (described as sensing in personality type terminology) tend to memorize descriptive terms and see grammar as a set of prescribed rules. The former are of course more at ease in college grammar courses; the latter tend to resist the theoretical models presented and to want to replicate traditional

grammar learning. These inclinations combined with another set of preferences, one for logical reasons to learn and the other for positive responses to
what is learned (thinking and feeling in personality type terminology), create
different kinds of learning preferences in the grammar classroom. Thus the
learner who has an intuitive feeling preference (most English and language
arts majors) will want a global, associative approach that includes positive
experiences and helps them to find ways both to enjoy learning grammar and
to help others do so as well.

Teaching preferences likewise reflect these differences. Most English
teachers enter the profession because they love literature, both reading it and
writing it. They prefer activities that will engage students and themselves in
important personal and social exchanges with the text and with one another.
They like to read and write about experience and meaningful relationships,
not about systematic studies of language or learning. Most English teachers
find linguistics and stylistics the least appealing part of the English curriculum because both have no "life" in them. Both are cold, cerebral studies that
either systematize what they think should be felt or analyze what they feel
should be experienced. For teachers of this relationship-oriented preference,
grammar learning and instruction fail to appeal to their most fully developed
preferences. Grammar both at its theoretical level and at its applied level in
editing and usage tends to be cerebral and unemotional, thus losing the interest and enthusiasm of most English teachers. When this enthusiasm disap-
pears, classroom learning declines, both in college classes and in the middle
school and high school classes they will later teach. Ironically, university
teachers of teachers have in the past tended to be fascinated with the cerebral, analytical approaches to language learning. Most future middle and high
school teachers of language arts are left cold by such an approach.

Given that the need to engage future teachers with the subject is so
strong and that their resistance is often so powerful, teachers of teachers must
grapple with these issues. The schools will continue to require grammar
instruction of some sort, and the profession at large will continue to insist
that all meaning is language-based. Thus both on the practical and on the
advanced theoretical front, a pedagogy that will address the question of affect
in teaching and learning grammar must replace standard grammar instruction
at all levels. University teachers of teachers must forsake their fascination
with the highly theoretical and systematic study of language and learn to
meet future teachers on their own ground.

A general argument for the importance of engagement in teaching and
learning reinforces this need for a new pedagogy. That argument comes from
the recent work of psychologist Mihaly Csikszentmihalyi, who studied affective responses in people as they went about their daily lives. His original
research began with questionnaires asking about the experience of engagement with tasks of all sorts. Later he perfected a research methodology that
used beepers to ask participants to stop in the middle of activities such as

class (teaching and learning), sports, and artistic endeavor. The major results of the extensive research concluded that humans experience stress when the demands of a task exceed their skills and boredom when their skills exceed the demands of the task. In the middle lies a wonderful experience Csikszentmihalyi calls "flow," the sensation felt when skills and the concomitant challenges match. The levels of intensity increase as the challenges and skills increase. Thus a master chess player experiences more intense connection with the moment than does a student watching her favorite MTV after school, but both lock into the moment oblivious of time and tasks outside the current activity (Csikszentmihalyi).

The study argues that humans need more than anything else to be engaged with significant tasks; when schools ignore this need or set up circumstances that will occupy rather than engage, learning as well as meaningful experience declines. Specifically, then, Csikszentmihalyi argues that humans learn when they are interested and involved in what they are doing. They do not learn when they are bored or disengaged. It probably does not take a longitudinal, multi-thousand-subject study to persuade teachers of the truth of this concept, but oddly despite instinctive awareness of the need to engage students, most schools go on requiring grammar instruction that engages neither students nor teachers.

In our own research we have observed junior high school teachers who move quickly through a classroom hour in which they and their collaboratively-grouped students discussed stories and wrote about them with warmth and enthusiasm. We have then stayed on to the next class hour to observe the same teachers grimly ask students to open their grammar books and do the exercises on relative clauses or subject-verb agreement up and down the aisles for the entire class period. We have asked those teachers why they do not teach grammar in the same exciting and engaging way that they teach literature. The answers vary from "I hate teaching grammar" to "the school administration demands that we do it this way." Teachers tell us that they remember their own school grammar learning without pleasure or enthusiasm and tend to reinscribe that pattern in their own teaching. Teachers who remember school grammar with pleasure are few and far between, and most of them are not teaching below the university level.

Such a repetition of negative experience fits with the psychological research on affect. Positive role modeling is the predictor that provides the most assurance that an individual will acquire desirable traits. Self-sponsored writers write because they have seen their role models enjoy and profit from writing, as self-sponsored readers read because they have seen others enjoy and profit by reading. The few self-sponsored grammar students we know (linguists) usually recall lively debates on language among their original care givers, and none remembers being corrected without explanation and encouragement. Too often language instruction has included parents who say 'May I have a cookie, not can I have a cookie' and teachers who 'correct' papers with red pens that note only undesirable usage and never praise the clever phrase or the particularly stunning usage choice. It should not come as any surprise, therefore, that teachers of grammar would role model the same kind of grammar teaching they had experienced, albeit in this case negative experience. Future teacher responses in grammar journals confirm this conjecture.

It is clear, then, that while we have made progress in preparing English teachers to make the teaching of reading and writing exciting and effective, we have done little to enable them to accomplish the same goals with their teaching of grammar. Our research with prospective English and language arts teachers has persuaded us that improvement in the learning and teaching of grammar must begin with these teachers. For the past few years, we have gathered responses from our grammar students describing their past and present experience in learning grammar. These responses confirm the current assumption that students fear or are bored by grammar. Our students' journals at the beginning of their grammar classes abound with comments such as "I hate grammar," "I dislike it," "I'm very intimidated by the word *grammar.*"

We know what has caused this fear or aversion to grammar, so we are trying to change the affective context of our future teachers' classroom experiences with grammar. One student commented on her high school teacher, "my teacher skipped grammar because he didn't know how to do it any better than his students." One source of this fear and indifference may be a too narrow view of grammar. Given their experience both with workbooks and with paper marking, teachers and students think of grammar as rules of usage, mostly proscriptive, to be memorized and applied to writing. As one student said, "Memories of diagramming and memorizing bring feelings of frustration and confusion." For such students, the learning of grammar has been largely a matter of reciting rules and filling in tedious workbook exercises. Said one student of her grammar learning experience, "I felt I never really understood grammar. During junior high and high school, I would endure the six weeks of grammar without ever learning more than the easy parts, i.e., nouns, verbs, direct objects." Another summarized the problem this way, "I think a large part of my previous mistrust of grammar stemmed from experiences of the past. The old methods of rote memorization and unbending guidelines made grammar a dreadful experience." Clearly, these students all emphasize the negative affect they associate with grammar learning.

We have noted a change in attitude since we began studying students' personality preferences and adapting our methodology to suit those students. The grammar course for teachers, Traditional and Non-traditional Grammars, had for many years been taught as an introduction to traditional, structural, and transformational grammars. The course divided into even thirds with lectures on the concepts of each grammar, explaining with examples, assigning exercises from texts, and for the most part ignoring student teachers' experience with reading and writing.

The change in methodology in this course in recent years can be characterized briefly as a transition from the old progression from traditional to transformational grammars to a new progression from unconscious grammar to conscious grammar. Students learn that grammar is descriptive and that writers need to be aware that usage choices are a part of every stage of composing. The course begins by redefining grammar. Students' original view of grammar is that it is a collection of do's and don'ts for usage. We call these "rules" applied grammar and tell students that we will worry about these issues at the end of the course. In re-defining grammar first as unconscious grammar, our objective is to persuade them that they "know" grammar and to give them confidence in generating, analyzing, and making judgments about language data.

We then provide interactive group tasks, which enable students to generate patterns and structures using their unconscious knowledge of the language before they proceed to analyzing and making judgments about language data. These interactive tasks have proven to be the key to stimulating both interest and confidence in student teachers' handling of grammar. The activities provide partial clues to generating examples of particular structures or forms under consideration. For example, to generate examples of various types of modifiers for nouns, we give them an exercise for creating noun phrases by providing open-ended lists of different forms of modifiers and headnouns. Students have to use their internalized knowledge to decide what forms to use, what types of modifiers precede nouns and what follow, in what order they should occur, and how many modifiers are possible.

To teach relative clauses and other types of subordination, we use sentence-combining exercises so that students can discover the processes of embedding, deletion, substitution, and rearrangement of elements in a sentence. The response to this kind of activity has been extremely positive. One student says, "This class was totally different (from previous grammar classes). There were so many hands-on activities... When I become a teacher, I want my students to learn grammar in this way. I believe it would keep their attention longer, keep them motivated, and interested." Another student says, "This exploration of language is not only interesting; it can also be fun and exciting, as I realized when we did the exercises in class." Still another says, "Everything just 'fell into place.' I would like to use this approach when I teach grammar."

Besides finding this approach to grammar interesting and gaining confidence in what they know of the language, the students are further motivated by finding this grammar learning experience relevant and useful. Past research on students' time spent doing grammar activities and their editing or general writing ability may have shown little measurable connection, but students in our study comment on how they are able to use their insights from these experiential exercises when they compose, revise, and edit. One student says, "My ideas about grammar have changed in that I now think that grammar is an invaluable tool in helping me to sharpen up my writing skills. I do have an operational knowledge of grammar.'' Another student comments, ''I am beginning to really understand grammar and use it effectively. When I am writing a paper, I not only understand the ways in which I am writing, but I can also begin to analyze it, which allows me to improve my overall writing.''

Others make more specific comments about the usefulness of grammar for them. One student says, ''The exercises dealing with sentence combining and subordinate clauses were helpful because I am always looking for ways to revise sentences to achieve the optimum effects. Until this unit, I was never really aware of the conjunctions I selected, but I have learned to become more discriminating.'' Another student says, ''In this semester I have been able to fine tune my writing. I now understand the difference between subordinate and coordinate conjunctions. I have always instinctively known how to do things such as sentence combining. But now I consciously know which conjunctions will give me which effects.'' Whether in actual practice these students do apply their conscious knowledge of grammar or not seems irrelevant. The important point is that they **feel** that way, and this is what would motivate them to continue to be interested in understanding grammar.

Another major point brought up by the students which contributes to their positive attitudes about this grammar learning experience is that it now ''makes sense.'' Unlike most of their experiences in high school or earlier, which, as one student says, is ''unuseful (sic) and does not make much sense,'' many students comment on having a different understanding of what grammar is. The same student elaborates by saying, ''In the past I simply memorized terms and was able to match a definition to them but did not learn how to point things out in my own writing. Now grammar makes sense to me, and it makes me realize what a complicated language English is.''

This student may have pinpointed the core of the problem with the teaching of grammar in the schools. From our research and from students' reports, the teaching of grammar in the schools is mostly sketchy, unsystematic, and error-oriented. One student says, ''In high school I never spent more than three days discussing grammar, and that was usually only just before a standardized test.'' Another student says, ''In the past, when I thought about grammar, the first thing that came to mind was the prescriptive grammar that is drilled into students' heads in junior high and high school. Now I realize that grammar involves more than simple rules to follow; it involves a complete exploration of language.'' Perhaps another student puts it best when she says, ''Before I enrolled in this course, I could not identify the whole picture of grammar. It is not only a subject that consists of rules. It is also a subject that contains unconscious knowledge that has come to life.'' Thus, in approaching grammar systematically, we have succeeded in giving students a better understanding of what it is as well as an interest in viewing it as a subject for continued study. One student says,

"Studying grammar is a life-long practice that we are constantly struggling to master. With practice and experience, I think that I will finally, while not mastering it by any means, come to grips with it." These students have learned that discussing and analyzing language can be an engrossing activity and that therefore they can enjoy discussing language as they enjoy discussing literature and writing.

Students' attitudes about the study of grammar have indeed changed even though not all the students in this one-semester course have succeeded in acquiring "the whole picture." Not all the students prefer the global theoretical assumptions that underlie all grammar instruction. Some of them finish the course still struggling with abstract concepts such as the difference between form and function, the recursiveness of structures, and the interpretations of different syntactic functions. But despite varying degrees of success in performance, student approval of the methodology and content of the course has been almost unanimous.

At least no one prefers to be taught grammar through mindless exercises and rigid rules. Even the few students who earn low grades have positive things to say about their experiences in the class. One such student says grudgingly, "As far as grammar classes go, this one was rather interesting. The way you taught the class made the subject more interesting than usual and didn't put me to sleep once." Finally, one student sums up how she feels about the course thus: "on 'How do I feel about studying grammar?' Simply put, I love it. Sounds rather crazy, but I really do enjoy learning grammar. I suppose that it has to do with the fact that I now am able to understand it more clearly. I started the semester with a fear and hatred of grammar, and now I am no longer scared, and I love it. I am glad that you had such great teaching methods to make me understand and love grammar." Another student adds her voice to the chorus, "Not only did I learn more than I thought there was to know about grammar, but I had a good time in the process." For many future teachers grammar loving is grammar learning. It remains to be seen what these students will do in their own classrooms, but since we know that teachers teach the way they were taught, we have faith and hope that this new generation will love what they do in the language classroom.

The negative affect caused great damage over the years. Our students say either they "can't remember very many rules" or they recollect vague rules of punctuation ("where the apostrophe goes"), spelling ("*i* before *e* except after *c*"), and usage ("don't use double negatives or *ain't*"). Even if some of these rules reflect present standard usage, many students report their instruction to have been so unimaginative and indiscriminate that students mixed useful descriptive algorithms with ridiculous "rules" ("never end a sentence with a preposition").

Strangely, some of the least useful classroom lore seems to stick most persistently ("don't start a sentence with *because*"), even when the best writers of the times consistently use these forms. Students therefore memorize indiscriminately to pass tests, easily forget important structures, and retain details that are often either useless or wrong. They then quake in fear when teachers mark their papers because they do not "know" grammar.

Such uses of grammar certainly explain the research that indicates a negative connection between grammar and writing. If grammar instruction has been used only to punish students for their language choices, then certainly they are right to want to avoid grammar. This fear of punishment must be replaced with an anticipation of success and enjoyment if future teachers are to be successful in their grammar classrooms. The new methodology described here will change the nature of grammar instruction. Then perhaps writing instruction will profit from the positive affect whether or not students actively monitor usage choices when composing, revising, or editing. Certainly they will not carry with them false information gleaned from misremembered or misapplied grammar instruction. They will not bear the marks of red pens, nor carry the weight of misinformation and absurd usage rules. They will learn instead a love of language nurtured by teachers who themselves love grammar.

15

Taking Computer-Assisted Grammar Instruction to New Frontiers

Eric H. Hobson

Discussions of the formal role prescriptive and descriptive grammars should play in writing instruction have been founded on the presupposition that written language is produced and transmitted on/via paper. Until recent years, this assumption has held. Given the rapid and ongoing developments in computer technologies, however, this assumption is no longer viable in the broader societal context or within the boundaries of education. Every day, more writers work almost entirely without pens or paper, via keyboards attached to powerful word processors, affixing language to no other page than the electronic. Likewise, much writing takes place in temporal relationships heretofore inconceivable: for instance, the explosion in electronic communications technologies in the past two decades has created a substantial amount of written language that exists nowhere except in a virtual space created and maintained by systems of interconnected computers.

What the changing face of writing technologies means for traditional views of grammar instruction within writing instruction is not yet determined. Educational publishers and many educational software designers would have us believe that the current generation of "grammar" software is a pedagogical panacea. These programs' virtues, notwithstanding, the proliferation of computer-assisted instruction (CAI) programs designed to "teach" and "test/check" grammar, editing, and writing skills, provides a glimpse into the probable directions in which grammar instruction as part of CAI educational environments is moving.

But current levels of sophistication at the nexus of technology and pedagogy do not allow more than armchair speculation about the future of CAI aimed at helping students develop an understanding of and an agility with the grammatical structures that undergird the languages they speak and write. Are we nearing a time when, as with the characters of *Star Trek: The Next Generation*, it will be possible to hold meaningful conversations with computers? In keeping with the flavor of this science fiction-influenced train of thought, are universal translators like those the crew of the U.S.S. Enterprise uses to engage speakers of other languages in syntactically-, semantically-, culturally-acceptable oral and written discourse possible? No. However much we wish for computers sufficiently advanced to work effectively and efficiently at processing and generating natural languages, however much we might like computers to assist students in developing agility and familiarity with the prestige dialects and grammars of English, we are just beginning to develop a sense of the enormity of such a task in terms of hardware technologies, software sophistication, and research and development investments of time and money. In the meantime, we continue to try to integrate into writing classrooms, writing centers, and writers' processes the rather crude, extremely varied, and limited computer resources available to most language educators.

If we believe that resolution to major pedagogical and technological questions does not exist somewhere over the horizon, this chapter fits in nicely at the end of a collection of essays that themselves foreground a similar lack of resolution to a question of educational policy: what role should grammar instruction play in the teaching of writing? While this issue typically elicits polarized responses from educators, parents, and community members, the question of how best to implement the instructional programs that result from these responses, especially in conjunction with available technologies, resists instantaneous polarization. I suspect the reasons behind a lack of definitive stances have to do with:

1. a lack of familiarity among language arts and composition teachers about the abilities and limitations of existing computer-based educational technologies;

2. obvious limitations inherent in the current generation of computer-based grammar instruction/remediation programs because of the programming languages and structures through which these programs have been created; and,

3. ongoing developments in electronic-based educational research and development.

Working from these assumptions, I attempt to provide (1) a topographic overview of the state of development of current resources for computer-assisted grammatical instruction, and (2) an introduction to the directions that the leading edge of computer hardware and software may take computer-assisted writing instruction with regards to grammar instruction particularly.

I'm looking at the high spots in the terrain of educational computing in general and in language instruction specifically. For in-depth analysis of the specific programs developed for teaching natural languages, look to the trade literature and to the on-line discussion groups whose central concern is keeping on top of these developments.

Current CAI Applications

Software marketed as writing aids or guaranteeing to clean up a writer's prose tend to fall into two broad categories: grammatical drill exercises and text checkers.

Discussing the pedagogical limitations of computer-based drill exercises for second language instruction, Mark Larsen notes that for the most part, an old, less-accepted language- acquisition paradigm, one heavily influenced by behaviorist models of education, served as the foundation on which many early computer-based language education resources were developed:

> Few programmers had a specific methodology in mind when they wrote their first CAI drill. Inspired by the interactive potential of the computer, they dusted off their language workbooks from a bygone era and reworked the material as software . . .
>
> Most CAI packages are subsequently a throwback to the pre-proficiency era, when grammar rules and translation were believed to be the fastest path to second language acquisition. Indeed, they are often little more than electronic workbooks, with fill-in-the-blank, transformation, substitution, and matching exercises. (939)

Within such a developmental history, it is not surprising that (1) many of the computer-based educational materials on the market today are nothing more than old workbooks and handbooks in electronic form, and (2) many writing teachers react negatively to these products. They ask, "Why would these instructional practices work any more successfully housed in a computer than empirical and anecdotal evidence demonstrated they did when these activities appeared on paper?"

While the drill approach to language acquisition evidenced in many computer grammar instruction programs is nothing new, the same cannot be said for the programs available that claim to "clean up" writers' texts. Grammar, spell, and style checkers are unique programs that have made a noticeable appearance in educational settings. Existing under the ubiquitous heading "grammar checkers," these programs are omnipresent in commercial, personal, and educational computing. Every competitive word processing program contains a spell checking protocol, and many have added grammar/style checkers as standard subprograms. WordPerfect 6.0, for instance, includes Grammatik 5 as an active item in the program.

Grammatik 5 is a fairly standard example of the text checkers on the market; it contains a set of programs that scan a text looking for appearances of certain sets of defined "errors." Typically, these "errors" fall into three categories: spelling, usage, capitalization and punctuation. For our concerns these categories are more important than the other whistles and bells contained in these programs. Such items as readability analyses, word count, and word frequencies do not fall into what the public recognizes in the broad and amorphous category "grammar." Using protocols that scan the target document, these programs flag any item that does not conform to the set of rules that defines the program's understanding of acceptable prose.

Lloyd Rieber maintains that grammar checkers elicit the type of polarized response typical of all things associated with grammar. "The subject of numerous reviews and much discussion by software vendors," he writes, "grammar checkers are long on promises and, some would say, short on delivery." He continues,

> Writers and English teachers who have experimented with them tend to either love them or hate them, but one message is clear–grammar checkers cannot be relied on to correct grammar, only to point out possible problems, and then only in a narrow range. . . . they cannot check for meaning. Even gibberish will receive a favorable analysis if it doesn't violate one of the grammar checker's dictionary of questionable phrases or construction. (57)

Limitations of These Systems

The primary educational limitation for computerized grammar checkers and for drill-based grammatical exercises is that they only perform finite operations within tightly-bounded parameters. Such limits would be no problem if English—and every other natural language—were likewise constrained. Natural languages, unlike artificial languages such as mathematics and computer programming languages, however, are plastic. Hypothetically, they are infinite. Undoubtedly they are, to some extent, unpredictable. Many rules that govern natural languages are highly idiosyncratic, even to the point of being illogical and inefficient.

Given natural languages' resistance to the prescriptive and restrictive grammatical systems on which most computer writing programs aimed at student populations are built, Jerome Bump argues that

> the limitations of the stylistic analysis packages are pretty evident. They can only search and flag certain patterns which have been chosen, perhaps somewhat arbitrarily, by the software designer. The student and instructor must decide after they have flagged the particular patterns whether they are really problems or not. (126)

This situation is for some teachers a half-empty/half-full glass type of situation, a field-dependent good/bad situation: for instance, many writing center

personnel optimistically see this situation as an opportunity for individualized instruction.

The ambiguity of the situation leads Bump to note a more important
limitation with these programs and their inability to really do much complicated or meaningful interaction with and reaction to texts produced in
authentic situations. While programmers may write a set of rules by which
to identify passive constructions as an error (which most text checkers on the
market do), the program can in no way "fix" the "error" because the computer has no way to *understand* the author's intent in creating the sentence
in its original form. Rieber comments that students using grammar checkers'
passive voice protocols with his composition classes found that the programs
spotted

> any form of the verb *be* followed by a past participle, whether the passive
> was appropriate or not. . . . The decision about whether to use the passive
> voice or not hinged on what the writer *wanted to do*. No algorithm, no code,
> no program could be developed to analyze a writer's intent. (57–58)

Critiquing the inability of grammar checkers to deal productively with the
elasticity of English sentences—their ability of syntactically correct sentences to be semantically meaningless—Bump offers the following lesson:

> The program must first "'disambiguate" sentences before it can analyze
> them and is thus completely baffled by a sentence such as "the chair
> speaks." In other words it is up against its limits when it encounters meta-
> phor, paradox, or ambiguity, the ingredients of much of creativity as we
> know it. . . . To construct an invention heuristic which can manage paradox
> is the next frontier. (130)

The foundational problem here is the inflexibility of the majority of
educational computer software aimed at teaching students grammatical concepts in any of a number of natural languages (English, German, French,
Russian, etc.). I use "inflexibility" here on purpose for the multiple meanings it can bring to the current and following discussion. Based almost
entirely on traditional prescriptive grammars, most of the educational grammar software on the market interprets prose within tightly-controlled and
static boundaries: e. g., passive voice is incorrect, as are contractions, variant
spellings, and capitalizations of individual words. Likewise, these programs
are inflexible at the architectural level of their programming. Their programs
are based on a binary logic that is not capable of adapting to situationality,
contextuality, intentionality, any of the number of linguistic pressures that
help to determine the grammatical "correctness," and more importantly, the
semantic acceptability of a given utterance or textual string.

At a basic level, the underlying problem with computerized grammar
programs is simple: "Some errors in writing are more easily detected by
machine than are others" (Hull, Ball, Fox, Levin, McCutchen 106). Describing an attempt to construct a more complex program than spell checkers that

use basic algorithms, Glynda Hull, Carolyn Ball, James Fox, Lori Levin, and Deborah McCutchen explain that

> it is a much more complicated matter to detect most other errors, errors in syntax and agreement and grammar, for these errors have to do, not with single word forms, but with how several word forms are combined into larger units. To detect such errors, we are developing search algorithms that have a more sophisticated pattern-matching capability than do spell checkers; we call this approach "augmented pattern-matching." Our eventual package will also include a parser, a program that analyzes the grammaticality of a sentence, [because] pattern-matching has its limits. (106)

Issues for CAI Research

What is particularly interesting about this problem and its implications for language education is the amount of attention that is directed to the issue in foreign language education and in linguistic studies. Using grammar instruction to teach uses of and facility with written language, these disciplines are further along in researching the pedagogical and technical issues than are English scholars. While compositionists by and large, with a few notable exceptions, have not explored the issues of *why* and *how* one might incorporate the computer as an instructional tool for mastering a new language—be it Standard Edited English or French—foreign language educators are exploring both the practical and theoretical implications presented by the current and evolving computer technologies.

And yet, although they may be quite a bit ahead of much of the English community in their research into and development of software for language education, the foreign language education community, like English studies, has had to address questions of how, why, and if to use computers to work with grammar instruction. In their *EDUCOM REVIEW* article, Nina Garrett, James Noblitt and Frank Dominguez present a thesis about computers, grammar, and foreign language learning that mirrors discussions found in *College English, College Composition and Communication, Composition Studies/ Freshman English News*, among other journals interested in issues related to the teaching of writing and the role that formal instruction in grammar should play in that activity. They write:

> Although foreign language educators have studied, and heatedly debated the value of learners' acquisition of *grammar rules*, until recently neither our theory or our research tools have allowed research on learners' acquisition of *grammatical concepts*. If we work from the hypothesis, implicit or explicit in many approaches to language acquisition theory, that language learners structure their own idiosyncratic rules of thumb for connecting meaning and form in the language being learned, we can design language tasks to require the production or comprehension of meaningful language in

contexts that allow unprecedented insights into learner language processing. Exploring those individual rules, the ways they overlap with and differ from the "real" rules of the language, and the ways they confirm or challenge the prediction of linguistic and psycholinguistic theory could contribute to a radically ambitious research agenda for foreign language education—and again, the findings would be equally significant to the improvement of pedagogy and to the development of interdisciplinary theory. (41)

This emphasis on thinking of language instruction as an integrated and highly complex system of linguistic and extra-linguistic influences most closely joins the efforts of English and foreign language educators as they work to build an understanding of the potentials for CAI as more than the myriad types of computer packages currently dominating the CAI "grammar" market. There exists a chasm of ideology and philosophy between those investigating how best to integrate the computer in language instruction and those supplying the majority of the hardware and software for this educational activity. John Higgins sees the chasm as one of competing educational paradigms and limited foresight. At the root of the problem was an inability on the part of users and suppliers to work collaboratively to define the philosophical bases on which the educational materials would be developed for the computer environment. That working at cross purposes extended to understandings of what potentials were represented by emerging technologies. Continuing his commentary on problems observed in CAI applications for language education, Higgins recounts that, "A number of commentators assumed that this was an inevitable constraint of computers." Bringing the debate up to date, he writes

> The current view, however, is that it was a failure of imagination. Of course drill and practice have value, if for no other reason than that learners sometimes demand it and feel comfortable with it. But to assume that a computer is capable of nothing else is to misunderstand grossly the nature of computers. (169)

As Garrett, Noblitt, and Dominguez make clear, the issue of computer-based language instruction is more than a problem for isolated academic departments. The challenge is truly interdisciplinary, offering educators from across the curriculum opportunities to bridge disciplinary boundaries to learn more about how language works, how humans process language, how computers can emulate this process, how pedagogy intersects with technology. The transdisciplinary project that Garrett, Noblitt, and Dominguez argue for not only has implications for language instruction, but for how educational institutions conceive of themselves and allocate their resources. Positing that "the most fundamental shift implied by the disciplinary perspective afforded us by these technological possibilities is in the epistemology of the discipline," they remind us that, "Traditionally, knowledge of a foreign language consisted of mastering a number of items or facts about the language, just as knowing the literature consisted of knowing a body of facts about it" (42). Going into more detail, however, they move from a theoretical discussion of epistemologies and their influence on educational practice to discuss the role that computer technology can play in this interdisciplinary project:

> Although computers can certainly still provide instruction to students in those facts, they can also make the primary data directly available to students, give them the opportunity to browse and explore, and structure an environment within which they can organize and interpret the data for themselves. Knowledge so acquired is not a set of items or facts but is a process, a way of thinking or making connections, a dynamic and flexible structure of relationships. (42)

The Next Generation

It might be inferred from the information presented above that, although a great deal of energy has been spent producing computer programs for grammar instruction and checking, little of that work has been of particular value. I do find the majority of commercially produced educational computing materials targeted for language instruction redundant and based on questionable assumptions about differences between language competence and acquisition. However, the next generation of programs promises to be more complex in its language processing abilities, less structuralist and hierarchical, and more phenomenological and egalitarian in its philosophical and ideological assumptions.

But, to fault the current generation of programs is easy. And, as Larsen points out the problem is actually quite complex:

> Language is a human phenomenon that involves more than grammar; it entails sounds, feelings, and cultural nuances. But such things are not easily entered through a keyboard and displayed on a monitor. Until computers are provided ears and mouths, their language abilities will be severely limited. (938)

While the technology to give computers ears, mouths, possibly emotions and cultural sensitivity is, as far as I am aware, only available through science fiction, recent efforts by programmers and educators—linguists, psychologists, mathematicians, compositionists—are creating exciting results.

Working with developments in the field of artificial intelligence (AI), researchers are experimenting with programs which they hope to refine into "intelligent courseware," what Carol Chapelle describes as "software which uses encoded information to create a learning environment and to respond to students in a way that appears to be similar to what a person would" (59). "Intelligence" in this context is determined by the computer program's ability to carry out defined tasks; the more difficult the task, the more difficult it is to develop a program architecture sufficient to grapple with the increasing complexities of the task. When considered in the arena of computer-assisted language learning (CALL), the challenge of creating Intelligent CALL is immense. And yet, these researchers are integrating into their programs other extremely complex and powerful expert systems which include parsing technologies and microworlds within which a totally bounded environment can be programmed in sufficient detail to allow the computer to interact with a human user at levels approaching "intelligent."

In fact, the levels of "intelligence" currently being programmed into computers for educational use give one pause. Garret, Noblitt, and Dominguez suggest that beyond its sheer computational abilities,

> an even more intriguing role for the computer lies in its potential for inter-
> acting directly with the learner in the act of producing language, in addition
> to its ability to respond specifically to learners' input and thus to shape their
> subsequent utterances. The computer not only can track the processing but
> can also immediately analyze the product and present learners with the
> analysis as feedback—instantaneously, while they are still in the mind-set
> that produced it—and ask them to revise their processing with its help. The
> detailed data on these interactions provide extraordinarily interesting evi-
> dence of what the learners think their errors are and what they think they
> need to know to correct their errors– evidence of how they think language
> works. (41)

The appearance of Intelligent CALL is, however, a long way down the road. Most development in the areas of AI and interactive programming is not for the educational market. The major players in this area of development are outside of educational settings. Much of the cutting edge work at the moment is underway as part of defense contractors' efforts to produce military equipment—particularly fighter aircraft—that operate more rapidly and more precisely using combinations of interactive voice and visual commands between the pilot and computer.

Because the programmers developing this generation of hardware and software traditionally work outside educational settings, with procedures that achieve other goals than those typically ascribed to educational institutions, the theories, philosophies, and ideologies on which the resulting programming stands are not conducive to speedy transfer to the proactive classroom. Additionally, because the funding required to develop, test, and market these technologies is great, educational applications will not be high priority. Garret, Noblitt, and Dominguez note that "Vendors and distributors of hardware and software value the education market but have a generally inadequate understanding of the disciplinary structures and forces that shape it; the foreign language sector is a relatively small one and its needs are difficult to understand or predict" (44). We are talking about highly specialized markets.

Language instruction, regardless of the numbers of students in classrooms, is a relatively small, extremely risky market for computerized materials. There is the constant promise of little return on the investment necessary to create the instructional programs made possible by developing computer program architectures. Applications of expert systems, AI, and highly-interactive programming will most likely arrive in language instruction as trickle-down technology.

The New Frontier and Issues to Consider

The research underway in CAI and CALL is promising. With every promise, however, there lies a responsibility. And for language educators that responsibility is to use the lag time between development of these technologies and their classroom application to think through many questions that will be issues of critical concern such as the following.

What Implications Do These Emerging Technologies Have for Teacher Training?

Regardless of how far the programming capabilities come for creating CALL environments that are able to work with students in "intelligent" ways, teachers in first and second language instruction must be trained to work daily in classrooms that are computerized to varying extents. On the subject of teacher preparation for computerized learning environments, "Preparing English Teachers for the Virtual Age: The Case for Technology Critics," Cynthia Selfe forwards five goals for teacher education in the language arts:

1. Prepare English teachers to be lifelong learners in technological environments.
2. Prepare English teachers to see technology critically, as it functions within complex social, economic, and political contexts.
3. Prepare English composition teachers to be classroom researchers who systematically observe technology and its relationship to learning.
4. Prepare English composition teachers to be architects of computer-supported learning spaces and virtual learning spaces.
5. Prepare English composition teachers to be humanists.

There must be a cadre of teachers who can use computers in their writing and literature classes. The technologies are coming. The hardware, software, and support services are advancing at an exponential rate, making available opportunities for instruction that were once the stuff of science fiction and teachers' daydreams: interactive distance learning, community participation in class activities, global education, instantaneous and expansive access to entire libraries of information, real audiences for student writing, virtual collaborative projects. Whether these technologies are used in educationally responsible and consistent ways depends on how the generation of teachers whose entire careers will be spent in technologically advanced classrooms—physical and virtual—will not happen if left to chance.

Will Intelligent CALL Resist Prescription?

An issue of vital importance in thinking about the role of CAI and grammar instruction is whether, when packaged on hard or floppy disk, the instruction offered about grammatical structures and usage will become the new orthodoxy to supplant that of the handbook? Given the architecture of the developing programs, especially with their use of parsing protocols, it is possible to create intelligent CALL systems that would be pluralist in their approach to grammar and usage.

Most CALL programs under development have discarded prescriptive grammars as their foundational grammar and use transformational grammars in their programming. Transformational grammars are more consistent, and consistency is essential when programming a binary system. ("Fuzzy logic" protocols, however, offer the possibility of working effectively with ambiguity.) As a result, it would be easier to program instruction in Black English Vernacular (BEV) than in Standard Edited English because BEV's grammar is the more economical and consistent. Conceivably, an intelligent CALL program could work with a student to explore the writer's intent for the text under consideration, examine the intended audience, context, level of formality and familiarity, and rhetorical situation to determine what grammatical options would be most appropriate. Whether or not these egalitarian possibilities are enacted, however, is a political issue.

What Will Be the Response to Emerging Virtual Grammar(s)?

If the issue of what role grammar is to play in writing instruction has not been settled yet, when the majority of writing instruction is done in paper-based classrooms, the issue will only get thornier as writers write more often and to developing audiences in virtual spaces. Because usage controls a language's grammar, how English will be used in electronic communications *will* have a marked impact on English grammar.

Are we, as language educators and as a culture, prepared to accept what may be fairly abrupt changes in orthography, typography, syntax, and semantics made possible (or demanded) in virtual writing spaces by electronic communications technologies? This question is important because writers who participate in the communication along the "information highway" of

Internet are developing a virtual grammar uniquely suited to that communication medium. particularly striking about this emerging grammar is its blending of spoken and written forms of English, especially with its mixing of levels of formality and informality in address. Just as the invention of the printing press altered English by ushering in a desire to formalize and systematize the English language, so too may the invention and rapid spread of computer-based communication alter the language.

Current CAI grammar instruction is rudimentary. In many aspects, what is offered teachers, students, and the general public is little more than handbooks and workbooks transferred to disk. But even though the future for CAI and Intelligent CALL is bright, we should not go running to educational distributors just yet. There is a great deal of research to do. As Higgins sums up the situation,

> It is not possible to make natural conversation, in whatever medium, with a computer, as one would with a human being, and it is unlikely to be possible for many years. The friendly and chatty robots of Star Wars are creatures of fantasy. This is not an inherent limitation of the technology, but rather of our own ignorance of what is involved in understanding language, of how the human mind brilliantly draws on its diverse store of knowledge and uses it to make sense of what it hears and reads. (170)

16

Correctness or Clarity? Finding Answers in the Classroom and the Professional World

Neil Daniel and Christina Murphy

The Apparent Crisis in Literacy

With grim persistence the nation's educational leaders, or some group of them, declare one literacy crisis after another and in each crisis issue a call, by now a familiar chant, to teach the basics. A 1993 survey of private and public educators indicates "a near-unanimous worry" that students are inadequately prepared for college. Trustees of the state and city universities of New York promise to develop guidelines in each subject area and urge a return to teaching the basics (Bauder).

Our academic colleagues identify the problem simply enough: English departments are failing. Their solution comes from the Vince Lombardi school of instruction; drill the students thoroughly in grammar, preferably before they get to college, and test them carefully. With a rigorous program of grammar drill and testing, we can save those students capable of mastering their mother tongue. Better yet, we can get rid of those who never should have been admitted.

Yet the crisis never ends, regardless of the remedies. At the heart of the problem is the term *grammar* and what it signifies. Linguists, school teachers, and copy editors use *grammar* quite differently from one another and in ways that shed little light on the recurrent complaint. What we call grammar comprises at least three discrete levels of human behavior: (1) grammar as a field of inquiry, a branch of the social science of linguistics; (2) grammar as internalized language rules (Noam Chomsky's *competence*) or an abstract system (Ferdinand de Saussure's *la langue*) that enables us to create and utter spoken language; and (3) grammar as a set of conventions, collectively known as usage, that govern written discourse (Francis, Gleason, Crowley). Those who complain about student writing typically believe students have inadequate or defective grammar in the second sense. The linguistic truth is that all normal humans have full control of the grammar they use every day. When non-specialists talk about grammar as it relates to writing, they usually have in mind correctness of form and observing the rules—that is, usage conventions.

What non-specialists often fail to realize, however, is that usage conventions vary with the writing situation. Serious writing, writing that matters in educational settings or in the workplace, is done in a context, and the context provides the manuscript conventions as well as methods of presenting information that characterize proficient writing in each specialized area. What counts as appropriate style or correct grammar is different for a set of clinical notes, a review of journal articles, or a business letter.

Perhaps more damaging than not knowing what to call grammar or the basics is not understanding how writing skills are acquired. Writing develops as a learning behavior, as opposed to a performance skill. Many educators assume writing is a record of speech or a window into fully developed thought. The truth is that writing is a developmental skill, a part of learning (Russell, Vygotsky, Bruner). We acquire our ability to write the same way we acquire spoken language, by exposure and long practice, by error and repeated correction. In the matter of acquisition, what distinguishes written discourse from spoken language is that writing takes longer to master. The acquisition is still in progress when students enter college and often when they leave college to enter the workplace.

These two misunderstandings about language development and its relation to grammar account for what Mike Rose calls "the myth of transience" (1985, 355). According to this romantic misunderstanding, the crisis in writing is a temporary aberration, usually blamed on television, overcrowded and drug-infested schools, or the break-up of the American family. Before the collapse of academic values, students wrote well. We can return to that golden day by hiring specialists (usually English teachers) to train the students, and by allowing the scholars in other fields to conduct their research or to teach the content of their disciplines without being distracted by writing problems.

A collateral version of the myth of transience is the conviction that students can master writing skills the way they master the principles of accounting. Once they pass the proficiency examination, they can be "certified," as accountants or life underwriters are certified, can hang their certificates on the wall, and can get on with the real business of education.

These misunderstandings would be no more than a nuisance if they were confined to those outside composition studies. In fact they are institutionalized in writing programs across the nation. A substantial portion of writing instruction in first-year composition courses nation-wide is devoted to rooting out error and satisfying the demand for certifiable proficiency. In this chapter we argue that writing teachers must reconsider how the experts construct programs to teach writing either in the academic world or in the professional world. Putting instruction into a real context can transform education on our campuses and in corporate settings, changing writing from an occasional performance to a life-long learning behavior and blurring the distinctions among undergraduate education, postgraduate education, and professional training. Shifting the attention of writing instructors from error correction to achieving clarity and polish will allow writing professionals to set realistic goals and provide appropriate instruction.

College Classroom—The Quest for Correctness

We concentrate first on writing instruction in the classroom. We examine how writing is taught at the boundary between the upper reaches of secondary school and the beginning of college because the transition from high school to college is thought by many to be the critical screening stage. Students are expected to enter higher education well prepared for college writing. To the degree our students are not well prepared, it is the mission of first-year composition courses to correct the deficiencies and get the students ready.

To discover the underlying assumptions of writing instruction at this boundary, we turn to what one state education agency requires its high school students to know and how the state tests its students at exit. In adopting this approach, we follow the lead of Mike Rose, who blames our reductionist writing instruction on reductionist assessments. "For evaluation schemes reveal powerful assumptions about the object of evaluation" (1983, 1985, 325).

The statement of Essential Elements developed by the Texas Education Agency (TEA) is intended to inform the curriculum and instruction of Texas English teachers, grades 9–12. We take this statement of curriculum requirements, effective September 1992, to be typical, if not perfectly representative, of the requirements of state agencies across the nation (see Appendix 1).

The Essential Elements and the corresponding testing program in Texas make the outcome requirements of a typical writing program clear. Students are expected to understand the constituents of good writing and to perform on demand. Despite the gesture toward teaching and examining "writing process" (a concept without definition) and the rhetorical concerns of purpose and audience, the instructional guidelines and the testing program target the elements implied by a traditional taxonomic analysis of sentence-level grammar: classification of sentences and identification of parts of speech. The exit test does not require students to name such concepts or recognize the terminology, but it asks students to make usage choices that depend on them (see Appendix 2).

That the same requirements are repeated in every grade, with only slight changes between ninth and twelfth, might be taken as encouraging evidence that those who guide the teaching of high school English accept writing as a developmental activity that matures steadily throughout a student's learning years. Yet identification and elimination of error are high priorities for success at the pre-college level. This is the composition priority students bring with them as they cross the threshold of higher education.

History is on the side of this approach to teaching writing, often identified as "current traditional." For much of this century, writing instruction sought clarity and polish by attacking error at the sentence level and assuming beginning writers could find their way from correct sentence patterns to organized and lucid prose. *Descriptive English Grammar* (1931, 1950) by Homer House and Susan Harman represents the traditional grammar books that have shaped composition instruction for decades. *Descriptive English Grammar* presents morphology and syntax as these elements of grammar were taught before the field was captured by professional linguists—the structural linguists and the transformational grammarians. Typical of the approach, still apparent in most modern handbooks and the Texas testing program, is its taxonomy of sentences, classified according to clause structure—simple, compound, complex, and compound-complex (202–203)—or according to general purpose—declarative, interrogative, imperative, and exclamatory (13–14). The book includes a descriptive analysis of clauses and phrases and traditional parts of speech, illustrating syntactic relations by means of Reed and Kellogg diagramming. An important assumption of traditional grammar is that if students master the analysis of sentences—can label parts of speech and diagram the relations between clauses and phrases—they will have the tools to construct flawless sentences. Significantly, House and Harman do not mention what it might take to compose effective sentences.

At least three studies in recent years insist that studying grammar at the sentence level has no positive affect on writing skills (Hartwell, Hillocks, Crowley). Yet this taxonomic approach to language analysis characterizes nearly every handbook in current use in college classrooms. The demand for methods of correcting error is high, and the books sell well whether they are designed for college composition courses or for seminars in the corporate world. Two frequently cited studies of the 1980s reinforce the focus on error found in House and Harman's *Descriptive English Grammar* by providing statistical analyses of errors in real-world writing. Maxine Hairston sought to identify the errors most offensive in business and the professions. Although Hairston's study embodies the common sense wisdom that all errors are not equally damaging, the implicit agenda of this article and of her work revising the *Scott, Foresman Handbook* is to identify offending errors and correct them. The errors Hairston addresses are at the sentence level.

Robert Connors and Andrea Lunsford analyzed thousands of college themes to identify the twenty most frequent errors of college students. The crucial feature of this study, its ranking of error, is preserved in the introduction to the *St. Martin's Handbook*, edited by Connors and Lunsford. The premise of Connors and Lunsford mimics that of Hairston; no one can correct everything at once. It makes sense, given the limits of time and energy among developing writers, to concentrate on those flaws in usage that are most prevalent, the errors most students most often commit. If we accept that all writers are in some sense developing writers, we can leave the less frequent errors to some other time and rely on the writers to master them on their own.[1]

Yet the success of an error-centered approach is dubious. Our colleagues still complain that students are unable to write. They still cite punctuation errors, frequent misspelling, and confusion over the placement of modifiers as evidence that our system has failed. In the process they keep alive a college-level composition industry that repeats the instruction for students who have successfully completed their high school education. The best construction that can be put on college composition courses is that they continue the high school instruction, providing a transition to college education, raising the stakes, and reminding students that, no matter what their educational level, someone is always ready to snag them if they wander into error. At their worst, first- and second-year composition courses are bereft of content or context, unmoored to recognizable educational objectives.

This is not to say that correcting errors is the only activity in a college composition course or that we have learned nothing in the last thirty years. The discipline of composition has made important advances in understanding learning strategies, and many composition classes are based on collaborative learning techniques recommended by Kenneth Bruffee and others. Composition theorists have recognized the importance of individualized instruction, and many have adopted a conference model recommended by such masters as Donald Murray.

Yet the practical teachers, the hard-nosed realists, continue to assign exercises developed to help students correct errors. Mike Rose helps us to understand why. Rose suggests that we fail our students if we do not make them aware of how others view error (1983,1988, 327). We agree with Rose: correcting errors is a reasonable goal. It is not the same goal as writing well. But it may help the struggling student avoid the sharp red pen of the teacher in a college course. Similarly, avoiding error may protect the job of a manager in industry.

Professional World—Seeking Clarity

In the workplace as well as the classroom, correctness is a pressing concern. A symptom of this concern is a writing seminar we attended recently, a day-long professional workshop on business grammar and usage, conducted at an urban motel in Dallas by a national consulting firm. In the audience were some two hundred employees of nearly one hundred regional businesses— mid-level white-collar employees, for the most part, responsible for communications in their respective offices. Promotional materials for the seminar carried the legend, "Don't let grammar blunders ruin your message. Put an end to embarrassing mistakes today."

Toward the end of the workshop, the seminar leader mentioned that the four most common fears of American adults are (1) fear of speaking in public, (2) fear of heights, (3) fear of snakes, and (4) fear of writing. She offered no source to document this catalogue of fears. It was clear to us, however, that the seminar had been designed to capitalize on the fear of writing—indeed, to intensify that fear. The unspoken but unabashed goal of the seminar was to sell teaching materials—tapes, workbooks, and other aids on sale in the lobby outside the seminar room—to buyers who had been softened by hours of harping on the danger of making mistakes.

Often a firm will invite a writing expert to conduct a series of workshops during which a trainer/teacher pinpoints the errors, manuscript conventions, or other writing challenges that most plague office workers. Exercises for such training sessions are typically based on the written work done by the participants in the course. A good deal of the time may be spent encouraging the writers, teaching them to relax about their writing, stimulating ease and fluency in writing in the hope that a more relaxed and personal relation with composing will take some of the sting out of writing. A useful approach is to teach office employees to collaborate with one another, to seek each other's editing help, and to share possible solutions to common writing challenges.

Experience has taught us, however, that in such a setting, the attention of the participants will return again and again to avoiding error. Writers in the business world know that every piece of written work sends a subordinate message to those who read it, informing the reader whether the writer has command of the conventions of written discourse. A single error, whether of carelessness or of ignorance, can blast an otherwise useful and instructive document. Someone out there is judging us for every misspelled word the computer spelling checker fails to pick up.

Despite the nagging and persistent attention to error, newer paradigms of writing instruction in business and professional settings have shifted from sentence-level emphases to concerns with the broader organizational patterns of effective discourse. The most promising approach to effective professional writing in the last decade is reader expectation theory. Although the term was coined by George Gopen (1987, 1185), it grows out of work by Joseph Williams, whose consulting with lawyers and other professionals led to the publication of *Style: Ten Lessons in Clarity and Grace* and to the more recent *Style: Toward Clarity and Grace*. The virtue of this approach is that it departs from the preoccupation with the sentence as the single site of analysis. Without ignoring the sentence, clearly the fundamental unit of written discourse, reader expectation theory identifies patterns that control sentences in a paragraph and paragraphs in extended discourse. At the same time, the approach shifts the writer's and the teacher's attention from avoiding error to achieving clarity.

For classroom instruction, including seminars for law firms and corporations, Williams and his colleagues have developed *The Little Red Schoolhouse*. A fluid, circulating textbook and course syllabus, published only on computer disks, *The Little Red Schoolhouse* presents a method for teaching reader expectations in an advanced college course—or to seminars in business, law, and other professions. The introduction to the text makes its method clear: the Schoolhouse begins with understanding how readers read so that writers can discover how to engage their readers (4).

The Schoolhouse syllabus begins with subjects and verbs, agents and actions, elements discovered at the sentence level. The authors then move "up" to matters of information flow, from old to new, beginning to end. By the middle of the course the authors address matters of discourse structure beyond the individual sentence, and by the end of the program they are examining patterns at the highest level, discovering what makes whole essays hold together (6).

The *Little Red Schoolhouse* is an advance from studies of error at the sentence level. The writing examined in the course is by professionals—lawyers, scientists, and academic writers, rather than by college students or students of basic writing. Partly because of this difference, the study can move easily from the sentence level to the level of whole discourse. The same difference accounts for the focus on reader expectations rather than error. The writing of mature professionals is not without flaws that might be classified as errors, but the errors are not usually in understanding the linguistic code or the conventions of written English. They are flaws of construction that confound readability rather than violations of conventional syntax, morphology, or usage.

A corollary development in the quest for clarity is represented in professional writing by the plain language movement (see Gopen, 1988). The importance of plain language is explained in part by the developmental model of writing we have referred to several times. Most lawyers, engineers, accountants, and other professionals have postgraduate degrees and have spent years acquiring the vocabulary and idiom of their respective professions. Early in their careers most take pride in their ability to sound professional. As their careers advance, however, they discover their principal need is not to impress clients and colleagues with bookish terms but to communicate their meaning cleanly and efficiently. Sooner or later, most professionals strive to acquire a plain style.[2]

The move from avoiding error at the sentence level to achieving clarity at higher levels is an important move, reflecting a different audience of writers. The emphasis is on results rather than form. The interest in results accounts for the instructional method found in many professional offices—learning by doing, on-the-job scrambling, and collaboration. In many law firms, mentoring—either formal or informal—characterizes the production of documents. According to Tom Goldstein and Jethro Lieberman, junior members of a law firm write overly long documents, checking only for spelling and typographical errors, because they know every document will be reviewed, reduced, rewritten, and polished by a senior lawyer with the firm (76). The motives behind such review are both training for the junior associates and saving the firm possible embarrassment. Goldstein and Lieberman also recommend an alternative approach, present in some firms, in which a professional editor reviews the documents and imposes consistency and polish. The editor doubles as trainer.

One version of learning by doing is represented by the collaborative effort that goes into funding proposals in the scientific community. Greg Myers describes the process in his account of "The Social Construction of Two Biologists' Proposals." The combination of educational setting and practical purpose in the Myers study helps us make the point that context is crucial to serious writing. Chronicling the revision of one proposal, Myers explains,

> After about two dozen drafts (done using a text-processing program from his handwritten revisions), he [the principal investigator] gave a version to his research group. He included the guidelines and reviews of his earlier proposal, because he considered the proposal-writing process part of the education of the post-docs and graduate students working with him. (223)

The most concentrated revision of the research teams in the Myers study is focused on creating the ethos of the investigators—revising "to show that one is cautiously but competently scientific" (227). Yet the researchers are conscious of the conventions of usage and prevailing scientific style: "Both authors cut jargon wherever they recognize it . . . Both authors are cautious with neologisms . . . Both authors correct, with the help of their readers, dangling participles, faulty parallelism, and the like, although they do not identify these errors by these names" (226).

The learning method, probably unrecognized as such by the writers, is mentorship in its purest form—senior and junior members of a team collaborating on a joint project. Although the locus of the activity is the academy, the activity is not classroom teaching. It is instead a wholly practical appeal for funds. The context is desperately real.

In each of these work settings, where documents are produced by writers well out of high school or college, the pattern repeats itself. One person puts ideas in writing and seeks the help and approval of others. Often the more experienced writer okays the work or suggests corrections, and the less experienced writer returns to the draft to revise the document and get it right. Getting it right means both making the message clear and accurate and putting the message in a form that looks and sounds professional. The scribal conventions are important. The newer employee gradually learns the company style for formatting, punctuation, and forms of address. The young professional acquires the skills to write a persuasive proposal.

Individual coaching, whether conducted by a senior member of the firm or by an outside writing consultant, has two advantages over disembodied instruction that enlightened corporations and firms recognize. The first is that the instruction is focused directly on the weaknesses of the particular writer. No time is spent on matters of form the writer already has under control. The second advantage is that the work is always directed toward a specific project and therefore focused on work at hand. Moreover, the writer and the writing expert cooperate as colleagues, respecting each other's strengths, rather than as teacher and pupil. The carry-over of such training is greater than that of conventional classroom instruction.

Lessons for Composition Professionals

Our suggestions about how we should teach writing depend on three principles that have informed our chapter. The first is that when we talk about grammar as a writing issue we usually are referring to usage conventions that have little to do with logic or linguistic meaning. Writing conventions are essentially arbitrary and have more to do with class distinction, ethnic difference, apparent educational level, and professional field than they do with effective communication.

Our second principle is that writing conventions are learned the same way speech is acquired, by practice and error and correction. In practical terms, this means that every student becomes a good writer by writing with and for some audience, perhaps a teacher, who can monitor and correct the writing in progress. The implications of this claim are two: first, good writing depends on making errors in the presence of those who care about the results, and second, no one ever masters good writing once and for all.

Our third principle, implied rather than stated, is that students intelligent enough to be in college are capable of learning what they need to learn when the need is matched to their intellectual interests. The place to learn writing is in the context of learning a discipline or a profession. This pedagogical position suggests that universities should eliminate first-year composition or any other course that separates writing instruction from the disciplinary or professional context in which the writing is supposed to count.

Eliminating first-year composition would mean that, except for advanced writing-skills courses in English or journalism, the students would encounter no course dedicated to writing alone. The financial and political ramifications of such a move would be considerable, given that academic incentives are tied to course loads and credit hours generated. Funds currently used to support an industry of composition sections would have to be redirected to provide the incentive for teachers in every discipline to incorporate writing in every upper-division course. To make such a change would require a complicated arithmetic and would entail a shifting of power in the academy as well as a redefinition of responsibilities for much of the senior professoriate.

An important consequence of shutting down the first-year composition industry is that we would have to persuade faculty members in all disciplines to teach the writing of their disciplines. To teach writing in the disciplines means, in part, to teach the forms and surface conventions that characterize writing in that discipline. Teachers who concentrate on these matters teach correctness along with content—teaching both in a context that matters. What we are suggesting, of course, is writing across the curriculum. For writing across the curriculum imitates the mentoring that characterizes most professions; the professional in the discipline supervises the writing of the student until the engineering student begins to think and write like an engineer, the philosophy student begins to read, write, and think like a philosopher.

When it is successful, writing across the curriculum restores the context we have claimed is missing from the isolated, unmoored composition course. Various proponents of writing across the curriculum offer various justifications for the approach, some arguing that writing to learn overshadows learning to write, others arguing that only graduates who can write well in their disciplines will save the institution from embarrassment when the students enter professional life. Nearly all agree, however, that learning to write well is only possible if students learn "how disciplines are constituted through their discourse" (Russell 295). When students learn this, editing for correctness and clarity becomes important. Students only learn what they perceive is important. This is the strongest justification we know of for eliminating composition classes where two-thirds of the energy is devoted to inventing assignments so that students can demonstrate that they are "literate."

Removing first-year composition courses and their attendant machinery and expanding the role of writing in the disciplines would have an additional impact with funding ramifications: it would increase the role and significance of writing teachers/consultants at many university writing centers.

Since Stephen North's essay "The Idea of a Writing Center" in 1984, theorists have urged us to see the writing center not as a "house of correction" given over to remediation and functioning as a fix-it shop for poor writers, but as an integral component in the pedagogies of writing across the curriculum. The history of writing centers is largely one of expansion, with writing centers "constantly inventing new forms of instruction and reaching new audiences" (Hughes 39). "The outreach that writing centers offer at their best sends instructors into classes to teach brief units on writing, designed to help students write particular course papers" (Hughes 40). This instruction can be "a valuable tool for teaching composition strategies to students and composition philosophy to their professors" (Howard 39).

The in-process nature of writing center instruction ties writing center pedagogy to the apprenticeship learning that often characterizes business and the professions. As Stephen North states,

> Whereas in the "old" center instruction tends to take place after or apart from writing, and tends to focus on the correction of textual problems, in the "new" center the teaching takes place as much as possible during

writing, during the activity being learned, and tends to focus on the activity itself. (439)

In this way, writing centers come closer than the traditional classroom to establishing writing environments and writing demands that writers will encounter when they enter the world of work. Andrea Lunsford argues that collaboration is the norm for most professions and cites the writing center as the most natural academic domain for recognizing "the notion of knowledge as always contextually bound, as always socially constructed" (1991, 8–9).

The power of writing centers to transform college and university writing programs derives from their being "instructional hybrids" balanced between administrative aims and the traditional practices of academic departments (Murphy 284). This twofold effort, along with their ability to cross disciplinary lines unhampered, makes them saviors of a sort, offering faculty members relief from the realities of "already overburdened days" of teaching, scholarship, and committee work (Adams 73). Even in their harried environment, almost all faculty members care about teaching writing; they look for direction and support in carrying out their charge. With writing instruction shifted from made-up composition courses to the more real disciplinary contexts, writing centers will help faculty members from the whole range of disciplines with writing instruction and draw them into the structuring of writing curricula. As Stephen North suggests, "writing centers are simply manifestations—polished and highly visible—of a dialogue about writing that is central to higher education" (439).

The changes we are recommending—eliminating first-year composition, expanding writing in the disciplines and strengthening the role of writing centers—will not mean our universities will suddenly produce writers capable of flawless prose for any occasion. Outside the academy, we must teach business and the professions a similar lesson, that they should not expect what they cannot have. In every domain, those entering the field step into a foreign culture. Beginners have to learn the conventions of the workplace. Those conventions include the forms of writing as well as dress codes, office manners, and professional standards. There is this difference between writing and other routine skills: in writing, the learning goes on for the rest of every individual's life.

If institutions of higher education make the changes suggested here, we should not expect the popular press to stop proclaiming a literacy crisis every few years. But those charged with policing the crisis will spend their energies in useful ways. Eventually those responsible for writers and writing— the heads of professional firms, the trustees of state university systems, and our colleagues in every discipline—may stop wringing their hands and get to work. We'll solve the literacy crisis the only way it can be solved: writer by writer, document by document, doing the work writing is supposed to do.

Notes

1. A recent article by Parker and Campbell suggests a more sensible application of linguistic theory to the challenge of writing is to be found in the speech act theory associated with John Searle, John Austin, Paul Grice, and others. The direction suggested by Parker and Campbell would shift the attention of writing teachers from error recognition at the sentence level to applications and practice of principles borrowed from the philosophy of language. So far as we know, no wholesale shift to speech act theory has characterized writing instruction in classrooms or corporate offices.

2. Books available to help writers achieve a plain style include Wydick for lawyers, Lanham for writers in business, and Daniel for more general audiences, as well as classics by Strunk and White, Barzun, and Zinsser.

Appendix 1

Chapter 75 Curriculum

Subchapter D. Essential Elements—Grades 9–12

State Board of Education Rules
§75.61 English Language Arts
(a) English I (1 unit). English I shall include the following essential elements:

(1) Writing concepts and skills. The student shall be provided opportunities to:

(A) use the composing process to plan and generate writing;

(B) write descriptive, narrative, and expository paragraphs;

(C) write multiple-paragraph compositions incorporating information from sources other than personal experience;

(D) write informative discourse of a variety of types;

(E) write persuasive discourse of a variety of types;

(F) use the forms and conventions of written language appropriately;

(G) evaluate content, organization, topic development, appropriate transition, clarity of language, and appropriate word and sentence choice according to the purpose and audience for which the piece is intended; and

(H) proofread written work for punctuation, spelling, grammatical and syntactical errors, paragraph indentation, margins, and legibility of writing.

(2) Language concepts and skills. The student shall be provided opportunities to:

    (A) produce well-formed simple, compound, and complex sentences;

    (B) choose appropriate words to convey intended meaning;

    (C) use all parts of speech effectively in sentences;

    (D) recognize the meanings and uses of colloquialism, slang, idiom, and jargon; and

    (E) use oral language effectively in a variety of situations.

(b) English II (1 unit). English II shall include the following essential elements:

(1) Writing concepts and skills. The student shall be provided opportunities to:

    (A) use the composing process to plan and generate writing;

    (B) write descriptive, narrative, and expository paragraphs of increasing length and complexity;

    (C) write multiple-paragraph compositions incorporating outside information with documentation;

    (D) write informative discourse of a variety of types;

    (E) write persuasive discourse of a variety of types;

    (F) write literary discourse of a variety of types including character sketches, stories;

    (G) use a variety of sentence structures including simple, compound, and complex;

    (H) use the forms and conventions of written language appropriately;

    (I) evaluate content, organization, topic development, appropriate transition, clarity of language, and appropriate word and sentence choice according to the purpose and audience for which the piece is intended; and

    (J) proofread written work for punctuation, spelling, grammatical and syntactical errors, paragraph indentation, margins, and legibility of writing.

(2) Language concepts and skills. The student shall be provided opportunities to:

(A) produce well-formed simple, compound, and complex sentences;

(B) choose appropriate words to convey intended meaning;

(C) use all parts of speech effectively in sentences;

(D) use oral language effectively in a variety of situations;

(E) recognize the meanings and appropriate uses of colloquialism, slang, idiom, and jargon;

(F) vary word and sentence choice for purpose and audience; and

(G) produce sentences that convey coordinate and subordinate ideas appropriately.

(c) English III (1 unit). English III shall include the following essential elements:

(1) Writing concepts and skills. The student shall be provided opportunities to:

(A) use the composing process to plan and generate writing;

(B) refine sentences and paragraphs into compositions exhibiting unity, clarity, and coherence;

(C) write longer compositions incorporating outside information with documentation;

(D) write a variety of forms of informative and persuasive discourse;

(E) write at least one form of literary discourse;

(F) make rhetorical choices based on audience, purpose, and form;

(G) use the forms and conventions of written language appropriately;

(H) revise written work for content, organization, topic development, appropriate transition, clarity of language, and appropriate word and sentence choice according to the purpose and audience for which a piece is written;

(I) proofread written work for internal punctuation, spelling, grammatical and syntactical errors, paragraph indentation, margins, and legibility of writing; and

(J) evaluate one's own writing as well as that of others.

(2) Language concepts and skills. The student shall be provided opportunities to:

   (A) produce well-formed simple, compound, complex and compound-complex sentences;

   (B) choose appropriate words to convey intended meaning;

   (C) analyze the grammatical structure of sentences;

   (D) use oral language effectively in a variety of situations;

   (E) describe the history and major features of American dialects;

   (F) recognize the sociological functions of language; and

   (G) demonstrate facility with word analogies and other forms of advanced vocabulary development.

(d) English IV (1 unit). English IV shall include the following essential elements:

   (1) Writing concepts and skills. The student shall be provided opportunities to:

   (A) use the composing process to plan and generate writing;

   (B) refine sentences and paragraphs into compositions exhibiting unity, clarity, and coherence;

   (C) write longer compositions incorporating outside information with documentation;

   (D) write a variety of forms of informative and persuasive discourse;

   (E) write at least one form of literary discourse;

   (F) use each of the commonly recognized patterns of organization;

   (G) achieve precision in meaning through sophisticated language and rhetorical choices;

   (H) analyze the presentation of ideas in written discourse, including forms of logical reasoning, common fallacies of reasoning, and techniques of persuasive language;

   (I) use the forms and conventions of written language appropriately;

(J) revise written work for content, organization, topic develop-
     ment, appropriate transition, clarity of language, and appropri-
     ate word and sentence choice according to the purpose and
     audience for which a piece is written;

(K) proofread written work for internal punctuation, spelling,
     grammatical and syntactical errors, paragraph indentation,
     margins, and legibility of writing; and

(L) evaluate one's own writing as well as that of others.

(2) Language concepts and skills. The student shall be provided oppor-
     tunities to:

(A) produce well-formed simple, compound, complex and
     compound-complex sentences;

(B) exhibit sophisticated and precise word choice to convey
     meaning;

(C) analyze the grammatical structure of sentences;

(D) use oral language effectively in a variety of situations;

(E) describe the major features of the origins and development of
     the English language;

(F) recognize the sociological functions of the language; and

(G) demonstrate facility with word analogies and other forms of
     advanced vocabulary development.

Appendix 2

Texas Assessment of Academic Skills
Instructional Targets
English Language Arts
Exit Level

DOMAIN: Written Communication

**Objective 1: The student will respond appropriately in a
written composition to the purpose/audience specified in a
given topic.**

- Vary word and sentence choice for purpose and audience
- Write compositions incorporating information from sources other
  than personal experience
- Write informative discourse of a variety of types

- Write persuasive discourse of a variety of types
- Use various composition models as aids in developing writing skills
- Use formal and informal language appropriately
- Use aural and visual stimuli for writing
- Evaluate content

Objective 2: The student will organize ideas in a written composition on a given topic.

- Use the composing process to plan and generate writing
- Evaluate organization of writing
- Write descriptive, narrative, and expository paragraphs

Objective 3: The student will demonstrate control of the English language in a written composition on a given topic.

- Evaluate appropriate transition, clarity of language, and appropriate word and sentence choice
- Use the forms and conventions of written language appropriately
- Use parts of speech effectively in sentences
- Use the fundamentals of grammar

Objective 4: The student will generate a written composition that develops/supports/ elaborates the central idea stated in a given topic.

- Demonstrate clear and logical thinking in support and development of a central idea
- Evaluate topic development

Objective 5: The student will recognize appropriate sentence construction within the context of a written passage.

- Recognize complete sentences and avoid fragments and run-ons
- Combine sentence parts and sentences to produce a variety of sentence structures including simple, compound, and complex

Objective 6: The student will recognize appropriate English usage within the context of a written passage.

- Use common affixes to change words from one part of speech to another
- Use correct subject-verb agreement with nouns, personal pronouns, indefinite pronouns, and compound subjects, and use correct pronoun-antecedent agreement

- Recognize correct verb tense and correct form of tense of irregular verbs, and avoid faulty shifts in tense
- Use the appropriate forms of adjectives and adverbs and the correct case of pronouns, and avoid the use of double negatives

Objective 7: The student will recognize appropriate spelling, capitalization, and punctuation within the context of a written passage.

- Use the fundamentals of spelling
- Use appropriate capitalization
- Use the fundamentals of punctuation

Afterword: Repositioning Grammar in Writing Classes of the Future

Susan Hunter

In "Why I Write," Joan Didion distinguishes what Martha Kolln or Rei Noguchi might call her "natural" grammatical sense from an acquired knowledge of grammatical rules; she writes that

> Grammar is a piano I play by ear, since I seem to have been out of school the year the rules were mentioned. All I know about grammar is its infinite power. To shift the structure of a sentence alters the meaning of that sentence, as definitely and inflexibly as the position of a camera alters the meaning of the object photographed. Many people know about camera angles now, but not so many know about sentences. The arrangement of words matters, and the arrangement you want can be found in the picture in your mind. (139)

I wasn't "out of school the year the rules were mentioned," and so, while I learned how to diagram sentences expertly and how to manage the grammar of Latin and Old and Middle English classics well enough to translate them into modern English, I do not do so "by ear." Now as a writer and a teacher of writing, I feel a sense of disjunction: on the one hand, I subscribe to what Wendy Bishop has called the "examined process" classroom; on the other, I want to share my acquired knowledge of grammatical concepts with the writers in my classes. I suspect that many compositionists share my dilemma. And that was my motivation for inviting other college writing teachers to examine their attitudes about grammar and speculate about its place in writing instruction.

We have much to learn from these compositionists. Although they do not all advocate the same degree of emphasis or method for incorporating grammar into writing instruction, the eclectic mix of essays in this collection reveals positive attitudes, well-reasoned positions, and innovative approaches toward grammar in college writing classes. All these teachers believe that indeed there are many places for grammar—broadly and boldly defined—in writing instruction. And as they enact this belief in undergraduate and graduate writing classrooms across the country, these scholars validate the contemporary truism that grammar must be taught in the context of a student's own writing at the same time that they challenge another contemporary truism: that understanding and manipulating grammatical structures does not improve writing ability. In so doing, I believe that they have dispelled the sense of disjunction many writing teachers like me have hesitated to articulate in the past decade. Following the seemingly definitive interpretations of research put forth by such experts as Patrick Hartwell and George Hillocks, we rushed to divorce our process pedagogy from current-traditional concerns of many of our literature colleagues and to act on the research findings of the 1960s and 1970s. We had all but abandoned grammar—or at least we had driven it underground.

Now these writers have reunified the trivium, shown us language as "whole." For grammar separated out as a single entity with too much attention paid to the sentence in isolation remains a problem in teacher education classes, in grammar checkers, in freshman composition classes, in WAC, in exit or competency testing. Additionally, these college writing teachers transmute grammar into something other than mere correctness by connecting it back to its roots in classical times—by connecting it to style and rhetoric. To guarantee the place of grammar in writing classrooms of the future, these writers have convinced us that we must look to the past and the present, arguing for past practices that must be reclaimed and present trends that must be made to mature into viable traditions. This volume of essays reveals how the seeds of future connections between grammar and writing germinate in our past and current attitudes and practices. Further, these writers plant the seeds of future attitudes toward grammar as they teach the next generations of composition and rhetoric specialists, of secondary English teachers, of undergraduates preparing for careers other than teaching English—all of whom will educate future students and colleagues to perceive grammar and writing as interconnected. Although today's emphasis on whole language and literacies would seem to make grammar obsolete, the institutions where we teach and society at large still equate correct grammar with effective writing.

Reminding us that conversations about the place of grammar in writing have really been ongoing—indeed, quasi-Burkean—, these teachers acknowledge the questions that researchers like Martha Kolln, Rei Noguchi, Constance Weaver, Patrick Hartwell, Maxine Hairston, Joseph Williams, Robert Connors, and Andrea Lunsford have asked in the past decade. They resituate earlier discussions in the contexts of their own classrooms, institutions, and writing centers, showing us how past findings about the place of grammar hold true or require modification. In this collection almost every writer takes us into a classroom to hear students' voices engaged in negotiating rhetorical concerns in terms of style, usage, and grammar. For example, in Wendy Bishop's and David Blakesley's classes, we read how students write in what Winston Weathers calls "Grammar B." Or we listen to cognitive and social theories of language acquisition helping John Edlund understand how to work with ESL students. While theoretically and historically grounded, these teachers' insights are always aimed at practitioners. To adapt their methods and apply their insights in our own classrooms, we need to understand much about the teaching programs of past grammarians, about modern grammars and linguistics, and we need to be willing to ask students to take risks with language so that they can tap into grammar's "infinite [rhetorical and stylistic] power."

What will the next generation of college students, schooled in student-centered classrooms with multiculturalism, whole language, and electronic literacies need with Standard edited English or the rules of grammar? What does our reclaiming grammar do for our students? What it's always done, according to most of the contributors here: grammar empowers them and makes them owners of the language they use. For example, Jon Olson claims expansively that grammar gives students what it gave Frederick Douglass: the "intellectual and ethical power to sustain freedom within a community." In classical programs of language instruction and more recently in Edward P. J. Corbett's seminars, when grammar enhanced rather than displaced writing instruction, grammar was not a system of rules; instead, according to Cheryl Glenn, students learned grammar as part of the life of reading, writing, and speaking. About the power of grammar, Richard Boyd 's discussion of nineteenth-century handbooks implicitly warns us that teachers who behave as if they hold the keys to "correct" grammar exert a kind of power that makes students desire to imitate them. In today's student-centered classrooms, such gatekeeping with regard to grammar is inappropriate; instead, students make grammatical *choices* in process workshop classrooms.

If we heed these writing teachers' conclusions and examples, in the future we will include grammar in process workshop classrooms as Wendy Bishop and David Blakesley do, in creative writing workshops as Stuart Brown, Robert Boswell, and Kevin McIlvoy do. We will bring to the peer tutors and students in our writing centers a broad understanding of grammar as Carl Glover and Byron Stay do. As Gina Claywell and Cheryl Glenn suggest, we will revitalize grammar with ancient programs of language instruction. We will follow R. Baird Shuman's practical example to help our students understand how to manipulate essential grammatical structures by drawing upon their natural, unconscious knowledge of grammar. We will strive to understand the political and linguistic bases for rhetorical and grammatical choices as Garry Ross and John Edlund would have us do. As Donald Bushman and Elizabeth Ervin urge us to do, we must continue to include teachers of other disciplines in the discussions of the place of grammar in writing instruction. We also need to reach beyond the college writing classroom, as Neil Daniel and Christina Murphy recommend, to the worlds of professional writing where clarity, enabled by grammatical understanding, is paramount. As Joan Mullin and Irene Brosnahan and Janice Neuleib remind us, as we seek to inform all these college teachers, we must not overlook ways to educate future secondary educators about the integral importance of grammar to writing instruction. And, beyond these pedagogical arenas, Eric Hobson reminds us of the impact we can have by means of electronic literacy on writers actively engaged in literate behaviors for commercial and civic reasons..

Finally, how we decide what the future place of grammar in writing instruction should be depends on the future impact that compositionists decide to have on the faculty and writing curricula in English departments and beyond. We must continue to teach writing at all levels; to seek connections among the various genres of writing that we teach; to direct writing programs and writing-across-the-curriculum programs; to author the handbooks that guide other teachers of writing who are less experienced and less knowledgeable in composition, rhetoric, and linguistics than we are; and to design the technologies that will enable writers—both in the academy and in their daily lives—to share in what every writer knows is grammar's "infinite power."

Works Cited

Adams, Katherine H. 1991. Satellite Writing Centers: A Successful Model for Writing Across the Curriculum. In *The Writing Center: New Directions*, ed. Ray Wallace & Jeanne Simpson, 73–81. New York: Garland.

Altenbernd, Lynn & Leslie L. Lewis. 1966. *A Handbook for the Study of Fiction*. New York: Macmillan.

Applebee, Arthur N. 1974. *Tradition and Reform in the Teaching of English: A History*. Urbana, IL: NCTE.

Aristotle. 1991. *On Rhetoric: A Theory of Civic Discourse*. Trans. George A. Kennedy. New York: Oxford.

———. 1984. *The Rhetoric and the Poetics of Aristotle*. Trans. W. Rhys Roberts. New York: Modern Library.

Ascham, Roger. [1570]. 1888. *The Scholemaster*. Boston: Small.

Bache, Richard Meade. 1868. *Vulgarisms and Other Errors of Speech*. Philadelphia: Claxton, Remsen, & Haffelfinger.

Bakhtin, M. M. 1986. *Speech Genres and Other Essays*. Trans. Vern W. McGee & ed. Caryl Emerson & Michael Holquist. Austin: University of Texas Press.

———. 1981. *The Dialogic Imagination: Four Essays*. Trans. Caryl Emerson & Michael Holquist, & ed. Michael Holquist. Austin: University of Texas Press.

Baron, Dennis. 1992. Why Do Academics Continue to Insist on 'Proper' English? *Chronicle of Higher Education* 1 July: B1–2.

———. 1989. Going Out of Style? *English Today* 5.1:6–11.

Bartholomae, David. 1989. Freshman English, Composition, and CCCC. *College Composition and Communication* 40.1:38–50.

———. 1980. The Study of Error. *College Composition and Communication* 31:253–269. Reprint in *The Writing Teacher's Sourcebook*, ed. Gary Tate & Edward P. J. Corbett, 303–317. 2d ed. New York: Oxford, 1988.

Barzun, Jacques. 1985. *Simple and Direct: A Rhetoric for Writers*. Rev. ed. New York: Harper and Row.

Bauder, David. 1993. SUNY Presidents Fault Lack of Basics: Survey Reveals Concern That Students Entering College Are Academically Lacking. *Times Union* 28 April:1B.

Berlin, James A. 1984. *Writing Instruction in Nineteenth-Century American Colleges*. Carbondale: Southern Illinois University Press.

Berlin, James & Glenn J. Broadhead. 1981. Twelve Steps to Using Generative Sentences and Sentence Combining in the Classroom. *College Composition and Communication*. 32:295–304.

Bernays, Anne & Pamela Painter. 1990. *What If? Writing Exercises for Fiction Writers*. New York: Harpers.

Berthoff, Ann E. 1982. *forming/thinking/writing: The Composing Imagination*. Portsmouth, NH: Boynton/Cook.

Bingham, Caleb. 1832. *The Columbian Orator*. Boston.

Bishop, Wendy. 1994. Risk-Taking and Radical Revision–Exploring Writing Identities Through Advanced Composition and Poetry Portfolios. In *Portfolios in Practice: Voices from the Classroom*, ed. Kathleen Yancey. Urbana, IL: NCTE.

———. 1993. *The Subject Is Writing: Essays By Teachers and Students*. Portsmouth, NH: Boynton/Cook.

———. 1990. *Released into Language: Options for Teaching Creative Writing*. Urbana, IL: NCTE.

Bitzer, Lloyd. 1968. The Rhetorical Situation. *Philosophy & Rhetoric* 1:1–15.

Bizzell, Patricia &Bruce Herzberg, eds. 1990. *The Rhetorical Tradition: Readings from Classical Times to the Present*. Boston: Bedford Books of St. Martin's Press.

Bly, Carol. 1990. *The Passionate, Accurate Story*. Minneapolis: Milkweed.

Booth, Wayne. 1988. The Idea of a University—as Seen by a Rhetorician. In *The Vocation of a Teacher: Rhetorical Occasions, 1967–1988*, 309–334. Chicago: University of Chicago Press.

———. 1963. The Rhetorical Stance. *College Composition and Communication* 14:139–445.

Boyd, Richard. 1993. Mechanical Correctness and Ritual in the Late Nineteenth-Century Composition Classroom. *Rhetoric Review* 11:436–55.

Braddock, Richard, Richard Lloyd-Jones & Lowell Schoer. 1963. *Research in Written Composition*. Champaign, IL: NCTE.

Bridwell-Bowles, Lillian. 1992. Discourse and Diversity: Experimental Writing within the Academy. *College Composition and Communication* 43.3:349–68.

Brinsley, Richard. [1612] 1968. *Ludus Literarius*. Reprint. Menston: Scolar.

Britton, James, Tony Burgess, Alexander McLeod, Nancy Martin & Harold Rosen. 1975. *The Development of Writing Abilities, 11-18*. London: Macmillan Education.

Brooke, Robert. 1991. *Writing and Sense of Self: Identity Negotiation in Writing Workshops*. Urbana, IL: NCTE.

Brosnahan, Irene. 1992. Approaches to Teaching Teachers of Grammar. In *Proceedings of the Second National Conference of the Association of Teachers of English Grammar*, ed. Ed Vavra, 84–93. Williamsport, PA: Pennsylvania College of Technology.

Bruffee, Kenneth. 1984. Collaborative Learning and the ''Conversation of Mankind.'' *College English* 46:635–652.

Buber, Martin. 1958. *I and Thou*. New York: Scribner.

Bump, Jerome. 1987. CAI in Writing at the University: Some Recommendations. *Computers & Education* 11.2:121–133.

Burke, Kenneth. [1945]. 1969. *A Grammar of Motives.* Reprint. Berkeley: University of California Press.

Cazort, Douglas. 1992. *Under the Grammar Hammer: The 25 Most Important Grammar Mistakes and How to Avoid Them.* Los Angeles: Lowell House.

Chapelle, Carol. 1989. Using Intelligent Computer-Assisted Language Learning. *Computers and the Humanities* 2:59–70.

Chekov, Anton. 1965. Dunghills as Artistic Materials. In *The Modern Tradition*, trans. Constance Garnett, eds. Richard Ellman & Charles Feidelson, 244–245. New York: Oxford University Press.

Chomsky, Noam. 1965. *Aspects of the Theory of Syntax.* Cambridge, MA: MIT.

———. 1986. *Knowledge of Language: Its Nature, Origin, and Use.* New York: Praeger.

Christensen, Francis. 1963. A Generative Rhetoric of the Sentence. *College Composition and Communication* 14:155–161.

Christensen, Francis & Bonnijean Christensen. 1978. *Notes Toward a New Rhetoric: Nine Essays for Teachers.* 2d ed. New York: Harper and Row.

Cicero, Marcus Tullius. 1986. *Cicero on Oratory and Orators.* Trans. & ed. J. S. Watson. Carbondale: Southern Illinois University Press.

———. *Rhetorica ad Herennium.* 1981. Trans. Harry Caplan. London: Heinemann.

———. *De Oratore.* 1979. Trans. E. W. Sutton. 2 vols. 1942. Reprint. London: Loeb.

———. 1949. *De Inventione—De Optimo Genere Oratorium—Topica.* Trans. H. M. Hubbell. The Loeb Classical Library. Cambridge: Harvard University Press.

Clark, Beverly Lyon & Sonja Wiedenhaupt. 1992. On Blocking and Unblocking Sonja: A Case Study in Two Voices. *College Composition and Communication* 43:55–74.

Clark, Donald Lemen. 1948. *John Milton at St. Paul's School: A Study of Ancient Rhetoric in English Renaissance Education.* New York: Columbia University Press.

Clark, Katrina & Michael Holquist. 1984. *Mikhail Bakhtin.* Cambridge: Belknap Press.

Clifton, Georgia Elizabeth. 1951. A Survey of the Present Practices and Trends of the Teaching of English Written Composition in the Junior High School Grades of Texas. Diss., Univ. of Texas, Austin.

Cmicl, Kenneth. 1990. *Democratic Eloquence: The Fight Over Popular Speech in Nineteenth-Century America.* New York: Morrow.

Coats, Sandra. 1986. Teaching the Use of Connectors. *Journal of Developmental Education.* 10.3: 2–5.

Coe, Richard M. 1988. *Toward a Grammar of Passages.* Carbondale: Southern Illinois University Press.

————. 1987. An Apology for Form; or, Who Took the Form Out of the Process? *College English* 49:13–28.

Commission on the English Curriculum of the National Council of Teachers of English. 1965. *The College Teaching of English.* New York: Appleton Century Crofts.

————. 1963. *The Education of Teachers of English for American Schools and Colleges.* New York: Appleton Century Crofts.

————. 1956. *The English Language Arts in the Secondary School.* New York: Appleton Century Crofts.

————. 1954. *Language Arts for Today's Children.* New York: Appleton Century Crofts.

————. 1952. *The English Language Arts.* New York: Appleton Century Crofts.

Compton, Alfred G. 1898. *Some Common Errors of Speech.* New York: Putnam's.

Connors, Robert J. 1985. Mechanical Correctness as a Focus in Composition Instruction. *College Composition and Communication* 36.1:61–72.

Connors, R. & A. Lunsford. 1988. Frequency of Formal Errors in Current College Writing or Ma and Pa Kettle Do Research. *College Composition and Communication* 39:395–409.

Copeland, C. T. & H. M. Rideout. 1901. *Freshman English and Theme-Correcting in Harvard College.* New York: Silver, Burdett & Company.

Corbett, Edward P. J. 1990. *Classical Rhetoric for the Modern Student.* 3d. ed. New York: Oxford University Press.

————. "English 879: Stylistics." Course syllabus.

————. *Little English Handbook.* 5th ed. 1987. Glenview, IL: Scott, Foresman.

Covino, William A. 1988. *The Art of Wondering: A Revisionist Return to the History of Rhetoric.* Portsmouth, NH: Boynton/Cook.

Cramer, Carmen. 1986. Basic Grammar Through Cognitive Development." *Journal of Developmental Education* 9.3:22–24.

Crowhurst, Marion. 1983. Sentence-Combining: Maintaining Realistic Expectations. *College Composition and Communication.* 34:62–72.

Crowley, Sharon. 1989. Linguistics and Composition Instruction: 1950-1980. *Written Communication* 6 480–505.

Csikszentmihalyi, Mihaly. 1990. *Flow, The Psychology of Optimal Experience.* New York: Harper.

Daniel, Neil. 1992. *A Guide to Style and Mechanics.* Fort Worth: Harcourt Brace Jovanovich.

Davis, Frederica. 1984. In Defense of Grammar. *English Education* 16:151–64.

D'Avis, Greg. 1993. More Students Failing on Writing Assessment. *Arizona Daily Wildcat* 1 December:1, 6.

DeBeaugrande, Robert. 1984. Yes, Teaching Grammar Does Help. *English Journal* 73.2:66–71.

DeBoer, J. 1959. Grammar in Language Teaching. *Elementary English* 36:414–21.

D'Eloia, Sarah. 1977. The Uses–and Limits–of Grammar. *Journal of Basic Writing* 1:1–20.

Denogean, Anne T. 1993. UA Looking for Ways to Improve Writing. *Tucson Citizen* 7 December: 1B.

DeQuincey, Thomas. 1967. *Selected Essays on Rhetoric*. Ed. Frederick Burwick. Carbondale: Southern Illinois University Press.

Didion, Joan. [1976] 1992. Why I Write. In Chris Anderson *Free/Style*. 139. Boston: Houghton, Mifflin.

Douglass, Frederick. 1892. *Life and Times of Frederick Douglass*. Reprint. New York: Crowell-Collier, 1962.

———. *My Bondage and My Freedom*. [1855] 1987. Reprint, ed. William L. Andrews. Urbana: University of Illinois Press.

———. [1845] 1962. *Narrative of the Life of Frederick Douglass, An American Slave, Written by Himself*. Reprint, ed. Houston A. Baker, Jr. New York: Penguin.

Douglas, Wallace. 1976. Rhetoric for the Meritocracy: The Creation of Composition at Harvard. In *English in America: A Radical View of the Profession*, ed. Richard Ohmann, 97–132. New York: Oxford University Press.

Elbow, Peter. 1993. Ranking, Evaluating, and Liking: Sorting Out Three Forms of Judgment. *College English* 55. 2:187–206.

Ellis, Rod. 1985. *Understanding Second Language Acquisition*. New York: Oxford University Press.

Ellsworth, B. and J. Higgins. 1990. *English Simplified*. 6th ed. New York: Harper and Row.

Faulkner, William. 1987. "An Introduction to *The Sound and the Fury*." In *The Sound and the Fury*. Norton Critical Edition, ed. David Minter, 218–220. New York: Norton.

Finegan, Edward. 1980. *Attitudes Toward English Usage: The History of a War of Words*. New York: Teachers College Press.

Fontaine, Sheryl I. & Susan Hunter. 1992. Rendering the "Text" of Composition. *Journal of Advanced Composition* 12.2:395–406.

Francis, W. Nelson. [1954] 1973. Revolution in Grammar. Quarterly Journal of Speech 40:299–312. Reprint in *Linguistics for Teachers: Selected Readings*, ed. John F. Savage, 135–151. Chicago: Science Research Associates.

Freese, J. H. 1982. *The "Art" of Rhetoric*. By Aristotle. Loeb Classical Library. Cambridge: Harvard University Press.

Freire, Paulo. 1970. *Pedagogy of the Oppressed*. Trans. Myra Bergman Ramos. New York: Continuum.

Frey, Olivia. 1990. Beyond Literary Darwinism: Women's Voices and Critical Discourse. *College English* 52.9:507–526.

Fulwiler, Toby. 1993. A Lesson in Revision. In *The Subject Is Writing*, ed. Wendy Bishop, 132–149. Portsmouth, NH: Boynton/Cook.

————. Provocative Revision. 1992. *The Writing Center Journal* 12.2:190–204.

Gardner, John. 1985. *The Art of Fiction: Notes on Craft for Young Writers.* New York: Vintage.

————. 1983. *On Becoming a Novelist.* New York: Harper.

Garrett, Nina, James Noblitt, & Frank Dominguez. 1990. Computers in Foreign Language Teaching and Research: Part 2. *EDUCOMReview* 25(2):39–45.

Gates, Henry Louis, Jr. [1978] 1987. Binary Opposition in Chapter One of *Narrative of the Life of Frederick Douglass, an American Slave, Written by Himself.* In *Afro-American Literature: The Reconstruction of Instruction,* ed. Robert B. Stepto & Dexter Fisher. New York: MLA. Reprinted. in *Figures in Black: Words, Signs, and the"Racial" Self.* New York: Oxford University Press.

Gilyard, Keith. 1991. *Voices of the Self: A Study of Language Competence.* Detroit: Wayne State University Press.

Girard, René. 1987. *Things Hidden Since the Foundation of the World.* Trans. Stephen Bann & Michael Metteer. Stanford: Stanford University Press.

————. 1986. *The Scapegoat.* Trans. Yvonne Freccero. Baltimore: Johns Hopkins University Press.

————. 1977. *Violence and the Sacred.* Trans. Patrick Gregory. Baltimore: Johns Hopkins University Press.

Giroux, Henry A. 1988. *Teachers as Intellectuals: Toward a Critical Pedagogy of Learning.* Granby, MA: Bergin and Garvey.

Gleason, H. A., Jr. 1965. *Linguistics and English Grammar.* New York: Holt, Rinehart and Winston.

Glowka, A. Wayne & Donald M. Lance, eds. 1993. *Language Variation in North American English: Research and Teaching.* New York: Modern Language Association.

Goldberg, Natalie. 1986. *Writing Down the Bones: Freeing the Writer Within.* Boston: Shambhala.

Goldstein, Tom & Jethro K. Lieberman. 1991. *The Lawyer's Guide to Writing Well.* Berkeley: University of California Press.

Goodman, K. 1986. *What's Whole in Whole Language?* Portsmouth, NH: Heinemann.

Goodman, K., E. Smith, R. Meredith & Y. Goodman. 1987. *Language and Thinking In School—Whole-Language Curriculum.* New York: Richard C. Owen Publishers.

Gopen, George. 1988. The State of Legal Writing: *Res Ipsa Loquitur. Michigan Law Review* 86.2: 333–380.

————. 1987. Let the Buyer in the Ordinary Course of Business Beware: Suggestions for Revising the Prose of the Uniform Commercial Code. *The University of Chicago Law Review* 54.4:1178–1214.

Gould, Stephen Jay & Richard C. Lewontin. 1979. The Spandrels of San Marcos and the Panglossian Paradigm: A Critique. *Proceedings of the Royal Society of London, Series B: Biological Sciences* 205:581–598.

Grimaldi, William M. A., S.J. 1974. The Aristotelian Topics. In *Aristotle: The Classical Heritage of Rhetoric,* ed. Keith V. Erickson, 176–193. Metuchen, NJ: Scarecrow.

Gustafson, Thomas. 1992. *Representative Words: Politics, Literature, and the American Language, 1776–1865.* New York: Cambridge.

Hairston, Maxine. 1981. Not All Errors Are Created Equal: Nonacademic Readers in the Professions Respond to Lapses in Usage. *College English* 43:794–806.

Hairston, Maxine & John J. Ruszkiewicz. 1991. *The Scott, Foresman Handbook for Writers.* 2d ed. New York: HarperCollins.

Halliday, M. A. K. 1987. Language and the Order of Nature. In Fabb, Nigel, Derek Attridge, Alan Durant, and Colin McCabe, ed. *the Linguistics of Writing: Arguments Between Language and Literature.* 135–154. New York: Methuen, Inc.

———. 1978. *Language as a Social Semiotic: The Social Interpretation of Language and Meaning.* Baltimore: University Park Press.

Harris, Muriel. 1986. *Teaching One-to-One: The Writing Conference.* Urbana, IL: NCTE.

———. 1981. Mending the Fragmented Free Modifier. *College Composition and Communication* 32.2:175–82.

Hart, John S. 1883. *A Manual of Composition and Rhetoric.* Philadelphia: Eldredge & Brother.

Hartwell, Patrick. 1985. Grammar, Grammars, and the Teaching of Grammar. *College English* 47: 105–127.

———. 1984. The Writing Center and the Paradoxes of Written-Down Speech. *Writing Centers: Theory and Administration,* ed. Gary A. Olson, 48–61. Urbana, IL: NCTE.

Herbst, Jurgen. 1963. Introduction to *Our Country,* by Josiah Strong, ed., ix–xxvi. Cambridge: Harvard University Press.

Higgins, John. 1985. Grammarland: A Non-Directive Use of the Computer in Language Learning. *ELT Journal* 39.3:167–73.

Hill, A. S. 1895. *The Principles of Rhetoric.* New York: Harper & Brothers.

———. 1889. *Our English.* New York: Harper & Brothers.

Hillocks, George, Jr. 1986. *Research on Written Composition: New Directions for Teaching.* Urbana, IL.: NCRE/ERIC

Hirsch, E. D., Jr. 1987. *Cultural Literacy: What Every American Needs To Know.* Boston: Houghton Mifflin.

Holloway, Dale W. 1981. Semantic Grammars: How They Can Help Us Teach Writing. *College Composition and Communication* 32.2:205–218.

House, Homer C. [1931] 1950. *Descriptive English Grammar.* 2d ed. Rev. by Susan Emolyn Harman. Englewood Cliffs, NJ: Prentice Hall.

Howard, Rebecca M. 1988. *In-Situ* Workshops and the Peer Relationships of Composition Faculty. *WPA: Writing Program Administration* 12:39–46.

Howell, James F. & Dean Memering. 1993. *Brief Handbook for Writers.* Englewood Cliffs, NJ: Prentice Hall.

Hoyt, F. 1906. The Place of Grammar in the Elementary Curriculum. *Teachers College Record* 7: 467–500.

Hughes, Bradley T. 1991. Writing Center Outreach: Sharing Knowledge and Influencing Attitudes About Writing. In *The Writing Center: New Directions,* ed. Ray Wallace & Jeanne Simpson, 39–55. New York: Garland.

Hull, Glynda, Carolyn Ball, James L. Fox, Lori Levin & Deborah McCutchen. 1987. Computer Detection of Errors in Natural LanguageTexts: Some Research on Pattern-Matching. *Computers and the Humanities* 21.2:103–118.

Huntsman, Jeffrey F. 1983. Grammar. In *The Seven Liberal Arts in the Middle Ages,* ed. David L. Wagner, 58–95. Bloomington: Indiana University Press.

Huston, Jon Reckard. 1954. An Analysis of English Grammar Textbooks Used in American Schools Before 1850. Diss., University of Pittsburgh.

Isocrates. 1929. *On the Peace, Areopagiticus, Against the Sophists, Antidosis, Panathenaicus.* Trans. George Norlin, 160–10. London: Heinemann-Loeb.

Jaeger, Werner. 1939. *Paideia: The Ideals of Greek Culture.* Vol. 1. Trans. Gilbert Highet. 2d ed. New York: Oxford.

Jensen, George & John DiTiberio. 1989. *Personality and the Teaching of Composition.* Norwood, NJ: Ablex.

Johnson, Sabina Thorne. 1975. Some Tentative Strictures on Generative Rhetoric. In *Contemporary Rhetoric: A Conceptual Background with Readings,* ed. W. Ross Winterowd, 352–364. New York: Harcourt.

Joseph, Sister Miriam. 1947. *Shakespeare's Use of the Language Arts.* New York: Columbia.

Katz, Jon. 1993. The Media's War on Kids. *Rolling Stone* 25 November: 47–49, 130.

Kennedy, George A, trans. *On Rhetoric: A Theory of Civic Discourse,* by Aristotle. New York: Oxford, 1991.

———. 1980. *Classical Rhetoric and Its Christian and Secular Tradition from Ancient to Modern Times.* Chapel Hill: University of North Carolina Press.

———. 1963. *The Art of Persuasion in Greece.* Princeton: Princeton University Press.

Kiedaisch, Jean & Sue Dinitz. 1993. Look Back and Say ''So What'': The Limitations of the Generalist Tutor. *Writing Center Journal* 14.1:63–74.

Kinneavy, James L. 1983. Contemporary Rhetoric. In *The Present State of Scholarship in Historical and Contemporary Rhetoric,* ed. Winifred Bryan Horner. Columbia: University of Missouri Press.

Kitzhaber, Albert R. 1990. *Rhetoric in American Colleges, 1850-1900.* Dallas: Southern Methodist University Press.

Kitzhaber, Albert R., Robert M. Gorrell & Paul Roberts. 1961. *Education for College.* New York: The Ronald Press.

Kolln, Martha. 1993. An Open Letter to Janet Emig, Chair, English Standards Board, and Miles Myers, Project Co-director. *Council Chronicle* June: 14–15.

————. 1991. *Rhetorical Grammar: Grammatical Choices, Rhetorical Effects*. New York: Macmillan.

————. 1990. *Understanding English Grammar*. 3d ed. New York: Macmillan.

————. 1985. A Comment on "Grammar, Grammars, and The Teaching of Grammar." *College English* 47:874–77.

————. 1981. Closing the Books on Alchemy. *College Composition and Communication* 33.2: 139–51.

Krashen, Stephen D. 1982. *Principles and Practice in Second Language Acquisition*. New York: Pergamon.

Kroitor, Harry P. & Lee J. Martin. 1994. *The 500-Word Theme*. Englewood Cliffs, NJ: Prentice Hall.

Kutz, Eleanor. 1986. Between Students' Language and Academic Discourse: Interlanguage as Middle Ground. *College English* 48:385–396.

Labov, William. 1969. *The Logic of Nonstandard English*. Washington, D. C.: Georgetown University Press.

Lanham, Richard. 1992. *Revising Business Prose*. 3d ed. New York: Macmillan.

————. 1979. *Revising Prose*. New York: Scribners.

Larsen, Elizabeth Koehler. 1983. A History of the Composing Process. Diss. U of Wisconsin-Milwaukee.

Larsen, Mark D. 1987. Obstacles of Integrating Computer-Assisted Instruction with Oral Proficiency Goals. *Hispania* 7.4:936–944.

Lazere, Donald. 1992. Back to Basics A Force for Oppression or Liberation?" *College English* 54: 7–21.

Lee, Felicia R. 1994. Grappling With How to Teach Young Speakers of Black Dialect. *The New York Times NATIONAL* 1A January 5 :1, 8.

The Little Red Schoolhouse. n.d. Gregory Colomb, Frank Kinahan, Larry McEnerney & Joseph Williams, contributors. Available on disk from the University of Chicago.

Longinus. 1957. *On the Sublime*. Trans. G. M. A. Grube. Indianapolis: Library of Liberal Arts.

Lunsford, Andrea. 1991. Collaboration, Control, and the Idea of a Writing Center. *The Writing Center Journal* 12.1:3–10.

Lunsford, Andrea & Robert Connors. 1989. *The St. Martin's Handbook*. New York: St. Martins.

Maimon, Elaine P. 1986. Knowledge, Acknowledgment, and Writing across the Curriculum: Toward an Educated Community." In *The Territory of Language: Linguistics, Stylistics, and the Teaching of Composition*, ed. Donald A. McQuade, 89–100. Carbondale: Southern Illinois University Press.

Mathews, William. 1876. *Words: Their Use and Abuse*. Chicago: S. C.Griggs & Company.

Maurois, Andre. 1962. *The Art of Writing*. Trans. Gerard Hopkins. New York: Dutton.

Mayher, J., N. Lester & G. Pradl. 1983. *Learning to Write/Writing to Learn*. Portsmouth, NH: Boynton/Cook.

McGuire, William J. & Claire V. McGuire. 1986. Differences in Conceptualizing Self Versus Conceptualizing Other People as Manifested in Contrasting Verb Types Used in Natural Speech. *Journal of Personality and Social Psychology* 51:1135–43.

McQuade, Donald. 1992. Living In—and On—the Margins. *College Composition and Communication* 43.1:11–22.

Meckel, H. 1963. Research on Teaching Composition and Literature. In *Handbook of Research on Teaching*, ed. N. L. Gage. Chicago: Rand McNally.

Miller, Susan. 1991. *Textual Carnivals: The Politics of Compostion*. Carbondale: Southern Illinois University Press.

Mills, John A. & Gordon D. Hemsley. 1976. The Effect of Levels of Education on Judgments of Grammatical Acceptability. *Language and Speech* 19:324–342.

Mills, Joshua. 1994. In-Your-Faceism vs. Light, *New York Times* 4A January 9:19–20.

Montaigne, Michel de. 1957. *The Complete Works of Montaigne*. Vol. 1. Ed. and trans. Donald M. Frame. Stanford: Stanford University Press.

Moody, Patricia Ann DeLand. 1972. "Charles C. Fries on *Shall* and *Will*: An Episode in the History of Schoolroom Grammar." Diss., U of Texas, Austin.

Moore, Terence & Christine Carling. 1982. *Understanding Language: Towards a Post-Chomskyan Linguistics*. London: Macmillan.

Murphy, Christina. 1991. Writing Centers in Context: Responding to Current Educational Theory." In *The Writing Center: New Directions,* eds. Ray Wallace & Jeanne Simpson. New York: Garland.

Murphy, James J. 1990. *A Short History of Writing Instruction From Ancient Greece to Twentieth-Century America*. Davis, CA: Hermagoras Press.

Murray, Donald. 1979. The Listening Eye: Reflections on the Writing Conference. *College English* 41:13–18.

The Mustard Seed Garden Manual of Painting. 1978. Trans. and ed. Mai-mai Sze. Princeton: Princeton University Press/Bollingen.

Myers, Greg. 1985. The Social Construction of Two Biologists' Proposals. *Written Communication* 2.3:219–245.

National Council Teachers of English. *1992. Teaching Composition: A Position Statement.* Urbana, IL: NCTE, 1992.

———. 1991. *Position on the Teaching of English: Assumptions and Practices.* Urbana IL: NCTE.

NCTE Committee on the National Interest. 1961. *The National Interest and the Teaching of English*. Champaign, IL: NCTE.

Neuleib, Janice. 1977. The Relation of Formal Grammar to Composition. *College Composition and Communication* 28:247–250.

Neuleib, Janice & Irene Brosnahan. 1987. Teaching Grammar to Writers. *Journal of Basic Writing* 6.2:28–35.

Newman, J., ed. 1985. *Whole Language Notebook—Theory in Use*. Portsmouth, NH: Heinemann.

Newmeyer, Frederick. 1986. *Linguistic Theory in America*. 2d ed. Orlando: Academic Press.

Noguchi, Rei R. 1991. *Grammar and the Teaching of Writing: Limits and Possibilities*. Urbana, IL: NCTE.

North, Stephen M. 1984. The Idea of a Writing Center. *College English* 46.5:433–46.

O'Hare, Frank. 1973. *Sentence Combining*. Urbana, IL: NCTE.

Ohmann, Richard. 1987. *Politics of Letters*. Middletown: Wesleyan University Press.

Olson, Gary A. 1984. *Writing Centers: Theory and Administration*. Urbana, IL: NCTE.

Parker, Frank & Kim Sydow Campbell. 1993. Linguistics and Writing: A Reassessment. *College Composition and Communication* 44.3:295–314.

Pattison, Robert. 1982. *On Literacy: The Politics of the Word from Homer to the Age of Rock*. New York: Oxford University.

Perl, Sondra. 1979. The Composing Process of Unskilled College Writers. *Research in the Teaching of English* 13:317–39.

Pinker, Steven. 1994. *The Language Instinct: How the Mind Creates Language*. New York: William Morrow and Company.

Pivar, David J. 1973. *Purity Crusade: Sexual Morality and Social Control, 1868–1900*. Westport, CT: Greenwood.

Plato. *Phaedrus*. 1956. Trans. W. C. Helmbold & W. G. Rabinowitz. Indianapolis: Bobbs-Merrill, 1956.

Quandahl, Ellen. 1986. Aristotle's *Rhetoric*: Reinterpreting Invention. *Rhetoric Review* 4.1:128–137.

Quintilian. [1920] 1969. *Institutio Oratoria*. 4 vols. Trans. H. E. Butler. 4 vols. London: Heinemann.

Richards, I. A. [1936] 1981. *The Philosophy of Rhetoric*. Reprint. London: Oxford University Press.

Rieber, Lloyd. 1992. Grammar Rules as Computer Algorithms. *College Teaching* 40.2:57–59.

Rose, Mike. 1989. *Lives on the Boundary: The Struggles and Achievements of America's Underprepared*. New York: Free Press.

———. 1985. The Language of Exclusion: Writing Instruction at the University. *College English* 47:341–359.

———. [1983] 1988. Remedial Writing Courses: A Critique and a Proposal. *College English* 45.2:109–28. Reprint in *The Writing Teacher's Sourcebook*, ed. Gary Tate & Edward P. J. Corbett, 318–37. 2d ed. New York: Oxford University Press, 1988.

Rudolph, Frederick. 1981. *Curriculum: A History of the American Undergraduate Course of Study Since 1636*. San Francisco: Jossey-Bass.

Russell, David. 1991. *Writing in the Academic Disciplines, 1870-1990: A Curricular History.* Carbondale: Southern Illinois University Press.

Rutherford, William E. 1987. *Second Language Grammar: Learning and Teaching.* New York: Longman.

Sanborn, Jean. 1986. Grammar: Good Wine Before Its Time. *English Journal* 75.3:72–80.

Sanford, Adrian B. 1982. Four Basic Ways of Working with Sentences. *English Journal* 71.7:68–70.

Sapir, Edward. 1921. *Language: An Introduction to the Study of Speech.* New York: Harcourt Brace.

Scharton, Maurice & Janice Neuleib. 1993. *Inside Out: A Guide to Writing.* Boston: Allyn & Bacon.

————. 1990. The Gift of Insight: Personality Type, Tutoring, and Learning. In *Expanding and Changing the Writing Center: New Directions*, eds. Ray Wallace and Jeanne Simpson, 184–204. New York: Garland Press.

Scholes, Robert. 1991. A Flock of Cultures—A Trivial Proposal. *College English* 53:759–772.

Schwartz, Mimi. 1984. Response to Writing: A College-Wide Perspective. *College English* 46(1): 55–62.

Selfe, Cynthia L. 1992. Preparing Teachers for the Virtual Age: The Case for Technology Critics. In *Re-imagining Computers and Composition: Teaching and Research in the Virtual Age*, eds. Gail E. Hawisher & Paul LeBlanc, 24–42. Portsmouth, NH: Boynton/Cook Heinemann.

Shaughnessy, Mina P. 1977. *Errors and Expectations: A Guide for the Teacher of Basic Writing.* New York: Oxford University Press.

Simmons, Sue Carter. 1991. Review of *A Short History of Writing Instruction From Ancient Greece to Twentieth-Century America*. Murphy, James J., ed. Davis, CA: Hermagoras Press, 1990; *College Composition and Communication* 42.4:516–518.

Smith, Frank. 1983. Reading Like a Writer. *Language Arts* 60:558–567.

Sommers, Nancy. 1992. Between the Drafts. *College Composition and Communication* 43(1):23–31.

————. 1980. Revision Strategies of Student Writers and Experienced Adult Writers. *College Composition and Communication* 31.4:378–388.

Spellmeyer, Kurt. 1993. *Common Ground: Dialogue, Understanding and the Teaching of Composition.* Englewood Cliffs, NJ: Prentice Hall.

Steiner, George. 1975. *After Babel: Aspects of Language and Translation.* New York: Oxford.

Stern, Jerome. 1991. *Making Shapely Fiction.* New York: Norton.

Streed, John. 1993. Labeling for Form and Function. *English Journal* 82.5:85–87.

Strong, Josiah. 1963. *Our Country.* 1886. Cambridge: Harvard University Press.

Strunk, William, Jr. & E. B. White. 1972. *The Elements of Style*. 2d ed. New York: Macmillan.

Stull, William L. 1983. Sentence Combining, Generative Rhetoric, and Concepts of Style. In *Sentence Combining: A Rhetorical Perspective*, ed. Donald A.Daiker, Andrew Kerek & Max Morenberg, 76–85. Carbondale: Southern Illinois University Press.

Sutton, G. 1976. Do We Need to Teach a Grammar Terminology? *English Journal* 65.12:37–40.

Tabbert, Russell. 1984. Parsing the Question "Why Teach Grammar?" *English Journal* 73.8:38-42.

Taylor, Sharon J. 1986. Grammar Curriculum—Back to Square One. *English Journal* 75(1):94–98.

Texas Education Agency. 1992. "Chapter 75 Curriculum: Subchapter D. Essential Elements—Grades Nine–12." 97–107. Austin: Texas Education Agency.

———. 1990. "Texas Assessment of Academic Skills: English Language Arts Writing Objectives and Measurement Specifications, 1990–1995, High School— Tested at Exit Level." Austin: Texas Education Agency.

Thurber, James. 1942. *My World—and Welcome to It*. New York: Harcourt.

Tierney, Robert J., Mark A. Carter & Laura Desai. 1991. *Portfolio Assessment in the Reading-Writing Classroom*. Norwood, MA: Christopher-Gordon.

Tubbs, Gail Lewis. 1991. A Case for Teaching Grammar to Writers. *Writing Lab Newsletter* 15(1): 1–3.

Tufte, Virginia. 1971. *Grammar as Style*. New York: Holt.

Vavra, Ed. 1987. Grammar and Syntax: The Student's Perspective. *English Journal* 76.6:42–48.

———. 1993. Welcome to the Shoe Store? *English Journal* 82 .5:81–84.

Vico, Giambattista. [1708] 1965. *On the Study Methods of Our Times*. Trans. Elio Gianturco. Indianapolis: Bobbs-Merrill.

Volosinov, V. N. 1973. *Marxism and the Philosophy of Language*. New York: Seminar Press. [Note: Although *Marxism and the Philosophy of Language* was published under the name "Volosinov," Clark and Holquist argue that it is clearly Bakhtin's, and also that the "Marxism" of the title was added to the book in a superficial manner to aid publication (166).]

Vygotsky, Lev Semenovich. 1962. *Thought and Language*. Trans. and ed. Eugenia Hanfmann & Gertrude Vakar. Cambridge, MA: MIT.

Wabnik, Alisa. 1993. Writing Skills Weak at UA, Exam Reveals. *Arizona Daily Star* 30 November: 1B, 2B.

Wallace, Ray & Jeanne Simpson, eds. 1991. *The Writing Center: New Directions*. New York: Garland.

Warner, Ann L. 1993. If the Shoe No Longer Fits, Wear It Anyway? *English Journal* 82.5:76–80.

Washington, Booker T. [1901] 1965. *Up from Slavery*. Reprint in *Three Negro Classics*. New York: Avon.

Weathers, Winston. 1980. *An Alternate Style: Options in Composition.* Rochelle Park, NJ: Hayden.

————. 1976. Grammars of Style: New Options in Composition. *Freshman English News* Winter: 1976. Reprint in *Rhetoric and Composition: A Sourcebook for Teachers and Writers,* ed. Richard L. Graves, 200-214. 3d ed. Portsmouth, NH: Boynton/Cook.

Weaver, Constance. 1979. *Grammar for Teachers: Perspectives and Definitions.* Urbana, IL: NCTE.

Weidner, Heidemarie Z. 1991. "Coeducation and Jesuit Ratio Studiorum in Indiana: Rhetoric and Composition Instruction at 19th-Century Butler and Notre Dame." Diss., Univ. of Louisville.

Whissen, Thomas. 1982. *A Way with Words.* New York: Oxford.

Wiebe, Robert. 1967. *The Search for Order, 1877–1920.* New York: Hill & Wang.

Williams, Joseph M. 1990. *Style: Toward Clarity and Grace.* Chicago: University of Chicago Press.

————. 1989. *Style: Ten Lessons in Clarity and Grace.* 3d ed. London: HarperCollins.

————. 1985. Four Comments on "Grammar, Grammars, and the Teaching of Grammar." *College English* 47:641–643.

————. 1985. *Ten Lessons in Clarity and Grace.* 2d ed. Glenview, IL: Scott Foresman.

————. 1981. The Phenomenology of Error. *College Composition and Communication* 32.2:152–168.

Winterowd, W. Ross. 1986. The Grammar of Coherence. In *Composition/Rhetoric: A Synthesis,* 221-228. Carbondale: Southern Illinois University Press.

————. 1986. *Dispositio*: The Concept of Form in Discourse. In *Composition/ Rhetoric: A Synthesis,* 245–252. Carbondale: Southern Illinois University Press.

————. 1975. *Contemporary Rhetoric: A Conceptual Background with Readings.* New York: Harcourt.

Woods, Marjorie Curry. 1990. The Teaching of Writing in Medieval Europe. In *A Short History of Writing Instruction From Ancient Greece to Twentieth-Century America,* ed. James J. Murphy. Davis, CA: Hermagoras Press.

Woolf, Virginia. 1957. *A Room of One's Own.* San Diego: Harvest-Harcourt.

Wydick, Richard. 1985. *Plain English for Lawyers.* 2d ed. Durham: Carolina Academic Press.

X, Malcolm. 1965. *The Autobiography of Malcolm X.* New York: Grove.

Zawacki, Terry Myers. 1992. Recomposing as a Woman—An Essay in Different Voices. *College Composition and Communication* 43.(1):32–38.

Zinsser, William. 1980. *On Writing Well: An Informal Guide to Writing Nonfiction.* 2d ed. New York: Harper & Row.

Contributors

Wendy Bishop is Associate Professor of English at Florida State University where she teaches writing and rhetoric. Her books include, *Something Old, Something New: College Writing Teachers and Classroom Change* (Southern Illinois UP, 1990); *Released into Language: Options for Teaching Creative Writing* (National Council of Teachers of English, 1990); *Working Words: The Process of Creative Writing* (Mayfield, 1992); and the edited collections *The Subject Is Writing: Essays by Teachers and Students* (Boynton/Cook, 1993) and *Colors of a Different Horse: Rethinking Creative Writing, Theory and Pedagogy* (coedited with Hans Ostrom; National Council of Teachers of English, 1994). In addition, she and Hans Ostrom are editing a collection of essays for the MLA series, Research and Scholarship in Composition, entitled *Genres of Writing: Mapping the Territories of Discourse.*

David Blakesley is Assistant Professor of English at Southern Illinois University, Carbondale. He has published articles on literacy and rhetoric, most recently an essay entitled "He/Man and the Masters of Discourse" in *Gender Issues in the Teaching of English* (Boynton/Cook 1992). He is presently completing a book on Kenneth Burke's rhetoric

Robert Boswell is Associate Professor of English at New Mexico State University where he teaches creative writing, contemporary literature, and the theory of the novel. He has an MFA from the University of Arizona. His writing includes the novels *Crooked Hearts* (Knopf, 1987), *Geography of Desire* (Knopf, 1989), and *Mystery Ride* (Knopf, 1993)—all recently reissued by Harper Collins—as well as the collection of stories *Dancing in the Movies* which received the Iowa School of Letters Award (U of Iowa P, 1986). *Crooked Hearts* was made into the film of the same name starring Peter Coyote and Jennifer Jason Leigh. His newest collection of stories is *Living to Be a Hundred* (Knopf, 1994). He is currently working on a novel and a play.

Richard Boyd is Assistant Professor of English at the University of California, Riverside and directs the Freshman Composition program there. He has published essays in *Rhetoric Review* and *Journal of Advanced Composition* and is currently at work on a manuscript tracing the operation of mimetic desire in the current-traditional classroom.

Irene Brosnahan is Associate Professor of English and Director of the English Language Institute at Illinois State University where she teaches linguistics and English grammar. Her research interests in the learning and teaching of grammar have led to several publications and presentations on the subject. She has published in *College English, The Journal of Basic Writing,* and *English Quarterly,* among others. She also works with TESOL and was a Fulbright Senior Lecturer in Shanghai, People's Republic of China, from 1980 to 1982.

Stuart C. Brown is Assistant Professor of Rhetoric and Professional Communication at New Mexico State University. He has both an MFA in Creative Writing and a Ph.D. in Rhetoric and Composition from the University of Arizona. His writing includes articles and book chapters on professional communication, rhetorical theory, and ethics and the coauthored textbook, *Becoming Expert: Writing and Thinking Across the Disciplines* (Kendall/Hunt, 1990). He is currently coediting with Carl G. Herndl *Rhetoric and the Environment: New Essays*. Other works include *Defining the New Rhetorics* (Sage, 1993) and *Professing the New Rhetorics* (Blair, 1994) with Theresa Enos. He has published poetry and literary nonfiction in a number of literary magazines.

Donald Bushman is Assistant Professor of English at the University of North Carolina at Wilmington, where he teaches courses in composition and rhetoric. Formerly he taught at the University of Arizona, where he was an Assistant Coordinator on the University Composition Board, a unit of the English Department, that is charged with the administration of the University's writing program. He supervised testing and placement at the first-year level and proficiency testing at the upper-division level, as well as campus-wide WAC support and outreach activities to area schools and community colleges.

Gina Claywell is Assistant Professor of English at East Central University in Ada, Oklahoma where she teaches usage, technical writing, and composition. She is pursuing a Ph.D. in English, with a specialization in Rhetoric/Composition, from the University of Tennessee, Knoxville, where she formerly served as a Graduate Teaching Associate. She received her M.A. from the University of Tennessee in 1991; her thesis was "Grammar Instruction Trends in the Composition Classroom: A Historiographic/Bibliographic Essay." She has also been an instructor at Somerset Community College in Kentucky.

Neil Daniel is Professor and Chair of English at Texas Christian University. Among the courses he teaches are modern grammar, professional writing and editing, and a course for teachers on teaching writing. He has served as director of composition. His work with writers in business and the professions includes consulting with the law department of Exxon Corporation and with several banks and insurance companies in Fort Worth. His publications include *A Guide to Style and Mechanics.* (HBJ, 1992), *Flexible Pacing* (Council for Exceptional Children, 1987), and *Educating Able Learners* (U Texas P, 1985).

John R. Edlund teaches writing at California State University, Los Angeles, and is currently the Director of the Writing Center. He has a Ph.D. in English from the University of Southern California, with the option in Rhetoric, Linguistics, and Literature.

Elizabeth Ervin is Assistant Professor of English at the University of North Carolina at Wilmington, where she teaches a variety of courses in composition, rhetoric, and women's studies.. She received her Ph.D. in Rhetoric Composition, and the Teaching of English from the University of Arizona and has previously published essays on historical scholarship in rhetoric, collaboration, and feminist mentoring.

Cheryl Glenn is Associate Professor of English at Oregon State University, where she teaches courses in rhetorical history and theory, composition theory, British Literature, and grammar. In 1992, she won OSU's Burlington Foundation Resources

Award for her outstanding classroom teaching. She has co-authored, with Robert Connors, *The St. Martin's Guide to Teaching Writing* and has published on literacy, composition, medieval literature, and women's contributions to the history of rhetoric. At present, she is writing *Rhetoric Retold: Regendering the Tradition from Antiquity through the Renaissance.*

Carl W. Glover is Assistant Professor of Rhetoric and Writing, director of the Writing Center, and coordinator of the freshman seminar at Mount Saint Mary's College in Emmitsburg, Maryland. His work has appeared in *Composition Studies*, and he has given numerous papers on classical rhetorical theory, writing center administration, and the rhetoric of the American civil war at CCCC and other regional conferences. In addition to his scholarly work, he writes the satirical "Ask Carl" misadvice column for the *Writing Lab Newsletter.*

Eric H. Hobson directs the Writing Center and Coordinates the Writing Programs at St. Louis College of Pharmacy. He holds a Ph.D. from the University of Tennessee and has published widely in writing center and composition journals. The author of *Reading and Writing in High Schools: A Whole Language Approach* (NEA, 1990), his book on writing center theory and practice is forthcoming from Boynton/Cook.

Susan Hunter is Associate Professor of English and Director of Writing Programs at Kennesaw State College in Marietta, Georgia. Her essays on gender and pedagogy and on professional issues appear in *Journal of Advanced Composition, Rhetoric Review, Freshman English News,* and *The Writing Instructor.* She has edited with Sheryl I. Fontaine *Writing Ourselves Into the Story: Unheard Voices from Composition Studies* (Southern Illinois University Press, 1993). She is a founding editor (with Ray Wallace) of *Dialogue: A Journal for Writing Specialists.* She is currently researching editorial review practices in composition journals.

Kevin McIlvoy is Associate Professor of English at New Mexico State University where he teaches creative writing, contemporary literature, and theory of fiction courses. He has an MFA from the University of Arizona. His writing includes the novels, *The Fifth Station* (Algonquin, 1988) and *Little Peg* (Athenaeum, 1990). He is editor of the literary magazine *Puerto del Sol* and former president of the Coordinating Council of Literary Magazines. He is currently working on a new novel, *The Distance,* and a collection of short stories.

Joan Mullin is Director of the Writing Center and the Writing Across the Curriculum Program at the University of Toledo. Since beginning both programs in 1988 she has presented papers on writing center theory and practice, classroom pedagogy, critical hermeneutic theory, and educational philosophy at such conferences as MLA, CCCC, ECWCA, Midwest Philosophy of Education, Bergamo, and NCTE. She has published in *Composition Studies, American Journal of Pharmaceutical Education, The Sociology Teacher, The Writing Lab Newsletter,* completed a guide to writing across the curriculum for the American Association of Colleges of Pharmacy, and coedited *Intersections: Theory-Practice in the Writing Center* (NCTE, 1994). Her current work includes creating a cross-disciplinary hypertext stack for WAC instructors and investigating the uses of visual literacy in the teaching of writing. She co-established the annual Ohio Conference on Learning Enhancement and serves on the Executive Board of the National Writing Center Association.

Christina Murphy is the Director of the Writing Center and Associate Director of the Center for Academic Services at Texas Christian University. She is the editor of *Composition Studies* and of *Studies in Psychoanalytic Theory* and has published articles on rhetorical theory, teaching writing, and writing centers in a range of academic journals. Her textbook on critical thinking skills was published by Prentice Hall in 1990 with a revised edition in 1991, and she is editing, with Joe Law, *Landmark Essays on Writing Centers* to be published by Hermagoras Press.

Janice Neuleib is Professor of English at Illinois State University where she directs the University Center for Learning Assistance and the Illinois State Writing Project. She has participated as codirector in two multi-year NEH projects and has published and presented on composition research and pedagogy. Her publications have appeared in *College Composition and Communication, College English, The Journal of Basic Writing*, and in numerous collections. She has recently co-authored a book, *Inside/ Out: A Guide to Writing*, and *Writing with the Masters*.

Jon Olson is the Writing Center Coordinator at Oregon State University where he also has served as the acting director of the Writing-Intensive Curriculum Program. He participated in the University of Southern California's Model Literacy Project which targeted members of the California Conservation Corps in Los Angeles. He has published pieces on the psychology of composition and on individual differences in *The Writing Instructor*, on the literacy of American slaves in *Vox Ecclesia*, and on writing across the curriculum in *Teaching with Writing*.

Garry Ross is Associate Professor and Head of Language and Communication at Northwestern State University of Louisiana. He has also been the Director of Writing in the Hankamer School of Business at Baylor University and in the Department of English at Henderson State University. He hjas recently published "Linking Freshman English to Western Civilisation" in *The Core and the Canon: A National Debate*. His research interests are in sociolinguistics, particularly the origins of BEV, and his current research is on the rhetoric of the new history.

R. Baird Shuman is Professor Emeritus of English at the University of Illinois at Urbana- Champaign, where he served as Director of English Education, Director of Freshman Rhetoric, Director of Development, and Acting Director during the establishment of the Center for Writing Studies. Shuman has taught at Drexel University, the University of Pennsylvania, San José State University, and Duke University. He is the author or editor of twenty-seven books, the most recent of which are *Resources for Writers* (1992), *American Drama, 1918–1960* (1992), and *Georgia O'Keeffe* (1993).

Byron L. Stay is associate professor of rhetoric and writing and chair of the department of Rhetoric and Writing at Mount St. Mary's College in Emmitsburg, Maryland. He is also President of the National Writing Centers Association and co-chair of the National Writing Centers Conference. His articles have appeared in *The Journal of Teaching Writing, The Writing Center Journal, Writing Lab Newsletter, Studies in the Novel*, and in a 1992 anthology, *Constructing Rhetorical Education*.

Ray Wallace is the Director of the Louisiana Scholars' College, the state's designated liberal arts honors college, located at Northwestern State University. His collection *The*

Writing Center: New Directions (Garland, 1991) won the book-of-the-year award from the National Writing Centers Association, and *Intersections: Theory-Practice in the Writing Center* has been recently published by NCTE. He is a founding editor (with Susan Hunter) of *Dialogue: A Journal for Writing Specialists.* He holds a Doctor of Arts degree in Rhetoric and Composition from Illinois State University.